LIBRARY

Children, Teachers and Learning Series
General Editor: Cedric Cullingford

Children and Primary Geography

Titles in the *Children, Teachers and Learning* series

Children and Primary Geography

Patrick Wiegand

CASSELL

Cassell

Wellington House	PO Box 605
125 Strand	Herndon
London WC2R 0BB	VA 20172

First published 1993
Reprinted 1997

British Cataloguing-in-Publication Data
A catalogue record for this book is available from the British Library.

Library of Congress Cataloging-in-Publication Data
Applied for.

ISBN 0-304-32604-6 (hardback)
      0-304-32592-9 (paperback)

Typeset by Colset Private Limited, Singapore
Printed and bound in Great Britain by Redwood Books, Trowbridge, Wiltshire.

For Katherine and Christopher

Contents

Foreword

The books in this series stem from the conviction that all those who are concerned with education should have a deep interest in the nature of children's learning. Teaching and policy decisions ultimately depend on an understanding of individual personalities accumulated through experience, observation and research. Too often in recent years decisions on the management of education have had little to do with the realities of children's lives, and too often the interest shown in the performance of teachers, or in the content of the curriculum, has not been balanced by an interest in how children respond to either. The books in this series are based on the conviction that children are not fundamentally different from adults, and that we understand ourselves better by our insight into the nature of children.

The books are designed to appeal to *all* those who are interested in education and take it as axiomatic that anyone concerned with human nature, culture or the future of civilization is interested in education; in the individual process of learning, as well as what can be done to help it. While each book draws on recent findings in research, and is aware of the latest developments in policy, each is written in a style that is clear, readable and free from the jargon that has undermined much scholarly writing, especially in such a relatively new field of study.

Although the audience to be addressed includes all those concerned with education, the most important section of the audience is made up of professional teachers, the teachers who continue to learn and grow and who need both support and stimulation. Teachers are very busy people, whose energies are taken up in coping with difficult circumstances. They deserve material that is stimulating, useful and free of jargon and that is in tune with the practical realities of classrooms.

Each book is based on the principle that the study of education is a discipline in its own right. There was a time when the study of the principles of learning and the individual's response to his or her environment was a collection of parts of other disciplines – history, philosophy, linguistics, sociology and psychology. That time is assumed to be over and the books address those who are interested in the study of children and how they respond to their environment. Each book is written both to enlighten the reader and to offer practical help to develop understanding. They therefore not only contain accounts of what we understand about children, but also illuminate these accounts by a series of examples, based on observation of practice. These examples are designed not as a series of rigid steps to be followed, but to show the realities on which the insights are based.

Most people, even educational researchers, agree that research on children's learning has been most disappointing, even when it has not been completely missing. Apart from the general lack of a 'scholarly' educational tradition, the inadequacies of such study come about because of the fear of approaching such a complex area as children's inner lives. Instead of answering curiosity with observation, much educational research has attempted to reduce the problem to simplistic solutions, by isolating a particular hypothesis and trying to prove it, or by trying to focus on what is easy and 'empirical'. These books try to clarify the real complexities of the problem, and are willing to be speculative. The real disappointment with educational research, however, is that it is very rarely read or used. The people most at home with children are often unaware that helpful insights can be offered to them. The study of children and the understanding that comes from self-knowledge are too important to be left to obscurity. In the broad sense real 'research' is carried out by all those engaged in the task of teaching or bringing up children.

All the books share a conviction that the inner worlds of children repay close attention, and that much subsequent behaviour and attitudes depend upon the early years. The books also share the conviction that children's natures are not markedly different from those of adults, even if they are more honest about themselves. The process of learning is reviewed as the individual's close and idiosyncratic involvement in events, rather than the passive reception of, and processing of, information.

Cedric Cullingford

Acknowledgements

I am grateful to several cohorts of PGCE and MEd students for the opportunity of discussing with them matters relating to primary geography. I am especially grateful to Geraldine Riley, Pauline Ward and Hilary Britton for some of their material described or reproduced in this book.

Professor Rosalind Driver introduced me to several helpful references on physical geography and environmental education; and Alan Wolinski and Carole Bennett, of the Leeds City Council Road Safety Unit, introduced me to some of the literature on children and traffic.

Thanks are due to Oxford University Press for permission to reproduce Figure 2.1b and Figure 2.8, and to R. Abler, J.S. Adams and P. Gould for permission to reproduce Figure 5.2.

I am also grateful to Sally Beveridge for reading the manuscript and for her comments.

CHAPTER 1
Primary Geography

Geography is good for you. It has a potentially significant role in creating a better world.[1] Geography explores the relationship between the Earth and its peoples, through the study of *place, space* and *environment*.[2]

The distinction between space and place is a significant one for geographers. Children are frequently first attracted to geography through an encounter with *place*. That encounter need not be direct and local – for example through play in a stream or on a beach or up a mountain; it could as well be an encounter with a distant place through a film, or a picture book or a story. The importance of place in human experience goes deep. To be human is to live in a world that is filled with significant places: to be human is to know and to have *your* place.[3] Places have meaning for us. They are individually experienced. We see them through our own unique set of attitudes, backgrounds and circumstances. Places are an important part of children's development. Corners of the house or garden or neighbourhood form a 'private geography' often remembered long into adulthood and which forms part of the identity of self. The development in children of a 'sense of place' is a fundamental aim for geography teaching – to help children develop a feeling for the unique identity of a place; what the places they already know mean to them and what it might be like to be in places that are as yet remote. Places derive their essential character therefore not only from the human and physical processes that create or influence features on the surface of the Earth but from our unique responses to them.

The study of *space*, on the other hand, seeks to explore the relationships between places, patterns of activity arising from the use people make of the physical settings where they live and work. The study of how places are linked by movements of people, materials and information is a contrasting, objective and 'scientific' way of looking at the world. This aspect of geography is concerned with building theories in order to explain patterns of human activity.

The study of *environment* links Earth and people. It is concerned with the resource base for human existence and the varied ways in which societies with different technologies, economic systems and cultural values have perceived and used that resource base. In so doing, new environments have been created.

It seems obvious therefore that geography is necessary and worth while.

1

After all, it deals with some of the most basic values of all – such as survival and the quality of life. And yet strangely we find that primary school geography had, by the early 1990s, suffered a sustained period of great neglect.

Cinderella subject

Like the curate's egg, geography in primary schools before the introduction of the National Curriculum was good only in parts. The 1978 HMI survey, *Primary Education in England*,[4] found some successful work based on the locality of the school but that insufficient attention was given to the basic skills of the subject: in particular, maps were used only infrequently. In all, much work in geography tended to be superficial and there was little evidence of progression. The survey of first schools four years later[5] was similarly disappointing. The most successful topics observed were those that focused on the home area but 'too many schools' did 'too little' to draw children's attention to the wider world and too often radio and television programmes were used with insufficient preparation and inadequate follow-up. There was a general lack of appreciation of the range of work that could be provided for young children and although potentially imaginative play materials such as models and plans of farms, roads, railways, runways, docks, etc. were present in classrooms there was little appropriate intervention by teachers in order to develop children's spatial concepts through such material.

At about the same time, almost all the geography lessons of a sample of children in primary schools in one particular town (Lichfield) were found to be somewhat limited in their pedagogical scope. Most lessons consisted of an explanation of the lesson topic by the teacher followed by discussion between teacher and children with the pupils then writing up the lesson material in their own words and drawing a picture to illustrate what they had written.[6]

Findings from an HMI national monitoring survey from 1982 to 1986 indicated that 'overall standards of work in geography were very disappointing'[7]. Geography was most frequently taught as topic work in conjunction with other areas of the curriculum and only occasionally as a separate subject, and then mainly to older classes. There was 'a tendency for geography to lose its distinctive contribution' to the curriculum and pupils achieved 'satisfactory or better standards in map work, including the use of atlases and globes, in only a quarter of the schools'. There was 'an almost total absence of a national and world dimension' to the work done and the majority of schools had 'a barely adequate level of resources for geographical work'.

The independent evaluation of Leeds City Council's Primary Needs

Programme[8] provides an illustration of the position of primary geography in one local authority. The City Council sought to transform classroom and curriculum practice by investing in enhanced staffing, school refurbishment, increased capitation and inservice support. The evaluation data illustrated how large amounts of time were devoted to language (about a third of children's time) and mathematics (about a fifth) and only 2 per cent to 'humanities/environmental studies'. The point made here by the evaluation report is not that environmental studies or geography should necessarily have equal time with other subjects but that the quality of the experiences offered should not be subject to such apparent variation. However little time is actually allocated to each of the subjects in school 'each of them should be fully staffed and resourced, carefully planned, seriously treated and delivered in the classroom in a convincing, stimulating and challenging manner'.[9] For 'humanities' or 'environmental studies' in Leeds, there proved to be very little local authority INSET, no specific support programme and a very small share of the Primary Needs Programme development funding. Most work was in the form of topics and there was 'evidence of relatively undemanding work, sometimes used to free the teacher . . . to concentrate on other curriculum areas'.

Why should geography have been in such a poor state in so many schools?[10] At least part of the answer may be found in the prevailing primary teaching ideology of the time, in which primary teaching was principally viewed as a 'child-centred' activity rather than a 'subject-centred' one. Robin Alexander[11] has identified a number of misunderstandings, paradoxes and contradictions resulting from this commitment by many teachers to 'child not subject'.

One problem is the apparent confusion between the notion of a subject as a label by which the work of the school day and week can be divided up and the notion of a subject as a discipline with its inbuilt structure of a progressive sequence of concepts and skills. But this distinction appears to have been applied inconsistently across different parts of the school curriculum.

Prior to the introduction of the National Curriculum in England and Wales there appeared to be two *de facto* curricula in operation in most primary schools – consisting, respectively, of the 'basics' and 'the rest'. Typical of the 'basics' would be mathematics – taught predominantly (notwithstanding the ideology) as a separate subject, in a teacher-directed way, usually with a major timetable allocation and well resourced with highly structured materials stressing the progressive development of knowledge and skills and demonstrating a high level of match between the learning experiences offered and the abilities of the child. Typical of 'the rest' would be geography – rarely referred to by name, usually subsumed within 'topic' or 'project' work in which the learning experiences were more likely to be random or circular and for which few material resources were available.

So, although some subjects (such as mathematics, PE, music and some aspects of English) were taught *as* subjects, others (such as geography, history, art and, until more recently, science) were accorded a much weaker identity within the curriculum and therefore their distinctive conceptual structures were lost.

The 'two-curricula' thesis was acknowledged by Alexander to be an over-simplification of the state of affairs in primary schools. Nevertheless, the evidence for such a fundamental division remains substantial and consistent.[12]

This analysis does not of course do justice to the exceptions. Indeed, in the 1989 report[13] HMI identified more than 50 schools as a result of the illustrative survey referred to above where 'good practice' was observed. Characteristics of such good practice were associated with situations where schools set out to achieve a balance both within and across the subjects that constituted topic work, where good, comprehensive documentation was available for staff in order to achieve a consistency of style and approach in the planning of work and where there was some leadership in the form of a teacher with responsibility for the oversight and co-ordination of topics in school. In the best schools, styles of learning were open and investigative; children proceeded from what they knew to what they did not know; basic concepts and skills were clearly identified by teachers in advance of teaching taking place and specifically incorporated in the work undertaken. The whole enterprise was also supported by a range of quality experiences and resources (such as books, maps, visits, visitors, information technology, broadcasts, etc.) and the outcomes carefully recorded and children's progress monitored.

Primary geography and the National Curriculum

The National Curriculum geography working group[14] believed that geographical education should:

(a) stimulate pupils' interest in their surroundings and in the variety of physical and human conditions on the Earth's surface;

(b) foster their sense of wonder at the beauty of the world around them;

(c) help them to develop an informed concern about the quality of the environment and the future of the human habitat;

(d) thereby enhance their sense of responsibility for the care of the Earth and its peoples.

In order to achieve these aims, the National Curriculum was structured around five Attainment Targets each of which forms the basis of the

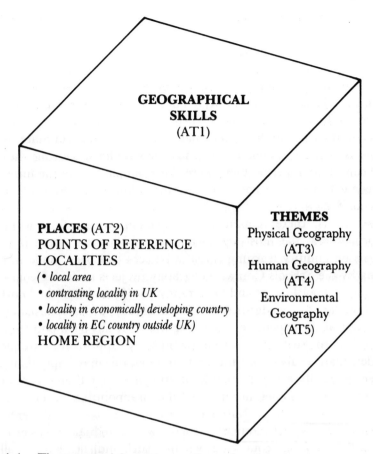

Figure 1.1 . *The structure of the Attainment Targets in primary geography.*

remaining chapters of this book. The Attainment Targets may be represented in the form of three faces of a solid cube, the contents of which would be the National Curriculum in geography (see Figure 1.1).

One dimension of geographical education is *geographical skills* (AT1): the techniques and competencies needed for enquiry, especially the making and interpretation of maps, the use of information technology and carrying out fieldwork. A second dimension is *knowledge and understanding of places* (AT2). This includes both the acquisition of a framework of knowledge about locations which will help pupils set local, national and international events in a geographical context and to develop a 'sense of place' of particular localities of varying types and at particular scales. The third dimension consists of geographical *themes*, specifically physical geography (AT3), human geography (AT4) and environmental geography (AT5). It is through the interplay of themes and places that children learn about the significance of location on human activities and physical processes and understand the relationships between people and their environment.

It is helpful to recognize that, by and large, the proposed National Curriculum for geography received a broad measure of assent from the geography education community. There *were* some significant changes made to the first draft document, incorporated in successive revisions and changed at the eleventh hour personally by the Secretary of State, but what remains is broadly acceptable to most geographers. During the (inadequate) consultation period there were, for example, few of the fundamental disagreements about the nature of the curriculum that were evident among historians.[15]

Nevertheless, there remain some objections to the final form of the statutory orders, the most significant ones being that there is too little emphasis on enquiry learning (great advances had been made in enquiry learning by the Schools Council geography projects such as Geography for the Young School Leaver and Geography 16–19) and that the 'world to be known' of place knowledge is somewhat arbitrary, overemphasizing Britain and Europe at the expense of the wider world. It has been pointed out that command words such as 'describe' or 'identify' appear more frequently in the orders than 'analyse' or 'interpret' and that this may imply that younger children especially are not capable of applying their thinking. Two other interpretations are sometimes made of the disappointing underemphasis on enquiry. One is that if the National Curriculum is to be legally enforceable then you have to specify content in such a way as to make it easier to determine, in the event of a court case, whether such and such has actually been taught – and that is easier to accomplish if the content is fact-orientated rather than process-orientated. The other interpretation is that enquiry approaches encourage children to question the world around them and therefore that politicians have a vested interest in a curriculum which accepts uncritically the existence of a body of facts to be transmitted at school.

The late adjustments made during the development of the National Curriculum led to some inconsistencies in the progression of statements of attainment. In a desperate attempt to reduce what was beginning to look to non-specialist primary school teachers like an impenetrable forest of statements of attainment, many such statements were axed at the last minute and the resulting gaps filled by some reshuffling. At the level of fine detail it becomes difficult in some cases to see how one statement progresses to the next. Why, for example, does 'demonstrate an understanding that most homes are part of a settlement and that settlements vary in size' (AT4 2a) come before 'give reasons why people change their homes' (AT4 3a)?

A further (technical) problem with the statements of attainment as they stand is that to some extent they link attainment to content. Level 5, for example, requires children to have studied a locality in a European Community country outside the UK. This would require an additional investment by primary schools in materials relating to such a locality for those pupils who might proceed to level 5. Children might therefore be prevented from attaining level 5 if their school had not so invested because particular skills have to be demonstrated within the study of a different *place*. In other words, highflyers in the top class of primary school would have to work on different content in order to attain level 5 and this necessarily implies some form at least of separation from the rest of the class. As a result, many feel that there is a strong disincentive for teachers in primary school to aim beyond level 4.

The haste with which the National Curriculum was put together and the way in which it was established, with the core subjects starting first and with little or no collaboration between working groups, has meant that the match between subjects is not always close. 'Weathering', in geography for example, is located at level 5 and in science at level 4. In fact much material that many people believe should properly be regarded as geography was incorporated into the first version of the science statutory orders. The status of physical geography is a particularly sensitive issue. There are strong feelings about the place of physical geography in the subject and at various times it has been thought to be under threat. The boundaries between geography and geology or other sciences are not always clear and the National Curriculum 'border dispute' reflects this.

The National Curriculum programmes of study represent, however, a valuable support for non-specialists. Teaching is, after all, a demanding enough job without having the responsibility for making a balanced selection from the content of subjects with which you are largely unfamiliar. But the support provided in the statutory orders is sometimes deceptive. Bill Marsden has pointed out that the statutory orders had their origins in a working party composed mainly of geography experts whose priority was academic rather than pedagogic and therefore the language that has found its way through to the statutory orders is still largely a technical one reflecting a 'set of *implicit* conceptual frameworks readily grasped by the specialist but opaque to the non-specialist'.[16]

Nevertheless, and despite the reservations pointed out above, the introduction of the National Curriculum must be welcomed if only because the situation beforehand appeared to be so dismal. Some concern still remains for the subject however. Decades of neglect mean that the resource base is low. Money needs to be spent on maps, atlases, visual material of all kinds, books and equipment, and I have attempted to identify some of the most useful resources available in the course of the text. But it is not just the material base of the subject that is weak. There is a very great absence of expertise. There are few well-qualified curriculum leaders for geography in primary schools, although their number is growing.

The global dimension

Of the five 'official' cross-curricular themes (education for economic and industrial understanding, health education, environmental education, citizenship, careers education), one – education for international understanding – is conspicuous by its absence. It is not even prominent in the theme of citizenship of which some think it is a part. This 'global dimension' has been called the 'missing link of the National Curriculum'.[17]

Although the geography working party strongly espoused the notion of geography as being the most suitable vehicle for environmental education, the part of geography in developing international understanding is greatly underplayed. It is important to recognize that education for international understanding is not a *subject* but a reform *movement* which consists of a number of identifiable conceptualizations of sub-movements, each with its own members, associations, literature, conferences, centres, etc. Many of these groups share the same general goals but they operate under different labels and have slightly different priorities.

World Studies, for example, emphasizes the interdependence of peoples and environments. Human and environmental problems are interconnected at a world scale and so world studies stresses the study of cultures and countries different from one's own, the major issues that face different countries and the ways in which our everyday lives are affected by the wider world. The World Studies Project set up by the One World Trust from 1973 to 1980 produced several publications such as the influential *Learning for Change in World Society* (1977). The project was followed by the joint Schools Council/Rowntree Trust project called World Studies 8-13. Two publications from this work are especially valuable for teachers: Fisher, S. and Hicks, D. (1985) *World Studies 8-13: A Teacher's Handbook*, Edinburgh, Oliver & Boyd; and Hicks, D. and Steiner, M. (1989) *Making Global Connections: A World Studies Workbook*, Edinburgh, Oliver & Boyd.

Also of significance in the field of world studies through its courses and publications is the Centre for Global Education at the University of York, which publishes the *World Studies Journal*. Two highly recommended 'global education' books are: Pike, G. and Selby, D. (1988) *Global Teacher, Global Learner*, London, Hodder & Stoughton; and Fountain, S. (1990) *Learning Together: Global Education 4-7*, Cheltenham, Stanley Thornes.

Development Education deals with the conditions of progress and the means to achieve a better quality of life. It had its origins in concern for the

Third World, but the term 'development' has increasingly been broadened from a narrow definition of economic development to one which includes human welfare expressed more comprehensively. Development education has largely been facilitated by a number of resource and information centres which provide speakers, courses, audio-visual aids and publications. The Development Education Centre at Birmingham (see Appendix 2) is especially active. It produces a newsletter, *The Elephant Times*, and set up a primary school project in 1983. A number of publications are based on ideas developed by the project team. Among those that can be recommended are: *Theme Work* (1991), *A Sense of School* (1986), *Hidden Messages* (1986); and a publication in conjunction with the World Wide Fund for Nature: *Where We Live: Exploring Local – Global Issues* (1992).

The Centre for World Development Education (see Appendix 2) aims to stimulate interest and awareness about development both within the education system and amongst the public at large. It plays a co-ordinating role for many non-governmental organizations and distributes publications.

Geography or topics?

The National Curriculum was set up around *subjects*. It need not have been. It could, for example, have been constructed from 'areas of experience' such as social, aesthetic, physical, spiritual, etc.[18] However, although the National Curriculum is defined in terms of subjects, there is nothing to prevent primary schools continuing to teach through topics; indeed the National Curriculum Council made it clear from the outset that this was anticipated, if not expected.

Topic work is usually associated with activity-based, investigative, autonomous learning. It has become associated in many teachers' minds with a way of teaching, stressing 'process' rather than 'content'. For example, the emphasis is on enquiry, using evidence and developing skills of observation and recording. Despite the rhetoric, however, on the basis of HMI survey evidence there appears no doubt that much topic work relating to geography is undemanding and often involves little more than copying from books. Much time is wasted by children on so-called 'collaborative' projects.

Supporters of topic work[19] argue that the division of human experience into subjects is inconsistent with the way children see the world. Children, it is said, should be allowed to construct their own meanings rather than have imposed upon them a received version of conventional wisdom. And yet, the counter-argument runs, education should not just be about the individual building a framework of personal experience and meaning but also about the interface between personal understanding and cultural tradition. Like it or not, several hundred years of human effort have been invested in an enterprise known as geography. It, and its community of scholars, writings, principles, concepts and boundaries, exists and it is part of teachers' responsibility to put children in touch with that way of understanding the world. No matter how the curriculum is organized, children must be able to understand the principles and procedures of each subject and be able to progress from one level of knowledge, understanding and skill to the next.

> If it can be shown that the topic approach allows the pupil both to make acceptable progress within the different subjects of the National Curriculum and to explore the relationships between them, then the case for such an approach is strong on both pedagogical and logistical grounds. If, however, the result is that the differences between subjects are extinguished, then the strategy is indefensible.[20]

This book does not take a definite view about whether geography is best taught through a separate subject approach or through topics. It seems likely that there is much to be gained from a mixture of approaches. Some parts of the geography curriculum could perhaps best be delivered by a 'geography-focused' topic, such as a locality in an economically developing country. In this case the locality chosen sets the framework for the work done and children concentrate on a limited number of Attainment Targets perhaps relating almost exclusively to the needs of the geography programme of study. In another case, a topic on 'transport' could usefully combine Attainment Targets from geography, history and technology. But all this implies a rigorous approach to planning and a whole-school policy rather than teachers choosing their own topics autonomously.

At the time of the introduction of the National Curriculum geography remains vulnerable. Priorities in inservice training are of course necessary but care needs to be taken that each subject is monitored and revisited in schools' development plans or those specific curricular experiences and skills will be lost to children.

Support for teaching geography

A full list of primary geography resources is beyond the scope of this book but reference can be made to a few significant sources of support. The Geographical Association is the principal subject teaching association for geography in England and Wales and has a growing primary membership (approximately 4000 in 1992). The association produces a magazine, *Primary Geographer*, which is closely related to the needs of the National Curriculum, and there is an annual conference at Easter. Admission to the conference is free. There is a specific 'primary day' with workshops, seminars and lectures, and a large exhibition put on by publishers.

The Geographical Association's best-selling handbook to primary geography, *Geographical Work in Primary and Middle Schools*,[21] was edited by David Mills before the advent of the National Curriculum. But that does not render the rich contents obsolete. In order to provide immediate support for non-specialists the Geographical Association has since produced an A4 booklet which shows exactly where guidance needed to implement the National Curriculum can be found in Mills's book.[22] In addition to a guide to each chapter there is a reworked index showing how information in the text can be rapidly accessed in terms of the National Curriculum requirements. There is also a helpful list of up-to-date resources. The guide is equally valuable for subject specialists and not-so-specialists who have responsibility for the development of geography in their schools. It is well worth buying if you have the book it refers to. Other booklets from the Geographical Association include guidance on planning for Key Stages 1 and 2 and planning for children with learning difficulties.

A further national source of expert guidance on geography is the *Geography in the Primary School Curriculum Project* (GIPP) based at the Department of Education, Liverpool University. It has published a number of useful guidesheets on various aspects of planning and implementing the National Curriculum.

The National Curriculum has stimulated a new generation of classroom publications, and a range of atlases and pupil materials is available from the major educational publishers, notably Oxford University Press, Heinemann, Collins-Longman, Ginn, Simon & Schuster, Oliver & Boyd, and Scholastic.

Recently published books for teachers on primary geography include: Bale, J. (1987) *Geography in the Primary School*, London, Routledge & Kegan Paul; and Wiegand, P. (1992) *Places in the Primary School: Knowledge and Understanding of Places at Key Stages 1 and 2*, London, Falmer Press.

The approach in this book

Time flies! I am constantly reminded when I talk with young children that their world is different from my own. Events which have shaped my view of the world – the postwar years, the Vietnam War, the South Atlantic War, the Gulf War – are unknown to them. I grew up in an age of liberalization of social values; they have known only the philosophy and values of Thatcherism. Also, they have grown up at a time when environmental issues are prominent; it is natural for them to 'think green'.

Throughout the text I have tried to assume that children are active learners who come to geography lessons already knowing a great deal about the world. Learning geography involves children not only in adopting new information and ideas but also modifying the knowledge and explanations they have established already. The view that children already have of other countries does matter and teachers have to take account of it. Children already have experience of the world – both direct and indirect – and they use this experience to interpret new experiences. Teachers have a responsibility therefore to establish what the nature of that prior knowledge and experience is, so that it can be built on.

This book is structured around the Attainment Targets for geography. It is hoped that this will make the text rapidly accessible to busy readers, but this approach is somewhat problematic because, as is indicated in the 'cube' diagram in Figure 1.1, the Attainment Targets themselves are closely interrelated. I have referred to work at both Key Stages 1 and 2 under each Attainment Target. I have tried in places to indicate how 'geographical' aims can be met by cross-curricular work. Sometimes this is explicit, sometimes I leave it to the reader to see the connections. The overall approach has been to attempt to identify the *evidence* for what children know and understand and from that to discuss appropriate learning activities for the classroom. However, hard evidence is often extremely limited and much trust has to be placed in what might seem reasonable to assume. There has rarely been serious funding for research in geography education or in children's understanding of geographical concepts. To some extent it is a problem of definition. Some aspects of 'geography' are in fact now much in vogue – such as understanding industry.

Teaching approaches change as new evidence comes to light. For example, it was widely believed about 30 years ago that map reading was generally too difficult for primary school children.[23] Many workers in this field in the last 10 years have, however, reported that very young children (as young as 3 years) can have considerable success using and making maps. It has also been widely believed that the best or only way to proceed in geography is from the local to the distant, from large scale to small scale and from the child's immediate and concrete experiences to more indirect ones. I try to show that this is not necessarily true – that children have indirect experience of distant places, for example very early in life through television, and that it is inappropriate to leave teaching about distant places until they fully understand the more immediate locality.

Throughout I try to stress what children *can* do, rather than what they cannot and how they make sense of the world through their previous experiences. I have also made a special effort to refer to children's literature in the text. This is because I believe that story is a powerful way to extend children's imagination and to connect their 'private geography' with the distinctive mode of enquiry and explanation in the subject.

NOTES AND REFERENCES

1. The 1986 conference of the Australian Geography Teachers' Association adopted the theme of 'teaching geography for a better world' to provide a co-ordinated professional experience for teachers who wanted to explore a socially critical approach to teaching and to develop their insights and skills in this area. The outcomes of that conference are to be found in Fien, J. and Gerber, R. (1988) *Teaching Geography for a Better World*. London: Oliver & Boyd.
2. Department of Education and Science (1990) *Geography for Ages 5 to 16: Proposals of the Secretary of State for Education and Science and the Secretary of State for Wales*. DES and Welsh Office, p. 6.
3. Relph, E. (1976) *Place and Placelessness*. London: Pion, p. 1.
4. Department of Education and Science (1978) *Primary Education in England: A Survey by HM Inspectors of Schools*. London: HMSO. For other evidence as to the nature and extent of geography teaching before the National Curriculum see also Cracknell, J.R. (1976) 'Geography in junior schools.' *Geography*, **61**, 3, 150–6; and Morris, J.W. (1972) 'Geography in junior schools,' *Trends in Education*, **28**, 14–23.
5. Department of Education and Science (1982) *Education 5 to 9: An Illustrative Survey of 80 First Schools in England*. London: HMSO.
6. Williams, T. and Richards, C. (1980) 'What geography do juniors learn? An investigation in Lichfield.' *Teaching Geography*, **6**, 1, 18–20.
7. Her Majesty's Inspectorate (1989) *Aspects of Primary Education: The Teaching and Learning of History and Geography*. London: HMSO.
8. Alexander, R. (1991) *Primary Education in Leeds*. Primary Needs Independent Evaluation Project, University of Leeds.
9. Alexander, 1991, op. cit. p. 46.
10. In this section, and that which follows, I am much indebted to a working paper of the Geography Inset Primary Project (GIPP) by its director, Bill Marsden. It and other excellent briefing and summary papers are available from GIPP, Department of Education, University of Liverpool, 19 Abercromby Square, PO Box 147, Liverpool L69 3BX.
11. Alexander, R.J. (1984) *Primary Teaching*. London: Cassell.
12. See, for example, Department of Education and Science (1978) *Primary Education in England: A Survey by HM Inspectors of Schools*. London: HMSO; and Galton, M., Simon, B. and Croll, P. (1980) *Inside the Primary Classroom*. London: Routledge & Kegan Paul.
13. Her Majesty's Inspectorate (1989), op. cit.
14. Department of Education and Science (1990) *Geography for Ages 5 to 16: Proposals of the Secretary of State for Education and Science and the Secretary of State for Wales*. DES and Welsh Office.
15. Compare, for example, the chapters by Patrick Bailey on geography and Elizabeth Foster on history in Wiegand, P. and Rayner, M. (eds) (1989) *Curriculum Progress 5–16: School Subjects and the National Curriculum Debate*. London, Falmer Press, which illustrate how the respective subject

communities responded to the challenges of the National Curriculum requirements.

16. Marsden, W. E. (1992) *Primary Geography and the National Curriculum*. Working paper of the Geography Inset Primary Project, University of Liverpool, p. 12.
17. For a development of this idea see Marsden, W. E. (1992) *'The one that got away?': Geography and International Understanding in the Primary Phase*, Project Guidesheet of the Geography Inset Primary Project (GIPP), University of Liverpool. See also a fuller exploration of geography and international understanding in Wiegand, P. (1991) *Places in the Primary School: Knowledge and Understanding of Places at Key Stages 1 and 2*. London: Falmer Press.
18. Her Majesty's Inspectorate of Schools (1985) *The Curriculum 5-16*. London: HMSO.
19. For an examination of the role of topic work and a theoretical overview of its aims, see Tann, S. (ed.) (1988) *Developing Topic Work in Primary Schools*. London: Falmer Press.
20. Alexander, R., Rose, J. and Woodhead, C. (1992) *Curriculum Organization and Classroom Practice in Primary Schools: A Discussion Paper*. London: Department of Education and Science, p. 22.
21. Mills, D. (ed.) (1988) *Geographical Work in Primary and Middle Schools*. Sheffield: The Geographical Association.
22. Morgan, W. (1991) *A National Curriculum Guide (for teachers) to 'Geographical Work in Primary and Middle Schools' (Mills, 1988)*. Sheffield: The Geographical Association.
23. See, for example, Satterley, D. J. (1964) 'Skills and concepts in map drawing and map interpretation.' *New Era*, **45**, 260-3.

CHAPTER 2

Geographical Skills

Pupils should demonstrate their ability to use skills to support work for the other attainment targets in geography, and in particular: (i) the use of maps; and (ii) fieldwork techniques. (Attainment Target 1, Department of Education and Science, *Geography in the National Curriculum (England)* HMSO, March 1991, p. 3.)

What skills and competencies are needed in order to be a 'young geographer'? There are of course *general* intellectual and communication skills which are common to many subjects in the curriculum and it is often difficult to separate these from curriculum content for the purposes of assessment. Some of these more general abilities (such as being able to extract relevant information from secondary sources like books, videos and other people's experiences) were included in the early drafts of the National Curriculum for geography. By the time the statutory orders were published, however, the Secretary of State had reduced geographical skills to those involving maps, photographs and fieldwork. In fact, references to fieldwork in the statutory orders remain fairly implicit, probably because any explicit reference would highlight the resource implications. This chapter therefore concentrates on skills in relation to maps and photographs.

What do primary school children need to be able to do in connection with maps?[1] Some suggested objectives are that they should be able to:

(a) find places on a map, using number and letter coordinates (required for AT1, level 3), four-figure coordinates (required for level 4) and six-figure grid references (required for level 5);

(b) understand the idea of direction by using terms such as left and right at first and then the points of the compass;

(c) orientate the map in the real world so that it is 'the right way round' and locate features in the real world represented on the map;

(d) understand that the map is a 'view from above';

(e) be able to interpret the symbols on the map and to realize that the information shown on a map is very selective;

(f) read and interpret the scale of the map so that they know how much of the world is represented on the piece of paper and what sort of distances are involved. They must also be able to measure the straight-line distance between two points on a plan (required for level 4);

15

(g) draw reasonably accurate sketch maps of an area known to them, such as their route to school (AT1, level 3b). They need to remember to give such maps a title (so the reader knows what the map is for and what it shows); a scale (so the reader can understand the area and distance represented on the map); a key (so that the reader can understand the symbols that are used); and a direction sign such as a north pointer (so that the map can be properly orientated).

Graphicacy

The term 'graphicacy' has been given to those forms of communication which use visual–spatial ability[2] to complement the abilities of literacy, numeracy and articulacy. Graphicacy refers to the communication of spatial information which cannot be conveyed adequately by verbal or numerical means *alone*, for example a plan of a town, a picture of a distant place, a block diagram, a drainage pattern; in other words, the whole field of cartography, photography, computer graphics, the graphic arts and much of geography itself. Grouping skills such as these under the umbrella term 'graphicacy' is useful. There is an important message here for primary schools because 'graphicacy is liberally present in young children'[3]. Many children seem to draw pictures and maps spontaneously long before they learn to read or write and so geography may be a way of exploiting skills some young children acquire very early on.

Many maps and plans

As they grow up, children are surrounded by maps and plans, even though they may not recognize them as such. Many road signs, for example, are plans of the junction ahead. There are small plans on kitchen cooker panels to indicate which hotplate is operated by which control. Children see 'You Are Here' maps in shopping malls, town centres and theme parks as well as more conventional maps on television (for example in the weather forecasts) and in newspapers. They use forms of maps and plans in board games such as Monopoly and Cluedo and in computer games.

Maps are, however, not always what they seem. Consider for example Figures 2.1(a) and (b). Both maps are recognizable as Great Britain, but whilst Figure 2.1(a) looks correct, there seems to be something 'wrong' with Figure 2.1(b). To understand more about these two maps it is necessary to know how they were made, and why. Figure 2.1(a) is the 'usual' way of representing the British Isles. Before satellite images were available, a map like this would have been made by triangulation: working from a measured

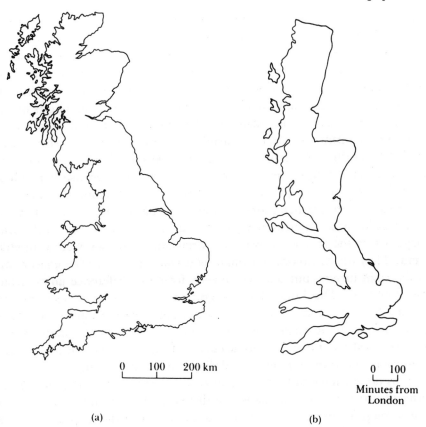

0   100   200 km

0   100

Minutes from
London

(a)   (b)

Figure 2.1   *Great Britain: (a) A conventional map of Britain; (b) A 'topological' map showing Britain as represented by train journey time from London. (From Fitzgerald, B. P. (1974)* Developments in Geographical Method. *Oxford: Oxford University Press, p. 49.)*

straight line surveyors covered the country by a series of triangles. Each triangulation (or 'trig') point marked the corner of a triangle and by sighting from one to the other and using simple trigonometry, the distances between each could be calculated. Each place on the resulting map was therefore accurately located with respect to every other place. The map has a scale whereby 1 centimetre on the map represents so many kilometres on the ground, and this scale holds true for every direction on the map. In other words, the map conforms to our common assumptions about the nature of straight and parallel lines, right angles and circles that form the basis of Euclidean geometry. Such a map can therefore be used with some confidence to find out exactly where places are in relation to each other.

The map in Figure 2.1(b), however, was drawn in a different way and for a different purpose. This cartographer wanted to make a map which

17

would illustrate how accessible different parts of Britain were by train from London. The scale of the map is related not to *distance* in the real world but to *travel time*. The cartographer took from a railway timetable the fastest train times from London to various cities in Britain. Each city was then plotted on its correct compass bearing from London on a scale where 1 centimetre represented so many minutes of train travel. Once the fixed points of, say, 20 cities were marked, the coastline was filled in by eye. The map is useful because it reminds us that in a shrinking world, some parts shrink more rapidly than others. A map like this might give some insight into the views of Scottish or Welsh (or even Cornish) nationalists, because it highlights the remoteness of those parts of Great Britain from London. Distance is in fact often measured much more effectively for day-to-day purposes by time or cost than by kilometres. Maps like this are called 'topological' maps. They look as though they have been stretched, as if they were printed on Lycra. They are 'correct', but only, as it were, in one sense. Places come 'in the right order', but only when seen from one reference point (in this case, London). The London Underground map is another example of a 'topological' map. The stations are in the 'right order' and spaced accurately as you follow along each line but distances shown on the map between stations on different lines are not accurate. Their true relationship has been distorted to make the Underground diagram easier to read.

Maps do not have to be transformed in order to show distortion. Many perfectly ordinary-looking maps are distorted, biased, misleading or just plain wrong.[4] Consider, for example, a series of pictorial maps like the ones available in postcard form for many parts of the country. These are usually available for whole counties or tourist regions (such as the 'West Country') or for national parks. There are also many map postcards of historic tourist-orientated towns such as Stratford-upon-Avon or Oxford. The postcards take the form of small (often water-coloured) maps on which are superimposed small pictures showing scenes or activities in the appropriate locations. Beware though, because these pictures place a great deal of emphasis in their selection of images on features that are historic and picturesque. The pictures show few of the factories, houses, motorways or warehouses that make up much of the real world and emphasize instead a tourist world rather than the 'lived-in' world that would perhaps be more readily recognized by the people who live and work there.

Map making is a subjective process. The cartographer has to decide what features of the real world to include on the map and what features to omit. In the case of the pictorial map postcards, the selection is on the basis of the various locations the postcard buyer might have visited on holiday. There's an advertising function too in that the postcards are serving as promotional material for the tourist attractions shown. The map readers or users determine to a large extent the content. When the bias is in the form of pictures and when the map readership can be clearly identified, the bias is easy to detect. Yet non-pictorial maps for general use can be biased too, in the selection of what is mapped and what is not.

The Ordnance Survey maps of Great Britain are among the best maps of their kind in the world, yet even they are not value-free. They include much 'middle-brow' cultural information about the landscape but omit other features. Historic sites, for example, are shown but not supermarkets. Scant detail is shown in Ministry of Defence property. Some forms of land ownership and management are shown (such as National Trust and Forestry Commission) but not others. All this may be entirely appropriate but the point is that a choice has been made on behalf of the map user.

This implies that children too must be aware of what maps show and what they do not. Maps have necessarily to offer a selective and incomplete view of reality. There is insufficient space to show everything. But teachers and children have to be able to develop a healthy scepticism about maps. Whereas pictures and words are able to reveal their biases more transparently, maps are rather like statistics: they *appear* to be more accurate than they may be. Good starting questions in mapwork therefore are: 'What does this map show?', 'How does it show it?', and (the critical question) 'What does this map *not* show?'

Using maps

'Everyone needs to be able to read and interpret maps.'[5]

But what does 'reading and interpreting maps' mean? It could mean at least three things.[6] Firstly, simply to find out where places are in relation to each other. You might use a map like this in order to understand the meaning of a TV news bulletin. It is difficult to make sense, for example, of the Middle East or Balkan conflicts without reference to a map. This use of maps for locational information is highlighted in the National Curriculum for geography in Attainment Target 2: locational knowledge. A second type of map reading and interpreting is to use a map to find your way. This is perhaps the most common form of map use in adult life and yet wayfinding has generally been neglected in school in favour of more abstract classroom-based mapwork. Nevertheless, this form of map using does appear in the National Curriculum (see AT1 2c). A third type of map reading and interpreting is using a map to solve problems. Looking at spatial associations on the map may give clues to what causes problems and suggest solutions. For example, why are some places more likely to suffer from flooding than others?

Each of these three uses of maps implies different yet interrelated skills.

To obtain information from a map you need to understand its symbols and conventions; to be able to navigate with a map, you need to be able to orientate the map to your surroundings; to solve problems you need to be able to identify patterns and to group information. Some of these skills are complex, but even very young children are able to do some of them, especially if the context in which tasks are presented is meaningful to them.

Children at the age of about 3 years will, for example, in free play, use blocks to represent houses and other buildings and assemble these into an imaginary large-scale environment such as a village or part of a town.[7] They are able to understand that the blocks stand for houses, shops and so on, as well as to solve simple problems such as finding short cuts from one part of the village to another, perhaps using toy cars to make representations of journeys. They can also make up stories about the people who live in the village or town, the work they do and the journeys they make, then recreate these using a map of the townscape they have constructed.

Children also appear to be able to recognize the more formal conventions of maps. When shown a map representing a possible urban environment and consisting of standard symbols representing roads, houses, churches, a river, etc., a group of children of ages 4–6 who had not previously had any formal training with maps appeared to be able to name the common conventional symbols that were shown – and yet the map itself had no key![8] The implications are that children do spontaneously understand the complexity of map 'pictures' if they are of places that they have some experience of (such as the urban environment).

It may be worth considering briefly what happens when children 'read' maps. Four processes are thought to be involved. However, these four activities are not necessarily distinct, neither do they necessarily happen in the following order.[9] At the simplest level the child must *detect* what symbols are on the map. This means that they have to be large or clear enough in order for them to be detectable. Light symbols on a dark background are more easily detected than dark symbols on the same background. It's hard to see a blue line (a river?) on a green background (an area of woodland?). Detection problems may also arise in the way that a map is scanned by the reader. The overall pattern of shape and colour on a map seems to influence the scanning strategy adopted for perception of detail. Visual acuity of the reader is also significant. If the map is used in poor light some small symbols may not be seen at all. Most maps are designed to be read at the same distance from the eye as a book and so maps displayed on the classroom wall may well be too distant for children to see the symbols clearly enough. Don't forget that in this situation the teacher's eye level may be much nearer the map than the children's.

Next, the child must *discriminate* between one symbol and another: for example a solid line and a pecked line, a large dot and a medium-sized dot. In order to discriminate between symbols children have to make judgements about their relative sizes and colours. Young children will probably find discrimination more difficult between two symbols which are close together in size than two which are more obviously different. There do not need to be too many variations in line thickness or dot size on maps for young users. More sophisticated symbols, such as proportional circles (often used to show population), are very difficult to differentiate between.

The next stage is that the various map symbols must then be *identified*: i.e. they must be matched to the legend (or key) so that they come to have meaning. If the legend contains all the symbols on the map then, theoretically, identification is a straightforward process. But this assumes that the image of, say, 'town' or 'national park' in the child's mind corresponds with the image in the mind of the map maker. Terms such as 'national park', for example, are quite misleading. Not only is the land not nationalized or owned by the state, the landscape does not look 'park-like'. Teachers therefore need a good deal of visual material in the form of pictures and videotape to ensure that children have a clear idea of what the phenomena represented on the map are like in real life. Some children's maps have pictures in the key to help make a stronger link between the symbols used and reality.

Children may, however, have some difficulties in using the key. Part of the process of identifying a symbol is recognizing it in its geographical context, and the symbols shown in the legend are not related to each other in a meaningful way; they are just arranged as a vertical or horizontal line of symbols and explanations. The key will typically show a short strip of blue line which is identified as a river. Another strip of black line is identified as a railway. But our identification of blue lines and black lines *on the map* depends as much on our expectation of where they are (e.g. rivers are found in valleys) and the way they bend (rivers tend to be wiggly whereas railways form smooth curves) as by reference to the key. The young children referred to above who had never previously used maps were able to recognize features on the map through their geographical context; they 'saw' patterns (for example of streets) and were therefore able to identify them as such.

All the information on the map needs to be processed in order to deal effectively with a map-using task. This is map *interpretation*. Interpretation involves calling on the child's prior knowledge and conceptual grasp of the phenomena shown on the map. Interpretation also depends on understanding the limitations of the map: what it shows and *what it doesn't show*. All maps are selective and make generalizations. Even plans, such as the Ordnance Survey 1:1250 plan, do not show everything. Much less is shown on the 1:50 000 map and far less still on atlas maps. There is a little evidence to suggest that children understand this principle but weakly, often believing that if it is not shown on the map then it doesn't exist.

We don't really understand enough about the skills needed to use and interpret maps or how those skills are acquired, and this lack has hindered the development of effective map-reading programmes in school. Nevertheless, some research is instructive and what follows in this chapter is an attempt to break down map reading and interpretation into a number of separate domains, accepting that the definition of some of these is still somewhat problematic.

The 'maps in children's heads'

Figure 2.2 shows some maps that were drawn by three children to represent their journeys to school. Maps such as these are often called 'cognitive maps'. But this term is rather problematic. It tends to imply, for example, that we all carry around maps in our heads, as a sort of mental atlas, and it is by no means certain that people all store information about places in this way. The term also tends to focus attention on the cartographic representation of place and neglects other important information that we have about places, such as feelings and associations. There is also a danger that children's efforts at representing their knowledge of places in this way will be compared with Ordnance Survey types of maps, whereas, as was shown earlier in this chapter, there are many ways of representing space in map form. It is also not at all clear to what extent knowledge or understanding of spatial relationships is related to ability to represent those relationships on paper.

Emma is 5 years old. The 'map' (Figure 2.2(a)) of her journey from home to school shows (in addition to a picture of herself) her house, the school and the road between the two. Home and school are shown iconically (as pictures) rather than in plan form and there is a certain amount of convention in her drawing of them. Her own house, for example, does not have a chimney, neither does the school. School (the building on the right) is bigger than home and has double doors, but apart from that bears little relation to the appearance of the real building. Emma's route is shown by a simple line. This is the simplest form of topological representation: home and school are 'joined' – like stations on an Underground map – but there is no representation of distance, direction, scale or orientation.

Paul is 9. His map (Figure 2.2(b)) is more complex. It shows his house (also with a smoking chimney), the homes of two friends (Steven and Tim) with whom he goes to school each day, a few familiar landmarks (the Kwik Save shop, the Caddie shop, the park and the farm) and the school itself.

Figure 2.2(a) *My journey to school, by Emma (age 5).*

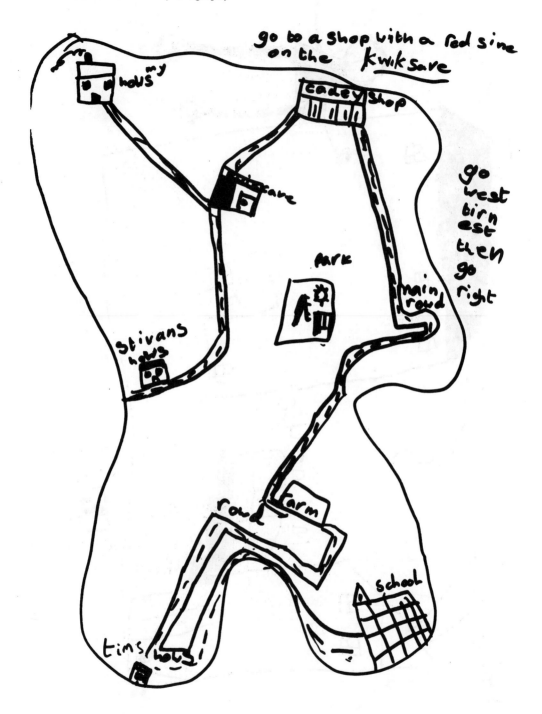

Figure 2.2(b) *My journey to school, by Paul (age 9).*

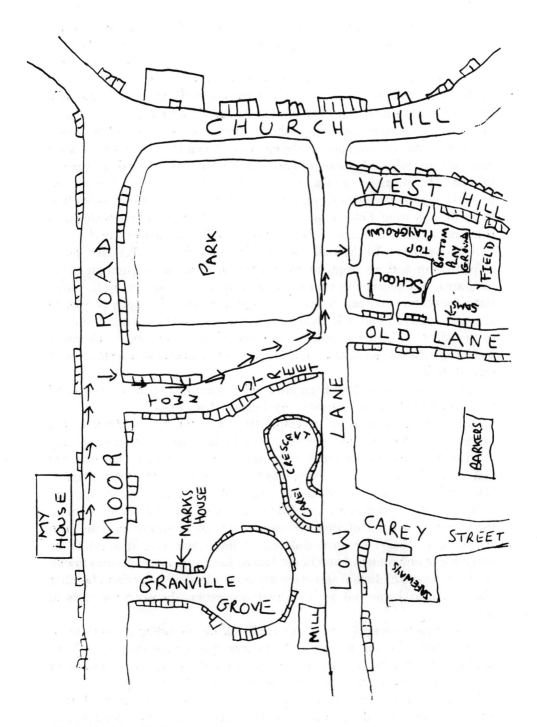

Figure 2.2(c) *My journey to school, by Anthony (age 11).*

Paul meets Steven under the red sign at the Kwik Save. They go past the Caddie shop, pass the park on the right and the farm on the left. They call at Tim's house before continuing the remainder of the journey. Paul has shown the road he takes in plan form (note the white lines in the middle of the road) but the houses are still picture-like. Considerable attention has been paid to direction. The landmarks are shown correctly (insofar as the park *is* on the right-hand side of the road between the shops and the farm). However, with the exception of the entry of Steven from the right at Kwik Save, we are really only aware of Paul's journey as along a winding corridor of road. The places on the way come in the correct order but they are not properly represented with respect to each other. Neither do we know how to get directly from Tim's house to Steven's. Note also that the whole map is bounded by a single line; this is the edge of Paul's 'known world'.

Anthony is 11. All the buildings on his map (Figure 2.2(c)) are shown in plan form and we begin to see a fairly accurate representation of his local area. The journey to school is clearly marked but so too are the other interconnections between roads. The houses of several friends as well as shops are marked and it is clear how a journey could be made from one to the other. Anthony is able to talk about alternative routes to school including a detour via Mark's house. Direction, distance and scale are well represented.

Maps such as these have been interpreted according to the concepts and terms used by the developmental psychologist Jean Piaget.[10]

In the *topological* stage of development (up to the age of about 7, i.e. including Emma) children are supposed to be able to understand only relative relationships between places in qualitative terms – for example that some places are 'near' each other whereas others are further apart. Children's understanding of spatial relationships at this stage is supposed to be *egocentric*; that is, they can only conceive of the spatial environment from their own point of view. Houses could not be drawn in plan form according to Piaget because children at this stage were thought to be incapable of imagining what a house looked like from above. Routes drawn on the maps of children at this stage are shown leading away from familiar places such as home but with no real connections between the ends of the routes.

In the *projective* stage (from about age 7–10, i.e. including Paul) children are supposed to be able to project themselves into another viewpoint. They can begin to imagine a route in their minds and recreate it on a piece of paper so that rights and lefts appear with reasonable accuracy.

In the *Euclidean* stage, supposedly reached at about the age of 10 (i.e. including Anthony), the relationships of objects in space are structured in the mind as though they were placed on a grid of horizontal and vertical lines – each object placed more or less in its correct vertical and horizontal position relative to the others. Size proportion and distance are shown accurately on their maps.

Unfortunately, although this sequence of development has now been fairly firmly established in books and articles on primary geography teaching, there is no agreement among psychologists that children do in fact pass through such stages. The basis for this analysis of children's maps must be seen therefore in the wider context of the critique of Piaget's work as a whole. Piaget saw children's thinking as essentially different from that of adults. A more modern view is that it is essentially the same but that children have not yet had enough practice to do it as well as adults. The distinction appears subtle but is important because the indirect effect of Piaget's work has been the widespread belief that young children are not yet 'ready' for mapwork, whereas a growing body of evidence suggests that in the right circumstances even very young children can have success with map skills.

Using maps for wayfinding

One of the prime functions of maps is to help you find your way. This is a major life skill. Most maps bought by the public are for this purpose and this is what children have primarily seen maps being used for in the real world. Parents will have been seen consulting a road map in the car or using a map to select somewhere to stop for a picnic on a family walk. Or they may have looked at a street map to find the address of a friend. Children may in fact have seen several sources of information used together: Yellow Pages and a street map to locate a shop, or the AA book for garage information followed by the road atlas. Schools, however, have traditionally not concentrated on such practical day-to-day purposes.

Using maps is not easy. Adults don't do it well. A number of studies indicate that when having to rely on map information adults have considerable difficulty in planning simple journeys or locating places. Many adults apparently find their way much more successfully with verbal instructions ('Second on the left, turn right at the pub', etc.) than they do if equipped with a map of the route.[11] Even primary school teachers are not very good at using maps![12]

However, the skills of using maps to find the way *can* be taught and can be taught to very young children. A key factor is being able to orientate the map to the environment it represents (see Figure 2.3). Not understanding this fairly elementary point seems to cause many difficulties with adult map users. (Adults generally assume that 'You Are Here' maps are correctly orientated, but this is not always the case and substantial errors have been found in map usage when 'You Are Here' maps have been

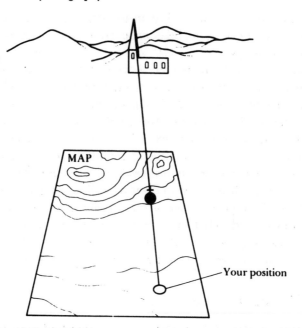

Figure 2.3 *Orienting a map.*

unsympathetically located with reference to the surroundings that they show.[13]

Most studies with very young children cannot use the real world and have therefore been restricted to maps of classrooms or playgrounds. As a result we don't know much about how children actually relate the real world to the piece of paper.

Even very young children (aged 3–5) can use simple maps to find an object in a room. An American investigation into young children's map-reading skills is worth describing because of the insights it gives into the nature of map reading and the ability of young children to do it.[14] Some 3–5-year-olds were asked to find a toy in a room with a map that showed where the toy was. Children were shown a room which was laid out with boxes and shapes of different colours. They had to find a small toy elephant, the position of which was marked on a map that showed the layout of the room using the same shapes and colours as the furniture in the room. In order to find the toy the children had to go through two, possibly separate, mental processes: firstly, the recognition that the symbols on the map stood for real, three-dimensional objects in the room; secondly, the ability to project the map onto the space it represented. This includes recognizing that the map and the room may not initially be aligned to each other and that the map may have to be orientated before the search for the toy can begin. Sixty children were involved in the experiment. None of the children involved had difficulty with the idea that the map and its symbols represented the room, the furniture and the toy. Younger children, however, were able to find the toy only when the map was given to them correctly aligned to the room, whereas the 5-year-olds were able to realign the map when it was given to them incorrectly aligned and then they were able to find the toy. Clearly this is very different from using a map to find your way in a real outdoor environment but it does give some pointers to useful map-using activities in class. Aligning the map is obviously an important step in the learning process. It is possible to imagine a similar teacher-made map game in which the children have to find an object in the classroom. The game is made more difficult when the map has fewer 'landmarks'. This in fact is closer to the real outdoor situation, as small-scale maps have far less information on them than large-scale maps.[15]

Can very young children (e.g. 4–6-year-olds) use a map to follow a route? It seems they can, although there have been very few studies in this area. This is especially so under conditions approaching those in which maps are generally used: i.e. to get to somewhere you can't see at the beginning of the 'journey'. Blades and Spencer[16] extended the American investigation referred to above into the outdoor environment by setting up a maze on a playground. Screens prevented children from seeing all the maze at once as well as the location of the 'roadblocks' which barred the way in parts of the maze. This actually is a realistic situation because when you are travelling through an area you see only part of it, whereas the map shows the whole area. The children were asked to find their way through the maze using a map and all but the very youngest (4 years) were able to do so, even though they had had no previous experience of maps. They were even more successful when 'landmarks' in the form of coloured buckets were placed at each of the junctions and marked in the corresponding colours on their maps. But what does 'no previous experience' of maps mean? Blades and Spencer suggest that as all the children in their experiment were able to follow the required route with their fingers on the map they may well be transferring their experience with board games to the map situation. The few children who couldn't navigate the maze were presumably unable to relate the map to the real environment or didn't understand that the map could help them.

Older children will want to learn to find their way using the common 'A–Z' or 'Geographia' type of street maps. These are particularly difficult for children to interpret and they need to be taught how to read them. There are a number of reasons for their complexity. The typeface is often very small in order to show a great deal of detail in a small area. The maps also use many abbreviations (such as Ave., Rd., St., Cresc., Mt., Bldgs., Gdns.,

Clo., La., Gro., Dri., Sq., Pl., etc.) and some of them may be inconsistent (such as Terr. and Tce.).

Many placenames are unfamiliar to children and popular British locality and street names are often difficult to read, spell and to pronounce (such as Grosvenor, Blenheim, Beaumont, Beaulieu, Berkeley, Wellesley, Vauxhall, Ranelagh, Montpelier, Marlborough, etc.). The orientation of streets on the map is such that lettering is rarely aligned horizontally, to be read from left to right. This means frequent movements of either the map or the head in order to read the street names. The lettering of each street is also frequently cut through with the labelling of the streets that cross it. The labelling of short streets may be tightly squashed together whereas that for long streets may be widely spaced. The small format of many books of street maps also causes problems of moving from one page to another. This is not at all to criticize the presentation of street maps of this type; they are excellent in many ways. It is simply that the very useful skill of being able to read such a map can pose learning difficulties for children and that teaching needs to take account of these likely difficulties.

Road atlas maps can pose similar challenges. One useful skill to practise with these maps is that of being able to read distances from the map. These are often shown in the form of numbers printed in between 'lollipops' marked at towns or significant junctions. This arrangement can be sometimes quite complex, with two or three levels of distances shown with the size of the numbers matching different-sized 'lollipops'.

A hierarchy of map skills

Although a number of writers have advocated different ways of teaching children about maps, there has been very little independent evaluation of the various approaches recommended, neither is there much agreement about the order in which aspects of map reading might best be presented. Nevertheless, the generally expressed view in contemporary map-reading literature is that children are able to develop map-reading and map-using skills much earlier than was previously acknowledged.

The National Curriculum documentation in its final version is less helpful on map skills than it might be. Although having more statements of attainment, earlier drafts were more supportive for the non-specialist teacher in that they provided more information. The points of the compass, for example (essential for map reading), were previously included but ended up being omitted from the statutory orders. Here is how they appeared in earlier drafts:

level 2: use north, south, east and west as directions[17]
level 3: use eight points of the compass[17]
level 5: use sixteen points of the compass[18]

Other aspects of map reading that were omitted at a later date include being able to use latitude and longitude to locate places on atlas maps (formerly at level 5) and being able to find the height of the ground from a layer tinted map using a simple key (formerly at level 4).

It is common to break down the complex skill of reading and using a map into a number of discrete elements, such as understanding scale, symbols, distance, etc., but there are some problems inherent in this approach. Lessons on maps have to synthesize all these separate elements because they are all needed at the same time, just as driving lessons have to deal with steering, accelerating, looking in the mirror and indicating rather than devoting a lesson to each of these in turn. Nevertheless, it *is* helpful to examine each element in order to consider progression in teaching and learning. Elements involved in map reading and interpreting are therefore grouped below under the following headings: perspective; symbols; location; direction; and scale and distance.[19]

Atlas maps will be dealt with separately because they have some special features that make learning about them distinctive.

UNDERSTANDING PERSPECTIVE

An important map skill is being able to look at something from a different perspective or viewpoint to your own. This skill is important in map using because maps are essentially a 'bird's eye view' which may be an unfamiliar perspective for the map user on the ground. It used to be thought that children had great difficulty in using maps precisely because they were constructed from an unfamiliar overhead viewpoint. This belief partly stemmed from Piaget's influential 'three mountain' experiment.[20] Children were confronted with a table top model of three mountains, each topped by a different feature (a cross, house, etc.), and were then asked to describe the model from the point of view of someone on the other side of the table. Very young children (i.e. before the age of about 7) frequently described their *own* view, rather than that of a person opposite, and this led Piaget to conclude that children could not 'decentre' or adopt a viewpoint that was not their own. Children were said to be 'egocentric': their own view is the only one they can understand. By extension, Piaget concluded that very young children would have difficulty understanding maps, because maps take the form of a 'view from above' which was thought to be an unfamiliar viewpoint for a child.

This work has had a number of important consequences. Few teachers have in recent years undertaken map work with children younger than age 7, in the mistaken belief that they are incapable of using or understanding maps, and few researchers have investigated young children's abilities with maps, under the impression that maps were too difficult.

However, it is now generally agreed that children are not so limited by their own viewpoint as Piaget suggested. The 'view from above' is nowadays much more familiar to children. Like ancient peoples, children are fascinated by flight – that's why so many children's heroes (from Peter Pan to Superman) can do it. Children have much experience of aerial views both directly and indirectly. Piaget's work was conducted before there was a television in every home. Many computer games involve flying in some form or another and offer the possibility of seeing the ground (often, unfortunately, in the form of a target) from above. Children may also have (limited) experience of their own holiday flights.

There have also been a number of studies which show that tests like the 'three mountains' experiment produce different results if the nature of the model is changed. More familiar content (such as shops or houses instead of mountains) and the opportunity to rotate the model often mean that even very young children are able to adopt the viewpoint of another observer.[21] Others have shown that the relationship between the child and the experimenter, the expectations that the child has of the experimenter's questions and the answers required can all influence the result. Even 3-year-olds appear to be able to adopt someone else's perspective. If photographs are used, for example, success may depend at least partly on being able to deal with the symbolism of the photograph itself. The success children have with this sort of test seems to depend crucially upon the materials used. The task is more difficult if the materials used are abstract or unrelated to children's interests.

Many schemes of work and books about maps start by introducing children to the 'view from above'. This is often in the form of a picture puzzle: 'What can you see in this drawing?' People with large (e.g. Mexican-style) hats often feature prominently in these puzzles because much of the activity can be concealed by the circle representing the hat. Close observational work also features in the development of understanding perspective. Children might be asked to compare the same (familiar) object seen from the side and seen from above. The aim is to notice how the shape changes from each different perspective. A tin of baked beans, for example, is circular when seen from the top but rectangular when seen from the side. There are obvious links in activities such as these with maths Attainment Targets 10 and 11: shape and space. Template 'silhouettes' for storing tools, musical instruments, cooking utensils, etc. in the classroom can provide excellent practice for very young children in identifying objects from their plan shape, and life-size drawing around familiar objects can form the basis for quizzes. The outlines of these objects (such as kitchen utensils, maths apparatus, etc.) can be coloured in according to a legend based on, say, the use of the objects or their height above the table top. Quizzes can also be devised using an overhead projector. Small toys, pencils, solid geometric shapes, etc. are placed on the projector to cast their plan shape on the screen.[22] (But note that it is important for the screen to be properly angled to avoid the distorting 'keystone' effect.)

As part of a project on the weather a class of 5-year-olds talked about appropriate footwear for rainy days and went on to draw the patterns on the soles of their shoes and to test different tread patterns for their grip in the wet. This led to drawing their shoes as seen from above – in other words making a 'map' of their shoes.

Play mats in the form of maps are often also used as a basis for imaginative play. These have road layouts with pictures of landscape features. The mats themselves vary significantly in quality; compare those available from the catalogues of educational equipment suppliers. Farm scenes are popular but there are some good materials available in the form of urban and industrial landscapes which may be more familiar to children. Some of these materials are more map-like than others in that all the features are shown in plan form. It's not too problematic if there is a mixture of plan and elevation on one mat as children generally seem tolerant of inconsistency, but some designs can be confusing. Mats like these might be used:

- to establish recognition of the features represented ('Show me the garage; show me a T-junction');
- to make up stories about the people who live and work in the area shown on the mat;
- to describe journeys made by these people using model cars ('This is the way X goes to work, she turns left here and right here . . .');
- to describe alternative routes, short cuts, etc. and compare lengths of journey.

Note also the learning of scale that takes place at the same time during this sort of work. Children will be aware of the size of model cars and trucks that 'go' (i.e. 'match') with each of these mats.

Lego and Duplo materials are also useful for developing aerial perspective, particularly those where a small scene is constructed on a base plate. Instructions with such kits often include a 'map' of each stage of the assembly as well as the finished scene. Children in nursery classes often assemble roadways or railways from commercially produced materials in the form of wooden or plastic panels. However, their layouts are often linear and they seem to have difficulty in completing circuits with the construction materials.[23] One way of helping children to develop building skills and a sense of perspective is for the teacher to photograph successfully built circuits so that they can be recreated on other occasions or copied by other children. It also seems better for children at first to have a limited selection of pieces. Too many curves of different radii can lead to frustration in not being able to complete a satisfactory circuit.

Commercially produced road layouts are not necessary to develop these sorts of understanding. Children are able to learn much about the development and control of three-dimensional space and its representation in two dimensions through blockplay.[24] Use large sheets of kitchen or wall lining paper and wooden blocks to create a 'village' or part of an urban area. Old white bedsheets are an alternative to paper. Different-coloured blocks represent houses, flats, shops, school, cinema, etc. These are arranged in 'streets', and cars and other models can be used for imaginative play. Then pose the problem: 'We have to tidy away now. How will we be able to set up the village again later so that we know where everything goes?' Draw around the blocks! The drawing can be used at first to reconstruct the layout on another occasion and then later to replace the blocks themselves. The model has now become a map. The outline shapes can be coloured to represent different land uses.

The sand table offers many opportunities for the development of perspective and mapping skills. Village layouts can be created with sand and building bricks. The entire sand table can then be covered with rigid transparent plastic sheeting (of the sort sold in DIY shops as a substitute for glass). The model layout can be recorded on the sheeting by looking down from above and using felt-tip markers of different colours. This procedure allows children to construct their own maps directly from a three-dimensional representation.

A more dynamic aspect to map making is introduced in mapping the journeys of 'minibeasts' across a white piece of paper. The animal is followed by a pencil (at a discreet distance) and the journeys of different insects compared.

Children's own plans of their desk or table top or the classroom or their bedroom have been popular learning activities over the years. Photographs from *Home and Garden* types of magazine can be used as the basis for workcards for drawing plan views. Magazines like these have lots of interior and exterior pictures which are suitable. Many of them feature 'ideal' teenagers' bedrooms with computer stations and music centres which add some motivation to the activity. Try also the brochures from companies that offer fitted kitchens and bedrooms. Some of these include pages with squared paper for your own kitchen planning and give the details of standard measurements of kitchen appliances. There are obvious links here with technology. Car manufacturers' brochures also usually have plan views of the cars advertised, together with their technical specifications. The free travel magazines provided by airlines and ferry companies also often have pictures in plan view of the aeroplanes and ships.

It is useful to engage children in a discussion of the arrangement and layout of their own classroom. Does the teacher always talk from the same point in the room? Does this mean that some children always have to swivel round in their seats? Many modern classrooms are arranged with children facing in different directions and yet the teacher may often make use of a chalkboard which is poorly placed for some children's viewpoint. Teachers might find such a discussion with the children on their own pedagogy useful – and revealing.

Children can also locate services (power points, radiators, lights) on a classroom plan. Are these in the best places? Where could extra power points usefully be fitted? Compare this classroom plan with the plan of another classroom. Consider the fire evacuation plan for the school. Which are the nearest exit points? What is the pattern of pedestrian traffic flows around the school? Which are the most congested points and when? Are there possible alternative routes? How could the younger children move around the school more safely?

Helping children to see the school as a whole from an aerial perspective presents something of a challenge. A model of the school is an ambitious project but one worth undertaking. Some schools have persuaded a talented parent or grandparent to build such a model. Some schools are also located near to high ground or high-rise buildings from which a view of the school can be seen or photographs taken.

SYMBOLS

Symbols stand for something. One symbol may stand for a number of quite different instances of the feature that is represented. The Youth Hostel Association symbol, for example, is displayed outside city centre youth hostels or simple mountain facilities. Similarly, a red dot on an Ordnance Survey map represents a station whether it's Clapham Junction or that place in Wales with the long name. In this way, some symbols can be misleading. Highest points are often represented by a triangular 'peak' symbol on maps even when the highest point itself is not at all peak like.

Symbols can be points (a cross to represent a church), lines (a black line to represent a railway line) or patches (a block of green to represent woodland). All three together on a map can merge into a complex pattern which creates a lot of 'noise' and makes the map hard to interpret. Maps can also exhibit the 'figure-ground' optical illusion whereby it is difficult to see which is the land and which is the sea, in the same way as the optical puzzle which is at one moment two faces looking at each other and the next a candlestick. Colours on maps are symbols too and can have a range of different meanings. Some colours simply differentiate between one area on the map and another. A map showing countries is like this – the colours simply show where one country stops and another begins. The colours in themselves on this sort of map have no other meaning. They are chosen and arranged so the map looks pleasant to read and, because the selection of colour is arbitrary, there is no need for a key. A map showing types of environment is different. Each environment (desert, cold forest, hot forest, etc.) is represented by a colour named and listed in a legend. Yellow represents desert on the map. Everywhere that is shown yellow is desert and therefore yellow cannot be used for any other phenomenon on the map. Other colours are used in yet another way. On some maps the colours mean 'more' of an attribute than others. Land height colours are like this. The patch of brown on the map means that the land is higher than that shown in green. The key to these maps usually shows colours arranged in blocks with a numerical scale up the side. Note that the numbers may rise evenly or not. It's quite common, for example, for land height tints on maps of the British Isles to have the following, uneven, range:

> more than 1000 metres
> 500–1000 metres
> 200–500 metres
> 100–200 metres
> less than 100 metres

This is done to bring out relief features which would be lost if the categories rose evenly in blocks of 200 metres. The North and South Downs, the Weald and the Chilterns would barely be seen if the first 'break' was at 200 m as only small parts of those areas rise above that height.

Point symbols tend to be of varying difficulty depending on whether they are iconic (picture-like) or conventional (more abstract); there is no clear distinction between the two. Picture symbols are generally easier to understand; a forest may be represented by a number of little drawings of trees or a public telephone may be represented by a picture of a telephone receiver. But a circle, cross or line is purely conventional and in order to be correctly interpreted needs a key. Nevertheless, it is important to establish early on that pictorial symbols are generalized representations of the phenomena, not accurate pictures of them. The telephone receiver symbols stands for a telephone – whether it's in an old-style red box or a modern grey one.

What sorts of understanding do children have of map symbols? Little work has been done in this area but 4–6-year-olds have shown a very high (up to 100 per cent) recognition rate of symbols such as those for parks, roads and rivers without needing to refer to a key.[25]

One starting point for classroom work on map symbols is to compare types of representation. The classroom is full of real boys and girls. Here are some things that stand for real children: dolls, photographs, drawings and symbols (like those used on lavatory doors). Children sort these into different types of representation and discuss the similarities and differences between them. Another popular early starting point is the recognition of common symbols (such as red or green lights, the pound sign, a smiling face, advertising logos, etc.) and discussion of their meaning. Once children know that symbols stand for things in the real world, there are two targets: for them to make their own maps with their own symbols, and to be able to recognize some of the standard symbols used by the Ordnance Survey. To establish the point early on that colours are symbols, children can colour on a plan of the school how the various parts are used: e.g. classrooms, offices, kitchen and play areas. Each type of area is coloured separately, so a key is needed to the plan. When two maps of the same area are compared it becomes apparent that the same phenomena can be represented in different ways. 'Susan has coloured the classrooms green whereas Judy has coloured them yellow. We can understand each map, though, because they have each provided a key to their maps.' However, it would make life difficult if every Ordnance Survey map were to use different symbols, so the same ones are used on each map.

Representations of the shape of the surface of the land are symbols. Children are required to interpret relief maps at level 5. They have to be able to read spot heights and identify hilltops and valley bottoms from contour maps. Experienced map readers are able to use the pattern of contours to form a clear image of the landscape, but reading contour patterns is a complex process. It involves visualizing the 3D landscape from a 2D map.

There may be at least three steps involved in this process.[26] First you have to spot the pattern of lines: whether they are close together or widely spaced or make circles or nesting V-shapes. Then you have to visualize the slope *across* the lines rather than following the shape of the lines themselves. In this way you can distinguish between steep and gentle slopes, convex and concave ones and between valleys and spurs. Lastly you have to be able to link small chunks of contour pattern together so that you can visualize a whole landscape such as a plateau or undulating hills.

There are many misconceptions at the age of about 11 in the interpretation of contours, and some of these appear to persist through to the age of 15.[27]

What is the best way to start children off with relief maps? The sand tray with acetate sheet overlay described above is again useful here. Children build a model landscape using sand and are then challenged with the problem of representing the shape of that landscape on the acetate sheet. They might, for example, devise a colour scheme to show 'flat areas', 'areas with gentle slopes', 'areas with steep slopes' and so on or use chevrons ($\gg$) to show where slopes are steep. They might find it interesting at this point to compare some of the methods used by mapmakers in the past to show relief – such as shading by 'hachures'.

Plasticene and cardboard relief models of hills and valleys are useful. Cut-out sets of thick coloured card can be used to 'assemble' a series of contrasting-shaped hills and the pattern made by the colours seen from above is a way of showing how contours indicate different sorts of slope. Children are given instructions to build two different-shaped hills and draw what they see from above. Models that build up height in this way should ideally be smoothed with some filling material as children are sometimes confused by the step-like structure of the model and think that contours mark real breaks of slope. Using card materials is rather easier to arrange in the classroom than an alternative technique recommended in many books on teaching which involves a Plasticene 'island' in a bowl. Water is poured into the bowl to a series of levels and the contour 'coastlines' progressively marked on the island with a (waterproof) felt-tip marker. A plastic bowl or dish *is* useful, however, to show the difference between convex slopes (bowl upside down) and concave slopes (bowl right way up).

Contours on maps of the locality around the school can also be investigated. The first step is usually to identify those parts of the locality that are higher than the school and those parts that are lower. This can be done by marking the results of field observations with a + or a − on a base map of the area and later colouring the map according to whether it is above or below school level. There emerges one contour line on a map made in this way: the boundary between the two colours, at the same height as the school. Slopes in the vicinity of the school can also be marked on a base map with chevrons; for example a single chevron ($>$) for a gentle slope or a double chevron ($\gg$) for a steep one.

Finally, mention should be made here of the symbols used on maps made for visually impaired people. These *tactile* maps use different-textured materials instead of colours for differentiating between areas on the map. Sandpaper in different grades and fabrics can be used to show roads, parks, etc. An activity in design and technology might be to devise a tactile map of the school for visually impaired people which would differentiate between classrooms, offices and so on as well as show the entry point to the school.

LOCATION

Location is always described in relation to some sort of reference system. This can be with reference to:

- oneself;
- some well-known concrete feature (such as a table);
- some more abstract feature (such as the tropics);
- a grid system (such as the National Grid or lines of latitude and longitude).

The starting point on work on location is usually to describe where you are relative to other people and objects (using terms such as 'next to', 'above', 'to the left of', etc.). Pictures can be used to describe the relative location of people and objects seen in the picture, and 3D materials can be used to model situations according to instructions given (e.g. 'Build a street. Put a shop next to a petrol station . . .'). The next stage is usually to describe location from the point of view of other people, either in real life or in pictures (e.g. 'Victoria is between me and Kerry. She's on my left but on Kerry's right'). Many children's picture books have hidden characters in the illustrations (see, for example, *Each Peach, Pear, Plum*, by A. and J. Ahlberg, Picture Puffin, 1989), and location can therefore be investigated from the point of view of the character found in the picture ('What can Tom Thumb see? What is to his left?').

Describing the location of countries involves much more abstract reference points, such as hemispheres, lines of latitude and reference to coastlines and other countries, as well as location within a larger land mass. Zambia, for example, is 'a landlocked, tropical African country'.

Maps can be used to solve simple *location problems* (e.g. 'Where – on a map of the school – is the best place to put a display or notice?'). Draw maps of an imaginary community, then discuss the best place for a fire station, a clinic, the rubbish dump, an airport, etc. Children then begin to realize one of the essential issues in planning: 'near, but not too near'. People usually want to be near essential services – but not too near them. Issues relating to 'not in my back yard' can be explored further through the programmes of study in human and environmental geography.

Very young children of ages 4–6 have shown they can understand coordinates and use them effectively if the task is made simpler by using *colour* codes rather than letters and numbers. Given one coordinate, most young children can read off the other from a simple line graph. They can also identify the colour 'grid references' of pictures shown in a grid. It is the numbers and/or letters that often appear to be the difficulty, not the task itself. With numbers you have just that bit too much to think about.

The implication here is that reception classes could benefit from such games, which contrasts with earlier findings which suggested that about 8 years old was more appropriate.[28]

A simple grid game can be made as follows.[29] You need pairs of small square pictures (like those used in Pelmanism or the 'memory game'). A square board is constructed with recesses for the pictures. Columns and rows on the board are identified by coloured squares and circles. The pictures are placed on the board, face down. Children search for each picture's twin on the board. They are helped in the search by the 'grid reference' in the form of a coloured circle and square on the reverse of each picture. Both pictures are turned over once the twin is found.

Alphanumeric grids can be used to show the positions of children sitting in rows and columns and extended to demonstrate the use of such grids in real-life situations – such as identifying a particular floor tile that needs replacing or finding a caravan on a crowded site or a pigeonhole or a grave in a cemetery. The game 'battleships' is well enough known but many teachers will find the nature of the 'game' inappropriate; also, some of the plastic commercially produced versions number and give letters to the coordinates 'the wrong way round', i.e. *not* from left to right and then from bottom to top.

Note that all the grid activities described so far involve identifying the 'spaces' in the grid rather than the 'lines'. When children can identify a square in the grid they are ready to identify points. 'Join the dots' games can be played with teacher-prepared grids. Each child has a numbered grid sheet and a series of reference points to mark with a dot. When the dots are joined they form an animal or toy or some other familiar shape. Children then make their own similar puzzles. They can then be introduced to the National Grid that is used on Ordnance Survey maps. Some find difficulties with terminology.

The National Grid consists of vertical and horizontal lines. The ones that go from west to east are called northings and the ones that go from north to south are called eastings! This is because the vertical (north–south) lines show you how far east you are from the point of origin of the grid, in the extreme south-west of the country. They are numbered progressively in kilometres eastwards, and in fact on an Ordnance Survey map you can read how many kilometres east of the Isles of Scilly you are. Similarly for the horizontal lines, which are numbered progressively in kilometres north of the point of origin. The method of identifying any point within each kilometre square on an Ordnance Survey map (by estimating tenths) is shown next to the legend on the map itself, but children need practice in estimating tenths before tackling this.

Locating places on the surface of the Earth probably involves the most

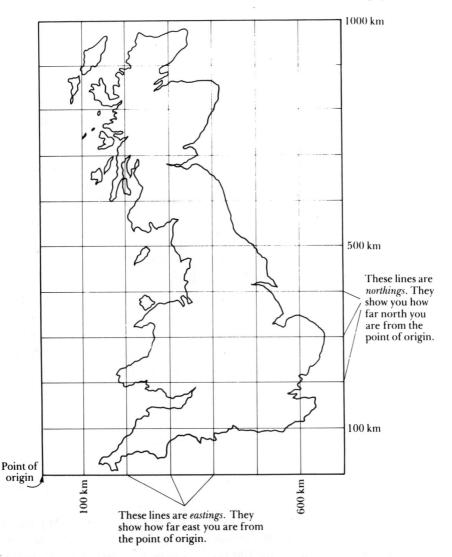

Figure 2.4 *Northings and eastings on the National Grid.*

demanding concepts. The Earth has no 'right way up' in space. However, an imaginary grid (or 'graticule') is used to pinpoint the position of any place.

The grid consists of lines called parallels of latitude and meridians of longitude. Parallels of latitude measure distance north and south of the equator. The equator is at latitude 0 degrees. The poles are at latitudes 90 degrees north and 90 degrees south. Meridians of longitude measure distance east or west of the prime meridian. The prime (or Greenwich) meridian is at longitude 0 degrees. The 180 degree line of longitude, on

41

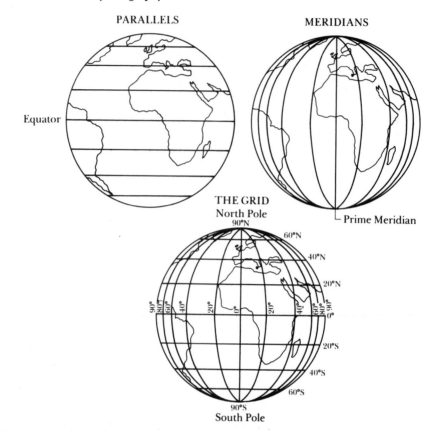

Figure 2.5 *Parallels of latitude and meridians of longitude.*

the opposite side of the Earth, is the international date line. When used together, lines of longitude and latitude form a grid.

Children can readily see the grid on a globe. The lines of latitude are parallel to each other – they never meet. Lines of longitude, however, meet at the poles. But whereas all the lines of longitude are 'great circles', that is, they go round the Earth at its maximum circumference, only one of the parallels of latitude is a great circle: the equator. All the other lines of latitude become progressively smaller towards the poles.

Theoretically, the most accurate way of locating a place on the surface of the Earth is to use a globe. But globes are inconvenient to use, especially one that is large enough for detailed work. An accurate world map may be made by 'unpeeling' strips from a globe along the lines of longitude (see Figure 2.6).

This can be easily demonstrated in the classroom by using a cheap inflatable globe. Cut along the lines of longitude and stick the strips

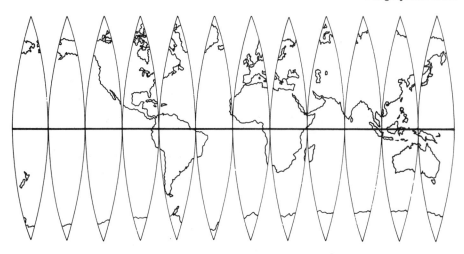

Figure 2.6 *'Unpeeling' a globe produces an accurate world map – but one that is impractical to use.*

together at the equator. This produces a map which, although it is a faithful representation of a sphere on a flat surface, has the great weakness of leaving large gaps in the land and sea areas and therefore would not be very practical to use. Grids of parallels and meridians which are used to turn a globe into a flat map are called map projections. It is impossible to flatten the spherical surface of the Earth without stretching or cutting part of it.

Some contrasting map projections are shown in Figure 2.7. Map projections either get the shape of the land masses correct and their relative areas wrong or the relative areas of the land masses right and the shapes wrong – or they get them both wrong! However, a map with both shape and area incorrect may be perfectly acceptable because the overall error is minimized. Mercator's projection (Figure 2.7(a)) was designed for navigators. A straight line on this map is a line of constant compass bearing. Just set your compass to the angle of the straight line on the map and sail on that bearing and eventually you get to your destination. This doesn't actually give the *shortest* route (readers might like to experiment with a world map and a globe by comparing straight-line routes on the map with straight-line routes using a piece of string on a globe). Although immensely useful on the high seas in the seventeenth century, the Mercator projection is much less use in schools in the twentieth. Nearer the poles the land masses are seen to get larger: compare the size of Greenland with Africa on a globe and compare with the way these are shown on a Mercator projection. A map such as this would be no use at all for showing, say, the extent of natural vegetation cover over the Earth because the area of ice or coniferous forest would

(a)

(b)

(c)

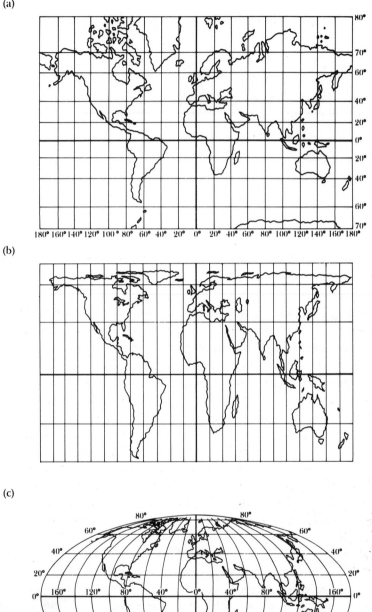

(d)

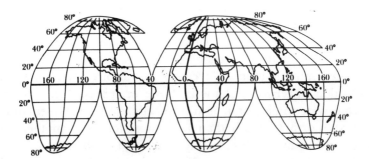

(e)

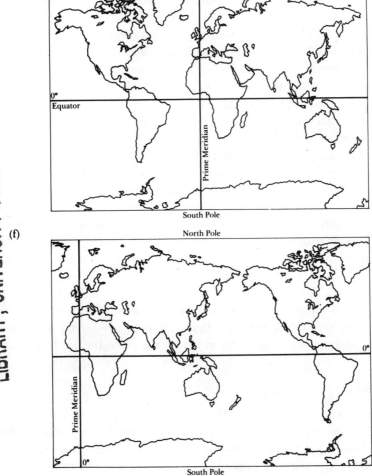

(f)

Figure 2.7 *Some contrasting map projections: (a) Mercator's projection; (b) Peters' projection; (c) Mollweide's projection; (d) Goode's Interrupted projection; (e) Gall's projection (centred on the prime meridian); (f) Gall's projection (centred on the Pacific Ocean).*

appear much larger in relation to, say, tropical forest as the relative areas of places are shown so distorted. For a purpose such as this, you need an *equal area* map, in which the relative areas of the land masses are shown correctly. Such a map is given by the Peters projection (Figure 2.7(b)), and has been much publicized recently by various development agencies. The distortion in terms of shape is, however, gross. Africa is, in reality, as far from west to east as it is from north to south. Greenland is much longer from north to south than from west to east. Another equal-area projection is that by Mollweide (Figure 2.7(c)). This gives better shape to the land masses in the centre of the map but the Americas and Australia are 'warped'. This problem can be solved by 'bending' the pattern of lines of latitude and longitude away from places where the map is not required, such as in the oceans. The result is seen in the Goode Interrupted projection (Figure 2.7(d)). This solution could also be adopted in reverse; that is, cuts could be made in the land areas if an ocean map was required.

General-purpose world maps make a compromise between shape and area. One such compromise can be seen in the Gall projection (Figure 2.7(e)) used for the National Curriculum maps. (Note, incidentally, that the National Curriculum documentation – at least to 1992 – stated, incorrectly, that this map was an equal-area projection.)

Most of the map projections that will be seen by British readers will centre the map on the Greenwich meridian and therefore on the British Isles. This convention is thought to give the misleading impression that 'we' are in the centre of the world and thereby to foster ethnocentric attitudes. (Ethnocentricism is a view of the world in which one's own group is the centre of everything and all others are judged with reference to it.) Maps in other parts of the world may be arranged differently. Consider Figure 2.7(f) for example. This is a map used in schools in New Zealand. Note that on this map it is the British Isles which are seen as two small and remote islands 'on the edge of the world' rather than New Zealand! Maps such as this can be helpful in reminding children that it is the *globe* which is the starting point for thinking about location in the world – not the world *map*.

DIRECTION

Many children will need practice in identifying left and right as well as making full, three-quarter, half and quarter turns. Practise this by playing 'Simon Says'. Then establish that left and right (as well as in front and behind) only relate to where *you* are and that left and right are reversed for a person facing you (as in the location activities described above). The fact that left and right can be reversed like this makes giving directions difficult. You need to have fixed points that remain the same no matter what your own position is. That's when the compass can be introduced.

Many teachers find introducing the cardinal points of the compass is best done by reference to the apparent movement of the sun. Try observing the course of the sun by noting how shadows move around the school during the day. Which parts of the school are in shade in the morning and which in the afternoon? Then record the length of the shadow made by a vertical stick. Children can make a simple graph showing length of the shadow set against time during the day. When is the shadow shortest? That's when the sun is highest in the sky. In Britain, the shortest shadow points to the north. That's because at its highest point in the sky, the sun is in the south direction. When children stand with their backs to the sun at the time of shortest shadow they are facing north. Children can make a permanent record of this direction and check it with a compass. Try painting a simple arrow on the playground to show north. The other three cardinal points of the compass can then be taught and similarly marked. Next, observe the directions of sunrise and sunset. In Britain, sunrise is only due east and sunset due west on 21 March and 21 September, but for practical purposes in school it is good enough to remember that 'the sun rises in the east and sets in the west'. Notice how direction is intimately linked to location in that with a compass children can orientate themselves to their position on a globe. It is also helpful to reinforce the notion of *vertical* direction on a globe ('up' is away from the globe, 'down' is towards the centre of the Earth). Children could do this with small figures showing the positions of children in other parts of the world. Many children have difficulty in visualizing how Australians 'can be upside down' and moving the small figure so that it jumps 'up and down', moves to the north, south, etc. can be helpful.

Once north and the other three cardinal points are fixed in relation to the school, a map of the school can be correctly aligned and playground exercises such as 'run to the west' can be practised. The *use* of compass points is surprisingly difficult for some children. It isn't just a matter of learning the positions of the points on a compass rose. Practise statements such as: 'Katy wants to go to Chris. She must move *towards* the north-west. Katy wants Chris to come to her. He will come *from* the south-east.' Children can then practise these direction skills with maps, for example: 'The church is north of the Town Hall'. Practice is also needed at a variety of scales: 'Liverpool is west of Leeds'; 'Portugal is west of Spain'. Playground exercises can also refer to compass points in order to describe a route on a map (e.g. to find hidden treasure using compass directions). The route can be marked on the map with right angle and 45 degree turns to help children find their way.[30] Some of these skills might be thought of as 'pre-orienteering' skills.

Some schools have made their own direction indicator in the form of a circle with arrows showing the direction to local landmarks that are visible. These can be more sophisticated by indicating the direction of more distant, unseen places whose distances and directions are worked out from maps and atlases. Point to a road leading in a particular direction and ask: 'Where is the first place you come to? Where do you come to after that? Where will you eventually end up?'

Further practice in direction might come from describing journeys using a road atlas and compass points, making a map from a narrative passage written by the teacher that contains reference to compass points and relating compass directions to the number of degrees in a circle. Programmable devices such as 'turtles' (used with LOGO) have applications for learning about direction.

It is also possible to set up directional investigations in the locality. Do gardeners, for example, have a preference for gardens facing in a particular direction? Investigate this using estate agents' property particulars. Do trees show evidence of 'wind sheer'? This is where the tops may be bent in the direction of the prevailing wind. Check the prevailing wind with the help of a home-made weather vane. Do lichen and moss grow especially on one side of trees in the area? Link the compass rose to weather records. What (stereotypical) images are associated in people's minds about 'the North', 'the South'?

Points of the compass are also related strongly to religious imagery. In Britain, Muslims pray to the east, the direction of Mecca, and Christians turn to the east to recite the creed to express the belief that Christ is the Dayspring and sun of righteousness. The altar is thus placed at the east end of a church. There was an old belief that only evil-doers should be buried on the north side of a churchyard, perhaps because of the lack of sun there. To 'go west' when referring to people means to die – perhaps because that's where the sun sets.

SCALE AND DISTANCE

Stories involving characters of different sizes can contribute to children's understanding of scale. 'Goldilocks and the Three Bears' and 'The Three Billygoats Gruff', for example, illustrate this theme. The home corner in the classroom may have cutlery, crockery and cooking utensils in different sizes and children can, through discussion, explore why relative sizes are important. ('Which knives and forks "match" these plates and saucers?') The suitability of different-sized toy vehicles for use with playmats and model road layouts has been discussed above in relation to developing a sense of plan. Similarly, what size dolls or figures are best with different-sized clothes or model cars? Models can also be arranged in order of size (the various versions of Russian-style nesting dolls are useful here as well as the differently sized repeat jigsaw puzzles).

Children's ability to grasp the notion of the separation of two points on a map or the comparative sizes of areas on a map depends to a considerable extent on their measurement skills. In this, children need to be able to use *relative* measures (such as 'smaller than', 'further than') as well as *absolute* measurements (for example centimetres and kilometres). Most primary school maths books are good sources of ideas for investigations of this sort. Children could be asked to estimate relative distances in familiar surroundings: say, finding which table is the nearest to the door and checking their answer with string. Understanding scale is closely related to understanding areas and shapes. In one investigation[31] children were asked to represent a simple model farm layout using a number of matching cut-out shapes. Their representation of the farm was to be one quarter the size of the original model and they were given a number of alternative cut-out shapes at varying scales. Only the oldest children could select the correct (one-quarter) scale shapes with which to make their own representation. However, the shape of the materials used had an effect on their ability to perform the task correctly. Circles and ovals presented little difficulty but few children could correctly choose squares and rectangles at one quarter of the original size. It would be worth making some hardware equipment to replicate this experiment, asking children to represent correctly, say, the school or the classroom.

Making a fairly accurate map to a certain scale, even of a simple area, is a difficult exercise and probably not a suitable one for most primary-age children. The whole range of practical measurement skills (for example, using trundle wheel, tape measure and ruler) needs to be mastered before it can be undertaken. It is best to make a map of somewhere very familiar if children *have* mastered the prerequisite skills – perhaps a part of the school. It's probably better too to have some credible reason for making the map, such as a map of the classroom to show parents where each child's work is set out for Open Day or a map of the school grounds to identify litter 'black spots' in order to find the best place for new wastepaper bins. Assuming children are confident in the prerequisite skills, what might be a suitable teaching sequence for making a scale map of this sort? Start with a rough sketch of the room or corridor or playground to be mapped. Measure the most significant parts with trundle wheels or tape measures. Decide on a suitable (*simple*, i.e. 1 cm to 1 m) scale and draw the final plan on squared paper. When making a plan of a room it is helpful to mark off metre lengths on a strip of paper fixed round the room. It saves rechecking measurements when children are drawing up their finished plans.

Enlarging and reducing drawings using squared paper is a good way of focusing attention on scale. Paper with two sizes of squares is needed – say 5 mm squares and 2 cm squares. A drawing on one piece of squared paper is transferred to the other, using the squares as a guide. Children who have difficulty with this may need to practise by simply transferring the drawing to another sheet of the same sized squares first. The exercise works well with country shapes not least because the effect of reducing the scale illustrates to children that detail in the outline is necessarily lost – a useful learning point for atlas use.

Another aspect of understanding scale is the ability to evaluate space according to appropriateness for particular activities ('Where is the best space in the school for a football game?; the best space for a reading group?', etc.). This activity might be a prelude to selecting maps at different scales for particular purposes. Children start this by comparing what things are shown on maps at different scales – and what things are not shown. Then they look at one particular feature – for example housing – and compare how maps of each of the scales available represent that feature. On an Ordnance Survey 1:50 000 map, for example, houses are shown as fairly generalized colour-filled blocks representing residential areas. The 1:2500 map in contrast shows the outline accurately of every single house.

Scale on maps can be represented in a number of ways. The most difficult to grasp is the expression of scale as a ratio (e.g. 1:50 000). Some teachers find it best to explain this as 'One of *these* (hold thumb and first finger apart) on the map stands for 50 000 of these along the road or across the fields'. Understanding scale expressed as a statement (such as 1 cm stands for 1 km) depends on a clear understanding of what those units look like in the real world. One centimetre is easily demonstrated but it is important for children to be aware of how far a kilometre is in their own locality; for example, 'from the school to the swimming baths'. (It is also valuable for children to have a clear idea as early as possible of how large a hectare is. The school and its grounds might occupy a hectare: 100 m × 100 m.) Note that it is incorrect and probably leads to confusion to write '1 cm = 1 km', because self-evidently one centimetre does not *equal* one kilometre. It is probably better to write the scale in full, as: '1 centimetre on the map measures 1 kilometre on the ground'. Scale can also be shown on a map as a linear scale: a straight line marked off in the units that the line represents. It is helpful to use this by marking off a long strip of paper with a straight edge against the scale line. The straight edge can then be used directly against the map to measure off distances required. Curved distances can be measured by using a piece of thin string and then holding it against the scale line. This is surprisingly difficult to do, however (the string won't always behave when laid along the roads, etc. on the map), and it may be simpler to use a map measurer (sometimes called an opisometer). This is a small device which is wheeled across the map and the distance travelled can be read off on a scale on the side of the instrument. Because they are often made for maps at a variety of scales, however, reading off the distance can be tricky.

Understanding scale becomes more demanding when small-scale (e.g. atlas) maps are used. It is very difficult to tell on a map showing countries how much of the Earth's surface is being shown. A reference is needed to a place the scale of which *is* known. How big is Britain? A useful figure to remember is that it is about 1000 km from John O'Groats to Land's End, as the crow flies. But of course this figure, although useful to know, and useful to compare with other distances at world scale, does not mean a great deal to children. It is usually better to start with time rather than linear distance. Talk about journeys that the children have made. How did they travel and how long did the journey take? Look at these journeys on a wall map of the British Isles and mark them on the map. How long would similar journeys to other parts of Britain take? How far could you go from where we are in two hours by bus?, by train?, on foot? Discuss how long the journey from John O'Groats to Land's End would take by air (probably about two hours). How long by car? (probably about two days). How long on foot? (probably about 40 days, on the basis of previous charity walks). Once this size has been established a *comparitor* map needs to be included with maps of other parts of the world. A comparitor map is one that shows how big Britain is compared to the part of the world you are looking at. That allows you to ask questions such as 'How many times bigger is Australia than Britain?'

Maps in the locality of the school

Children really need access to a range of maps at a number of scales, showing their own locality and the entire region. Minimally, this might include maps at the following scales (see Appendix 1 for further details):

1:2500
1:10 000
1:50 000
1:100 000

The 1:2500 scale map will show the school building itself clearly but probably not all the catchment area. That will most likely be contained on a single 1:100 000 map. Murphy's Law of Cartography, however, says that your school (or holiday resort) will always be located at the intersection of four Ordnance Survey maps. Nevertheless, it's worth assembling a montage of map sections so that the school is in the centre of a map that can be used as the basis for local investigations. Many schools display such a map in

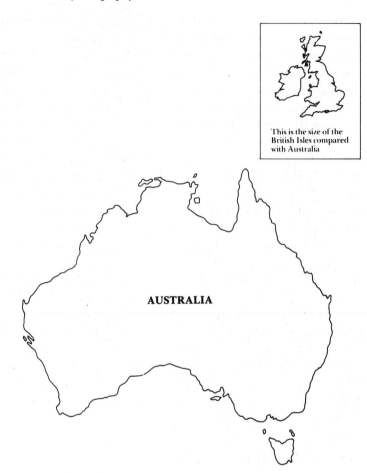

This is the size of the British Isles compared with Australia

AUSTRALIA

Figure 2.8 *A comparitor map of the British Isles to show the size of Australia. (Based on maps in the* Oxford Junior Atlas, *Oxford University Press.)*

the entrance hall. It is worth making sure that there is a map in school which shows as much as possible of the actual catchment area. The first time this is done makes a project in itself: that is, to identify the catchment area (see Chapter 5). In the light of the philosophy underpinning schools in the early 1990s this could even be presented as a marketing exercise! If the resulting map is laminated it can be used with worksheets prepared along the following lines. These activities are only roughly structured and are intended to illustrate a range of map skills but you should notice how they gradually increase in difficulty. The key concept in each task is shown in bold type.

Find our school in the centre of the map.
What is the **name** of the road that the school is in?

Find on the map the main entrance to the school. What building is **opposite**?
If you go out of the main entrance and turn **left**, what is the first road you come to on the **right**?
What is the name of the church to the **north** of the school?
Describe the quickest way **from** the school to the police station.
Describe the quickest way from the fire station **to** the school.
Which is **nearer** to the school: Westgate Newsagents or Eastgate Newsagents?
Measure the distance from the school to the cinema.
(Using a transparent overlay marked with a circle) How many shops are there within a **radius** of 50 m from the school?
In what direction is the public library from the school?

Mark on the map where the children live. Do this with small labels or coloured dots. These could be colour keyed to gender, mode of transport, etc. The dots could be numbered with a legend (key) to indicate who is who. Use a legend also to show addresses. The 'meaning' of addresses can be explored. Where on the map does the name of the town or district change? Compare the Ordnance Survey maps with a street map which shows postal areas. The assignments above can be developed to include:

Who lives **nearest** to the school?
Name anyone who lives **twice as far** away as Katy.
How many times further than Chris does Matthew live?
How many children live **south** of the school?
How many girls live within a **radius** of 400 m from the school?

An integrated environmental studies project which gives much information and many ideas about similar map investigations in the locality has been published by the Geographical Association.[32] One group of children established the progression of road building on their housing estate from the school's admission registers of 20 years previously. The inclusion of an address in the register indicated that the road was complete and that houses on that road were beginning to be occupied. Lists of roads, in chronological order of their appearance in the admissions register, were used to divide the history of the estate into a number of periods of building. Traced overlays were then made of each building period using the existing estate map as a base. The children thus established a comprehensive picture of the growth of the estate and presented their findings in map form.

Maps and children's literature

It is likely that children remember stories more if they are accompanied by a map. Many children's books contain maps. The stories about *Milly Molly*

Mandy by Joyce Lankester Brisley (1948), for example, centre on the village where she lives. Although many teachers seem to find these stories rather sweetly sentimental (in the village are: 'the nice white cottage with the thatched roof where Milly Molly Mandy lives'; 'the Moggs' cottage where little-friend Susan lives', etc.) they remain popular with young children. The stories are more understandable with the map, and important aspects of the plot, such as the short cut to school, are clearly shown. Like most maps in children's fiction, this is a pictorial map. Other classic examples are to be found in A. A. Milne's *Winnie the Pooh* (Methuen, 1926), Arthur Ransome's *Swallows and Amazons* (Cape, 1930), J. R. R. Tolkien's *The Hobbit* (Allen & Unwin, 1937) and C. S. Lewis's *The Voyage of the Dawn Treader* (Collins, 1952). Note also the maps in *The Weirdstone of Brisingamen* (Collins, 1960) and *The Moon of Gomrath* (Collins, 1963) by Alan Garner. Both these stories have maps of Alderley Edge, where the stories are set. *Summer in Small Street* by Geraldine Kaye (1989; Mammoth, 1990) also has a pictorial map showing the street and the location of the homes of the characters in the story.

In *The Last Bus* by William Mayne (1962; Red Fox, 1990), Peter spends too long playing with his cousin David and the kittens so he misses the last bus down the dale. To catch up with the bus he has to cross country, with the help of a pony, roller skates, a Land-Rover and a pole across the beck. The book has a map of the route, but what is different about this story is that this is a *real* journey, between Aysgarth and West Burton – real places in the Yorkshire Dales that can be looked up on the Ordnance Survey map! (Sheet 98).

It is not necessary, however, for authors to supply young readers with a map: they can construct their own. In Helen Morgan's *Meet Mary Kate* (1963; Puffin, 1965), Mary Kate is 4 years old. She lives in the country with her parents and the stories in this book are of an everyday kind. 'At the bottom of the garden was a little wood. It was so small that from her bedroom window Mary Kate could see right through it to the field beyond and the bridge over the stream. There was a winding path through the woods that led from the gate in the garden to the stile in the fence round the fields. It was a short cut to the village and to Granny's cottage.' Children can draw their own map of the short cut to illustrate the story.

Look out also for the maps that are occasionally published in relation to radio and TV soap operas. There is, for example, a map available of Ambridge from 'The Archers', and maps exist of Coronation Street, Ramsey Street ('Neighbours') and Albert Square ('EastEnders').

Some stories are easier to map than others. Postman Pat, for example, especially lends himself to being mapped because of the nature of the job. The 'Postman Pat' stories are concerned with everyday life in the village of Greendale, an imaginary Pennine village. The village has all the essential services and the inhabitants go about their daily business contending with difficulties such as the weather and various people needing help. All the characters in the village are linked by Postman Pat as he goes on his rounds and the structure of the stories therefore makes them an ideal subject for mapping.

Understanding aerial photographs

For the requirements of the National Curriculum, children have to be able to 'identify familiar features on photographs and pictures' (AT1, level 2) and 'identify features on aerial photographs' (AT1 level 3). For level 4, children have to be able to relate a map and aerial photograph of the same place by identifying features common to both.[33] The sequence is clear therefore: identify familiar features first at *ground* level, then proceed to the view from *overhead* and then relate this to *maps*. Note that there are two forms of aerial photograph: *oblique* aerial and *vertical* aerial. The former gives a view from above but sideways, as if looking out of an aeroplane window. Features on the ground are fairly easy to recognize because the sides of the features may be seen as well as their tops. Vertical aerial photographs show the view from directly above. They are therefore more difficult to interpret.

Addresses of some companies supplying aerial photographs are given in Appendix 2 but it is also worth trying the local newspaper offices as they often hold a selection of suitable photographs. Good-sized aerial photographs are fairly expensive to buy but the cost is less prohibitive if the outlay is seen as a long-term resource for the school as a whole. Aerial photographs, like maps, come in a range of different scales: each may show a different area of land. The terminology of scale for photographs is the same as for maps. A large-scale photograph shows a smaller area of land but the details are larger; a small-scale photograph shows a larger area but the details are smaller. Commercial companies will supply photographs with the scale marked. A measurement of 1 cm on a photograph with a scale of 1:10 000 will represent a measurement on the ground of 100 m.

If you request photographs from a commercial company you will usually be sent photocopies of the pictures they have which are good enough to help decide whether or not they will be suitable. Many schools have a framed aerial photograph, together with a selection of maps on permanent display. Although it sounds extravagant, the cost of a half or one hour pleasure flight with a flying club from a local airfield would probably not be outside the budget of many primary schools, particularly if two or three schools in the same locality each send a teacher who is reasonably competent with a camera. Thirty-six colour transparencies of places familiar to children in the locality of the school would be an extremely useful resource for Key Stages 1 and 2. It takes some planning, including a list in advance of places that need to be photographed, and it isn't always possible – but it is certainly worth considering. In addition to photographs of the immediate locality around the school it is helpful to have pictures of contrasting localities; for example an urban or rural area, a coastal or inland location.

Aerial photos are not the same as maps. The principal difference is that they show *everything* from above, not just those phenomena which the cartographer has selected to map. This includes ephemeral and transitory features such as traffic, snow and smoke. Neither do photographs have conventional symbols or boundaries or placename labels. There are other, more subtle differences, too. Consider an aerial photograph taken with the camera pointing directly downwards towards the Earth. The only truly overhead part of the photograph is in the centre; the outer edges present a view at least to some extent from the side. This means that even with a vertical aerial photograph you can see the sides of buildings the further you look from the centre of the photograph. A map, on the other hand, always shows a view directly from above, no matter where on the map you look. But there are similarities with maps too. An aerial photograph involves a reduction in scale and features are shown with some degree of abstraction: houses are shown only by roofs rather than by their three-dimensional shape. Because using an aerial photograph requires some of the skills involved in map using, it has often been suggested that mapwork can be most successfully introduced via aerial photographs.[34]

Quite young children are usually able to recognize many environmental and landscape features from aerial photographs. For example, when a group of 6-year-olds were shown vertical and oblique aerial photographs, each seemed able to identify readily on average half a dozen features in the photograph such as cars, roads, houses and grass.[35] But there will be limitations to what is recognized. Children may well not recognize an aerial photograph of their own locality for what it is and they will have difficulty recognizing features that are relatively unfamiliar to them.[36] Recognition of landscape features may also depend on the scale of the photograph; that is, from how high up it was taken.

It is claimed that recognizing features on photographs involves being able to undertake fairly complex mental operations such as adopting a view from above, reducing one's three-dimensional view of the world to a two-dimensional one, mentally reducing the scale of the environment and then abstracting it into semi-iconic symbols.[37]

Is children's ability to perform this complex task affected by their familiarity with TV and other media? Apparently not, for even children with no experience at all of seeing the world from above via such media have been able to recognize such features.[38] Nevertheless, even if children are able easily to recognize features on aerial photographs, they will probably have little experience of seeing their own locality from above and every effort should be made to obtain such photographs of the locality.

ACTIVITIES USING AERIAL PHOTOGRAPHS

The most appropriate first activity with aerial photographs is simply for children to look at a selection of different types of photograph. They will notice that some are oblique, others are vertical and that they vary in scale (i.e. the amount of detail they show and the area they cover). You need a set of magnifying glasses to use with the photographs – they really are necessary in order to see detail clearly. The better the quality of the photographs the more rewardingly they come alive with magnification. Looking at photographs can be either an open-ended activity ('Write down/tell me 10 things you can see in the photograph') or more structured ('Can you see these things in the photograph: a school, a factory, a garage, a car park?', etc.). It is especially helpful to discuss the criteria on which identification is made. 'How did you decide what things were shown in the photograph?' The most common criteria are colour (woodland is usually dark green); shape (buildings are usually regular); and size (factories are usually larger than houses). These criteria lay the foundation for *interpretation* of photographs.

Acetate sheet overlays (overhead projector transparencies are suitable) allow children to work directly on top of the photographs. Routes can be traced from one part of the photograph to another and the journeys thus made described with reference either to directions such as right and left or to compass point.. Overlays with alphanumeric grids allow reference to be made to parts of the photograph ('Look at the school in square C4'). Overlays can also be used by the teacher with an overhead projector. Part of the photograph is traced and projected onto a screen or wall to make a large map of the area which can be further developed with symbols following examination of the photograph. Distinctive parts of the area shown in the photograph can be coloured: for example, a residential area, industrial area, area of major public buildings, etc. Outline drawings from oblique aerial photographs can also be used as the basis for worksheets.

The most effective work is often done when maps and aerial photographs are used together. One source adds more information to the other. Maps can provide additional information for photographs, such as the names of roads and uses of buildings. Photographs can provide additional information for maps, such as where there is most traffic.

Globes

There are many sizes and types of globes and a primary school really needs a selection in order to fulfil the requirements of the National Curriculum. Reasonably priced globes for school use vary from about the size of a netball to that of a large grapefruit. There is much to be said for the smaller size because the scale is usually such that the globe can be compared directly with world maps at a similar scale in an atlas. This allows a much more effective way of comparing the representation of land mass shape than if you compare the atlas map with a much larger globe. The latter though has much more detail so it is worth making both types available. Mention has already been made above of inflatable globes and how they can be cut up in order to demonstrate map projections. Inflatable globes are also found in several sizes – the largest being the size of a large beach ball. They are much cheaper than conventional plastic globes although generally less accurate in their printing and sphericity.

Globes are available in political (coloured by countries) and environmental versions (coloured according to types of environment: deserts, forests, etc.). The latter often come without a legend, making interpretation difficult. The straightforward political globe is best for place finding. Especially valuable for teaching are globes that children and teachers can write on. These can either be black rubber which takes chalk or (better) clear plastic that will take washable felt-tip marker. There are also globes marked only in land and sea, with no placenames. These are useful for introducing the names of the continents and for testing.

Atlases

The small-scale maps found in atlases have a number of characteristics that make learning slightly more difficult than large-scale maps. Principally, the degree of abstraction is much greater and teachers need therefore to establish the thoroughness of children's learning about the phenomena that are mapped. One small dot on an atlas map can stand for an entire city. Young children *can* use atlas maps, but time has to be spent on developing some of the terms needed to understand the maps – such as city, coastline, ocean, desert, etc.

School atlases, unlike road atlases, tend to show whole countries or groups of whole countries on each page. This necessarily means (because countries are not the same size) that the scales of the maps must vary. Belgium, the Netherlands and Luxembourg frequently appear together on one page. So too do the countries of Scandinavia – and yet Scandinavia is at least ten times bigger than the Benelux countries. Road atlases show blocks of land at a uniform scale but this solution means that whole countries are rarely shown per page. If children become aware that their atlas is not an objective representation of the world but a subjective one in which decisions have been taken on their behalf by the editorial team of the atlas, they may develop a healthy criticality of maps.[39]

When choosing an atlas,[40] teachers may find it helpful to bear in mind that a school will probably need several atlases to allow for gradation and progression in the way small-scale maps are introduced at Key Stages 1 and 2. Good atlases will have clear, uncluttered maps that are simple and directly explained by title and by legend. Look for a clear typeface and not too many sizes of type on each map. There should be a good contrast between the style of lettering used for towns and cities, administrative areas and physical features. On atlas maps most features, such as towns, are usually shown in upper and lower case and administrative areas in capital letters. Physical features (mountains, rivers, etc.) are usually shown in italics and peaks are often printed in condensed type. The importance of places is frequently shown by the use of bold, medium or light type. All these conventions show how the way in which the words are printed give children more information about the places marked. A good atlas usually has a preliminary section which draws attention to the way the typeface has been used. Children can practise *scanning* the map for placenames more easily once they have cracked the code to the way the places are printed.

Symbols used on the map should be clearly described in the legend (or key). Some atlases provide small pictures as visual clues to the meaning of the symbol and the printed explanation. The legend needs to be prominent on *every* page – not restricted to a section of the atlas (such as inside the front cover) to which constant reference has to be made. National and international boundaries on the map should be shown boldly and clearly but without obliterating details underneath. Colours are also symbols and some atlases separate the legend into two: 'What the symbols mean' and 'What the colours mean'. The sea areas, usually coloured blue, need to be referred to in the legend as well.

Lines of latitude and longitude (the 'graticule') should be shown on the maps – preferably with an alphanumeric grid for younger children to allow places named in the gazetteer (placename index) to be found more easily. Note though that the numbers and letters of the grid need to stand out reasonably well in the margin or on the edge of the maps referred to. The ease with which children can use the alphanumeric grid will depend on, among other things, the coarseness of the grid pattern. If there are many lines and grid squares, then the numbers and letters at the edge of the map will be dense and possibly confusing. Too 'open' a grid, however, will mean too long a search for the required feature within the grid square once it has been identified. Children have to be able to 'use the index and contents pages to find information in an atlas' for level 4 so look for an atlas which is appropriately clear. Do *all* the places on the maps feature in the index? It's not necessary that they do; it depends on how the atlas will be used. Some atlases only have a gazetteer for places in the British Isles. That allows the skill of locating places to be practised but doesn't take up too large a part of the book with the index. Some gazetteers use different colour printing or type styles to differentiate in the list of placenames between towns, rivers, high land, etc. The gazetteer is of course a suitable vehicle for teaching alphabetical order, not least because of the potential complexity of the unfamiliar names. Note the progression in difficulty of the following for example:

> Bristol, Hull, Leeds, Manchester (first letter defines order);
> Ramsgate, Reading, Richmond, Rotherham (second letter defines order);
> Wakefield, Wallasey, Walsall, Warley (third/fourth letter defines order);
> Southampton, South Downs, Southend-on-Sea, Southern Uplands, Southport (sixth letter defines order but note the added complication of word breaks and hyphens).

The contents pages of the atlas are as useful as the index; especially so if a 'sheet line' map is included. This is a guide to the content and coverage of the atlas pages which takes the form of a map of the world or the British Isles on which the page layouts are marked. This graphic index also allows the teacher to demonstrate that overlap on the pages may occur, with the same place being shown on several pages, sometimes at different scales.

Children need quite a long 'familiarization' time with their atlas. Many children enjoy just browsing. There is a sort of paradox in atlas choice here. Because children like to look for places they know in the atlas and because those places tend to be local – and therefore small in size – there is a need to provide them with a large atlas with lots of placenames. Yet that is a difficult resource to use and they probably learn best about the world as a whole in a more structured way by having a much simpler atlas. The answer is that both are probably needed! Once children have some familiarity with their atlas then they can learn to differentiate between the maps in it. These will probably be of at least four types: topographic maps showing the most important features of the landscape, such as towns, rivers, major routes and the height of the land; environmental maps showing what the land is like and how it is used; political maps showing countries and capital cities, as well as smaller administrative units; and thematic maps showing special topics, such as information about farms, ports or food.

Children also need to note the date of their atlas. Times (and places) change. Countries split or join together. Boundaries change, often as a result of conflicts. An out-of-date atlas is still an important learning resource. But children ought to know where to find the date of publication. Most placenames in atlases are printed in black and that's fairly easy to keep up to date (it only means a change to the black film used in printing). Changes that mean changes in colour (and therefore changes to all three primary colours used in the printing process) are more expensive and usually wait until a new *edition* rather than a new *printing*. It is sometimes at least as helpful to have an older atlas as a new one. Modern atlases will show Germany reunified. But that may not help much if the only information (such as statistics) on a particular topic is available separately for the former Federal Republic and Democratic Republic. To illustrate the extent to which countries can change their names compare a map of Africa dated 1960 or earlier with the one in the school atlas. (I am assuming that this will be more recent!)

Drawing maps for children

From the discussion above of maps and children's understanding of them, it is possible to distil a number of principles that teachers may find helpful when producing their own maps (of the locality or of other parts of the world) for use in class.

Maps need a scale. This is often expressed best by comparison to somewhere the children know, such as a linear scale marked as 'the distance from our school to Safeway's' on a map of another locality in Britain. Or the scale could be shown as time, for example: 'It takes half an hour to travel by bus from place A to place B.' Small-scale maps of the rest of the world need a small inset comparitor map of the British Isles, once children have been taught how big that is.

Maps need a north pointer, and a title that is clearly expressed in a way children can easily read: 'This map shows where some important factories are in Britain' is clearly better than 'Distribution of industry in Britain'.

Because of the difficulties in separating out elements of the embedded placenames on maps, it is easier for children to read a teacher-prepared map if a consistent lettering style is used for different sorts of feature. Capital letters for country names and administrative areas, upper and lower case for other features. Or differentiation could be by colour. It simply helps children to separate the names of places into categories. Lettering on maps needs to be especially clear because of the unfamiliarity of the names; and as lettering often has to be small it's worth paying particular attention to 'a's and 'o's. Remember that the 'closed' form of printed 'a', as opposed

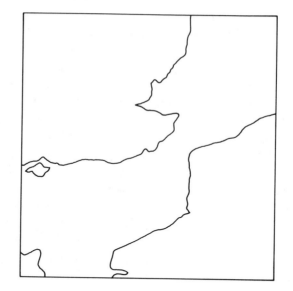

Figure 2.9 *Which is land and which is sea? Teacher-prepared maps need to differentiate clearly between the two by colouring or labelling land and sea areas.*

to the 'open' handwritten style, was developed to make it easier to distinguish from 'o'! Where possible placenames should be written horizontally and the amount of intercutting between one label and another reduced.

Where maps are to show land and sea, label the land and sea areas clearly. In Figure 2.9, for example, it is not at all clear which of the areas shown is land and which is sea. The map is of part of the English Channel but the sea area needs to be coloured, or shaded. Children may not recognize coastline shapes familiar to adults, and labelling towns may not be enough to establish the shape of the coastline. Use of an especially thick line for the coast helps.[41]

NOTES AND REFERENCES

1. This list of specific teaching objectives is derived from Simon Catling's list in Catling, S.J. (1980) 'Map use and objectives for map learning.' *Teaching Geography*, **6**, 1, 15–17.
2. Balchin, W.G.V. and Coleman, A.W. (1965) 'Graphicacy should be the fourth ace in the pack.' *Times Educational Supplement*, 5 November.
3. Balchin, W.G.V. (1985) 'Graphicacy comes of age.' *Teaching Geography*, **11**, 1, 8–9.
4. Monmonier, M. (1991) *How to Lie with Maps*. Chicago and London: University of Chicago Press.
5. Kenneth Baker, Secretary of State for Education and Science, announcing the terms of reference for the National Curriculum Geography working group, 5 May 1989, and quoted in a research review of children's understanding of maps by David Boardman in *Geography*, **74**, 4, 321–31.

6. See Keates, J.S. (1982) *Understanding Maps*. London: Longman.
7. Blaut and Stea (1974) 'Mapping at the age of three.' *Journal of Geography*, **73**, 7, October.
8. Blades, M. and Spencer, C. (1987b) 'Young children's recognition of environmental features from aerial photographs and maps.' *Environmental Education and Information*, **6**, 189–98.
9. What follows is a summary of the processes of map using and visual perception described in Keates, J.S. (1982) *Understanding Maps*. London: Longman.
10. For a description of Piaget's stages of children's spatial awareness see Piaget, J., Inhelder, B. and Szeminska, A. (1960) *The Child's Conception of Geometry*. London: Routledge & Kegan Paul. For Simon Catling's interpretation of children's cognitive maps see Catling, S.J. (1979) 'Maps and cognitive maps: the young child's perception.' *Geography*, **64**, 4, 288–98.
11. See, for example, Garland, H.C. *et al.* (1979) 'Transit map colour coding and street detail: effects on trip planning performance.' *Environment and Behaviour*, **11**, 162–84; and Streeter, L.A. and Vitello, D. (1986) 'A profile of drivers' map-reading abilities.' *Human Factors*, **28**, 223–39.
12. See Giannangelo, D.M. and Frazee, B.M. (1977) 'Map reading proficiency of elementary educators.' *Journal of Geography*, **76**, 63–5.
13. Levine, M., Marchon, I. and Hanley, G. (1984) 'The placement and misplacement of You Are Here maps.' *Environment and Behaviour*, **16**, 2, 139–57.
14. Bluestein, N. and Acredolo, L. (1979) 'Developmental changes in map reading skills.' *Child Development*, **50**, 691–7.
15. See Presson, C.C. (1982) 'The development of map reading skills.' *Child Development*, **53**, 196–9.
16. Blades, M. and Spencer, C. (1986) 'Map use in the environment and educating children to use maps.' *Environmental Education and Information*, **5**, 4, 187–204.
17. DES (1990) *Geography for Ages 5 to 16*. DES/Welsh Office.
18. DES (1989) *National Curriculum Geography Working Party Report*. DES/Welsh Office.
19. I acknowledge here the very helpful book: Winston, B.J. (1984) *Map and Globe Skills: K-8 Teaching Guide*. Macomb, Ill.: National Council for Geographic Education. I based the following structure on this.
20. Piaget, J. and Inhelder, B. (1956) *A Child's Conception of Space*. London: Routledge & Kegan Paul.
21. Liben, L.S. (1982) 'Children's large-scale spatial cognition: is the measure the message? In Cohen, R. (ed.) *New Directions for Child Development: Children's Conceptions of Spatial Development*. San Francisco: Jossey-Bass.
22. Pick, W. (1978) 'Teaching children to think and draw "plan".' *Bulletin of Environmental Education*, **91**, 11–17.
23. Billet, S. and Matusiak, C. (1988) 'Nursery children as map makers.' *Education 3-13*, March.
24. 'Blockplay, as a way of developing children's understanding of three dimensional space, can be regarded as a non-verbal symbol system, analogous with spoken language but with the scope for representing some ideas more powerfully than words' – Gura, P. with Bruce, T. (1992) *Exploring Learning: Young Children and Blockplay*. London: Paul Chapman Publishing.

25. Blades, M. and Spencer, C. (1987b) 'Young children's recognition of environmental features from aerial photographs and maps.' *Environmental Education and Information*, **6**, 189-98.
26. Sandford, H.A. (1979) 'Things maps don't tell us.' *Geography*, **64**, 4, 297-30.
27. Boardman, D.J. (1982) 'Graphicacy through landscape models.' *Studies in Design Education, Craft and Technology*, **14**, 103-8; Boardman, D.J. (1983) *Graphicacy and Geography Teaching*. London and Canberra: Croom Helm.
28. Piaget, J., Inhelder, B. and Szeminska, A. (1960) *The Child's Conception of Geometry*. New York: Basic.
29. Based on an idea from Blades, M. and Spencer, C. (1986) 'On the starting grid.' *Child Education*, December.
30. See Walker, R.J. (1980) 'Map using abilities of 5-9 year old children.' *Geographical Education*, **3**, 4.
31. Towler, J.O. and Nelson, L.D. (1968) 'The elementary school child's concept of scale.' *Journal of Geography*, **69**, 89-93.
32. Palmer, J.A. and Wise, M.J. (1982) *The Good, the Bad and the Ugly*. Sheffield: Geographical Association.
33. There are, as yet, few materials available for teaching about aerial photographs. A notable exception is the resource pack *Discovering Aerial Photographs* (1992) by Terry Fiehn with Sharon Wetton and Chris Gibson, produced by Geonex UK Ltd. (See Appendix 2 for address.)
34. Riffle, P.A. (1969) 'A new approach to teaching map reading.' *Journal of Geography*, **68**, 554-6; Muir, M.E. and Blaut, J.M. (1969) 'The use of aerial photographs in teaching mapping to children in the first grade: an experimental study.' In Stea, D. (ed.) *Place Perception Research Reports*, 2. Worcester, Mass.: Graduate School of Geography.
35. Blaut, J.M., McCleary, G.S. and Blaut, A.S. (1970) 'Environmental mapping in young children.' *Environment and Behaviour*, **2**, 335-49.
36. McGee, C. (1982) 'Children's perceptions of symbols on maps and aerial photographs.' *Geographical Education*, **4**, 51-9; Blades, M. and Spencer, C. (1987b) 'Young children's recognition of environmental features from aerial photographs and maps.' *Environmental Education and Information*, **6**, 189-98.
37. Blaut, J.M., McCleary, G.S. and Blaut, A.S. (1970) 'Environmental mapping in young children.' *Environment and Behaviour*, **2**, 335-49. See also several chapters in Downs, R.M. and Stea, D. (1973) *Image and Environment*. London: Arnold.
38. Stea, D. and Blaut, J.M. (1973) 'Some preliminary observations on spatial learning in school children.' In Downs, R.M. and Stea, D. (eds) *Image and Environment*. Chicago: Aldine.
39. For a discussion of the processes involved in atlas editing and how decisions taken may influence the final product, with implications for the use of the atlas in school, see Wiegand, P. (1991) 'A model for the realization of a school atlas.' *Geography*, **76**, 1, 50-7.
40. See Miller, J.W. (1982) 'Improving the design of classroom maps: experimental comparison of alternative formats.' *Journal of Geography*, March/April.
41. Jones, G. (1981) 'Perception of land/sea cartographic designs by urban students in grades 4, 8 and 12.' In Wilson, P. *et al. Research in Geographical Education*. Brisbane: Australian Geographical Education Research Association.

CHAPTER 3

Knowledge and Understanding of Places

> Pupils should demonstrate their increasing knowledge and understanding of places in local, regional, national, international and global contexts, particularly: (i) a knowledge of places; (ii) an understanding of the distinctive features that give a place its identity; (iii) an understanding of the similarities and differences between places; and (iv) an understanding of the relationships between themes and issues in particular locations. (Attainment Target 2, Department of Education and Science, *Geography in the National Curriculum (England)* HMSO, March 1991, p. 7.)

This chapter attempts to explore the concept of place, investigates the experience children have of places and suggests some approaches to teaching place knowledge and teaching about localities. A more comprehensive account of children's knowledge and understanding of places, particularly distant places, has been provided elsewhere.[1]

Place: the central concept in geography

People often feel strongly about places. Consider, for example, the widespread objections voiced in France in the early 1990s to the development of the EuroDisney theme park. What many perceived as the distinctive character of part of the Paris basin was considered to be under threat by the cultural imperialism of 'Disneyfication'. Places have value for people.[2] They are also the spatial expression of human values. National parks, for example, *become* national parks because of the value placed on leisure and landscape by the national community.

Teaching about places involves sensitizing children to the world in which they live. This means not only imparting facts but also discussing feelings and attitudes. In order to understand places you have to be able to think and feel yourself into them. You ought to be able to begin to answer the question: 'What would it be like to live there?' The study of *place* therefore is inextricably bound up with a consideration of children's attitudes to places and to *people*. Stereotypes and prejudice play an important part in geography and it is necessary to evaluate critically the way in which places and people are presented to children and to assess the potential biases in the classroom materials used.

The study of places in Attainment Target 2 can be viewed as a series of concentric circles. Children have to study their own locality, a locality in another part of the UK, a locality in Europe, a locality in an economically developing country, and so on. For a long time it was thought that this order was the most appropriate one for geography teaching. You taught 'from near to far'. But this meant that it might well be the later years of the primary phase by the time children learned about the wider world, and in view of the fact that they are, albeit indirectly, in touch with the rest of the world from a very early age, this now seems entirely inappropriate. Television and travel have served to bring the rest of the world much closer. Even if children are not themselves in contact with the wider world and other peoples, they are in contact with *attitudes* about the wider world and other peoples from a very early age. Even nursery-age children appear to display quite definite prejudices.[3] Teaching about the wider world needs therefore to begin early and there is some (but not as much as many would like) recognition of this in the geography statutory orders.

As well as the dimension of 'near to far', the study of places in the National Curriculum involves understanding that smaller places 'fit inside' larger ones. You *can* be in two places at once! That is to say, you can be in Leeds and Yorkshire at the same time. Young children typically find this difficult to appreciate.[4] They can be helped by teacher-made jigsaw-type materials which allow them to position a shape representing their town on top of a shape representing their county, on top of a shape representing their country and so on.

For Attainment Target 2, children must study *localities*, then *regions*, then whole countries. A locality 'should be a small area with distinctive features and in the case of the local area is the immediate vicinity of the school or of where the pupil lives'.[5] In practice this area is likely to be something between 1 and 4 square kilometres (between one and four squares on an Ordnance Survey 1:50 000 Landranger map). It is at this scale that the potential for developing the characteristics of 'place' is greatest.

The home region should be an area which is substantial either in area or population.[6] For children in Wales, the whole of the Principality is to be the home region. For England, the following list of regions might give some indication of what sort of area is intended: the Lake District, Fenland, the Weald, Yorkshire, Greater London, the Wirral, Tyneside, the South-West Peninsula, Wessex, the Potteries, the Midlands. Note that some of these regions are formal or official (such as county boundaries) and therefore they are clearly defined on maps. Other regions may be informal. You know when you're in the heart of the 'West Country' but it's difficult to define precisely where the edge of it is. Nevertheless, there usually exists in informal regions some 'shared view' (often held over many generations) of the characteristics of the area. The notion of an informal region might be reinforced by the circulation pattern of local newspapers (for example the *Western Mail* or the

Northern Echo) or television companies or tourist promotional literature. Each of the regions listed above is large enough to have some internal variety whilst retaining some sense of identity.

How do children know about places?

Children have both direct and indirect experience of places. *Direct* experiences of places are those which result from first-hand encounters – for example of their own locality through their journey to school or to the shops. Experience of the local environment is explored more thoroughly in Chapter 6. But children also have their own direct experiences of more distant places, primarily through holiday travel.

Indirect experience of place is 'second-hand' experience, which comes primarily through television, film, books and hearsay. The boundary between these two sorts of experience is not clear cut, however. One informs the other and the result for the child is a unique constellation of information, images, associations and attitudes towards the wider world. What seems to be clear is that children are better informed about places (both near and far) than ever before, particularly as a result of their own widespread travel and increased access to television and video.

CHILDREN'S TRAVEL

We know very little about the extent of primary school children's foreign travel because data are not collected nationally for children as a separate subset of all travellers. Travel companies that do have the information are reluctant to release it for commercial reasons. Some reasonable guesses can be made, however, about children's holiday destinations based on the national pattern of adult travel.

About a third of all package holidays are destined for southern Spain and the Balearic islands of Majorca, Minorca and Ibiza. France and Greece make up about another third. In the rest of the world, North American destinations (especially Florida and California) are growing rapidly. As package holidays are very often cheaper than holidays in the UK, particularly for those who book early and go out of the high season, it is not surprising to find large numbers of children who have been to southern Spain, even in schools where it is sometimes claimed by teachers that 'these children never go off the estate'. Admittedly, the *nature* of the experience of, say, Spain, gained from a week or two in Torremolinos may be open to question. After all, holiday resorts are there to provide relaxation for the tourist rather than authentic geographical experiences. Nevertheless the fact remains that many children have been to such resorts and that in itself provides a foundation for teaching.

At the very least, children may have some idea of distance (it took two hours in an aeroplane) and route (we flew over the English Channel), as well as some knowledge of a few words of a foreign language, some idea about the type of food and drink available and some familiarity with a foreign currency. However, it seems very likely that some children at least gain far more than that from their travel experiences.[7] Children who have travelled do, in many cases, seem to be able to achieve a sense of balance in the way they describe places. They have learned that places are not always what they seem and that the stereotypes held about them previously may not be true after all. Some children also seem able to project this experience onto places which they themselves have not visited, so that they are able to question stereotypes in general. Travel may, therefore, be said to have broadened their minds. A small but significant number of children in Britain have substantial experience of travel in the Indian subcontinent, often living in the community where their family originated for up to six weeks or so. The experience of these children is invariably more 'authentic' when contrasted with the holiday travel of others, and that experience could usefully be explored in the context of geography teaching.

TELEVISION AND FILM

Children obtain a great amount of their information about the wider world from film and television.[8] The most influential programmes appear to be soap operas, many of which are set in distant locations (principally, at the time of writing, in Australia and the United States, as well as fairly specific locations within the United Kingdom, such as the East End of London). Advertisements are also powerful image formers with respect to other countries, particularly when stereotypes are exploited. TV commercials, like jokes and cartoon drawings, have to set the scene rapidly. This almost inevitably leads to the use of stereotypes so that we can recognize situations and anticipate how people will react in them. The most likely source of information about the world – television news programmes – appears not to be attended to by children even though the programmes may be 'watched'.[9] The formal presentation, the level of abstraction of many of the items (for example politics and economics) and the presentation of material in the form of unconnected items causes them to 'switch off' their minds, if not their sets. News items about particular individuals do seem, however, to be rather more memorable. Children do appear to remember items that deal with the exotic tours, balloon flights, polar crossings, ocean rowing boats, etc. of colourful and prominent people.

BOOKS

Some information about the wider world will come from books. However, there is disappointingly little contemporary children's fiction set in foreign countries. I stress contemporary because classics such as Erich Kaestner's *Emil and the Detectives* or Meinert de Jongh's *The Wheel on the School* do not give an indication of what life is like in Germany or the Netherlands *today*. Neither do folk tales. Although they enrich children's literary experience,[10] they provide little contemporary sense of place for the reader. There are suggestions for stories to use in the classroom in connection with near and far places in the *Books for Keeps Guide to Children's Books for a Multicultural Society*, compiled by J. Elkins and edited by P. Triggs. It is in two volumes: for ages 8-12 (1985) and ages 0-7 (1986). A further selection of stories, with discussion points and ideas for activities, is to be found in Anne Gadsden's *Geography and History through Stories: Key Stage 1* (Sheffield: The Geographical Association, and Cheshire County Council, 1991).

Personal favourites of mine are the parallel picture books by Nigel Gray and Philippe Dupasquier in which what happens in Britain at home is mirrored by events far away. The stories, with no or little text, are presented in two horizontal strips across the page. In *Dear Daddy* (Picture Puffin, 1990), life in Britain is shown season after season while Daddy (a merchant sailor) visits other parts of the world. The story is told through simple letters written by his daughter, telling about what is going on at home. In *A Country Far Away* (Picture Puffin, 1990) children's everyday life – swimming, shopping, school, etc. – is compared in Britain and tropical Africa.

Fiction is particularly effective in establishing for children the feeling of 'what it might be like to live there'. In Suzanne Fisher Staples' *Daughter of the Wind* (Walker Books, 1991), for example, Shabann and her family live in Pakistan's Cholistan desert. She's a free-spirited girl in a country which denies women's independence. At 12 years old, she's already betrothed and her sister Phulan, who is a year older, is about to be married. Then tragedy strikes . . . Stories like this focus the reader's mind on the circumstances of the individual. Once you begin to *identify* with someone in a story you're led into an imaginative reconstruction of how *you* might respond in that situation. Another good example from the same country is Anita Desai's *The Peacock Garden* (Mammoth, 1991). It is 1947: the country of Pakistan has just been created. It is a time of terror for many Muslims in the Punjab who have fled to an unknown future in the new country. This is the story of Zuni, whose family sought refuge in a local mosque. Zuni lives in secret in the mosque garden and is enthralled by the peacocks . . .

A slightly different approach in fiction dealing with other cultures is to consider those cultures as they are experienced in another country. There is now much good fiction dealing with British children whose families have strong Asian and Caribbean roots. In one of the stories in the collection *Imran's Secret* by Nadya Smith (Walker Books, 1992), Shaleen wants to go swimming with the rest of her class but she's not allowed to wear a swimming costume. So, one day she gradually edges closer and closer to the edge of the pool until she ends up in the water fully clothed . . .

For West Indian stories, the series of books published by Macmillan Caribbean can be recommended. In C. Everard Palmer's *The Cloud with the Silver Lining* (Macmillan Caribbean, 1987), Milton and Timmy's grandfather has had a leg amputated. The boys decide to set up a stall in their Jamaican village market to make enough money to buy him a buggy. Other West Indian stories by the same author include: *The Sun Salutes You*; *My Father Sun-Sun Johnson*; and *A Cow Called Boy*. Popular Caribbean stories in the same publisher's series include P. Sherlock's *Anansi the Spider Man* and T. Turner's *Once Below a Time* and *Climbing Clouds*.

Many of the images children hold about far-away places will come from information books. There is a great range of books available, each of which deals with a particular country, but, as yet, few that address themselves to the scale of the individual locality. 'Country' books tend to have an inbuilt structure to them that makes them effective in one dimension, but less so in another. Many books, for example, show the country in question through the eyes of one child or family or village. This has the merit of some depth of treatment but raises problems of the 'typicality' of the case study selected. How representative is the person or place described of the country as a whole? The end result is that in order to be recognizable, the person or place selected for the book runs the risk of being a stereotype.

An alternative approach is to present the country through the eyes of a larger number of people, but given a book of finite size there is less space available for each person and so the risk in this case is of shallowness of treatment. Good teaching needs therefore to rely on a wide range of resources: some in-depth, some which attempt to place the case study in its wider context.

What do children know about places?

As we have seen, children accumulate information about places from a number of different sources. Some of this information will be specific to particular children; for example, a 6-year-old might know about a distant, but rather obscure, place because that's where her father happens to have gone to work for a short while. This particular place is highly unlikely to be known by other children in the class and perhaps not by her teacher. But some places in the wider world are known by many children. There seems to be a shared 'known world' that emerges during childhood.

What are the first places that young children come to know about? The evidence is slender, but Spain, France, Africa, 'America' and Australia are often 'known' by children as young as 4 years old. At this early age real places such as these are often muddled with fantasy places (such as Disneyland or Never-Never Land). There is also much confusion between places which are near and places far away. Nevertheless, these five places seem particularly strong in the minds of nursery children. Learning about the wider world begins early.[11]

The 'known world' of primary-age children was investigated just before implementation of the National Curriculum in a study involving 222 children in Yorkshire.[12] By the age of 7 the world view of children had widened to consist of something like France, Spain, Greece, Russia, China, India, Australia, America/United States and Africa. By age 11, most of western Europe seems to be known, together with the larger countries of the Middle East. Countries which were commonly known at age 7 are by age 11 frequently paired with others on the basis of their closeness to each other or on perceived cultural similarities: for example, 'America' with Canada, Australia with New Zealand and China with Japan. Although children (boys particularly) at age 11 make frequent mention of Argentina and Brazil (presumably because of football connections), much of South America remains unknown. The constituent countries of Africa also remain largely unknown. Other blank areas on the map of children's known world at age 11 are South-East Asia and eastern Europe.

Knowledge of the world varies with children's experiences but these results seem to indicate that it is possible to make some generalizations about places that come to be known. A complex series of factors are at play here. Some countries, for example, promote themselves more vigorously. The larger and wealthier countries are rarely out of the news. But representation of countries in the news is not enough for them to be 'known' by children. At the time of the investigation described above, all the countries of eastern Europe were in the news constantly for the preceding year. Some countries (such as those of the Middle East) are rarely out of the news and yet these places appear not to capture children's attention. It seems to be that some countries loom very large in the public imagination and these are repeated in early years' reading and teaching materials. Some places seem to be used almost as icons for the distant and exotic, much as people refer to 'Timbuktoo' when they mean 'a long way away' rather than making a specific reference to a city in the Republic of Mali.

Perhaps the most inaccurately referred to place of all is Africa. 'Africa is always producing some novelty', said Pliny, quoting a Greek proverb alluding to the belief that Africa abounded in strange monsters. 'Africa' is almost universally referred to by children as a homogeneous land. It is seen as a place where people are starving, live in 'huts' and where life is 'primitive'. Unfortunately this reflects a comparable view held by many adults, and one of the priorities in geography teaching might be to develop in children's minds the differentiation of places and people in the continent and to make a serious effort to eradicate pejorative language from teaching materials. 'The darkest thing about Africa has always been our ignorance of it.'[13]

Children's knowledge and understanding of the world can be explored through their own, freehand maps of the world, drawn from memory. Lucy's map of the world, for example (Figure 3.1(a)), seems to indicate that although she is aware that the places she has heard of are real units and that they are in some way joined, she has little idea of the relative size of the places she knows, nor how they fit together. Towns, countries, islands, continents are all pieced together in a random jigsaw puzzle. Steven's map, on the other hand (Figure 3.1(b)), is strongly influenced by his study of the globe. Europe, North America and Australasia form clusters of countries and he has identified the poles correctly. He has a weakly developed understanding of the position of Asia and can't quite see how the countries he knows in the Middle East fit with the rest. He does know, however, that you can't see all round the globe at once, and Japan and Thailand are shown 'round the corner'. Orlando (the self-styled 'Entertainments Capital of the World', with its Walt Disney World, EPCOT centre, Circus World, Sea World and the Kennedy Space Centre) figures prominently on his map.

Teaching place knowledge

The maps in the National Curriculum documentation indicate that children are required to know the names and the locations of the continents by level 3. The Earth's land surface comprises seven continents. Europe, Africa and Asia, although culturally distinct, physically form one land mass which could be called Afro-Eurasia and which forms almost 60 per cent of the Earth's land surface. Central America is usually included with North America as a continent separate from South America, although they are of course joined. Many geographers prefer the term 'Oceania' (to include all the non-Asian Pacific islands as well as Australia and New Zealand) to the term 'Australasia', which is found in the National Curriculum documentation. The seventh continent is Antarctica.

Learning about continents is necessarily linked to learning about the ways in which the spherical Earth can be transferred to a flat map (see Chapter 2). For that reason, the best place to start teaching the names of the continental land masses is to use a globe.[14] 'Blackboard' globes or globes that will take a felt-tip pen marker and which have only land and sea marked are

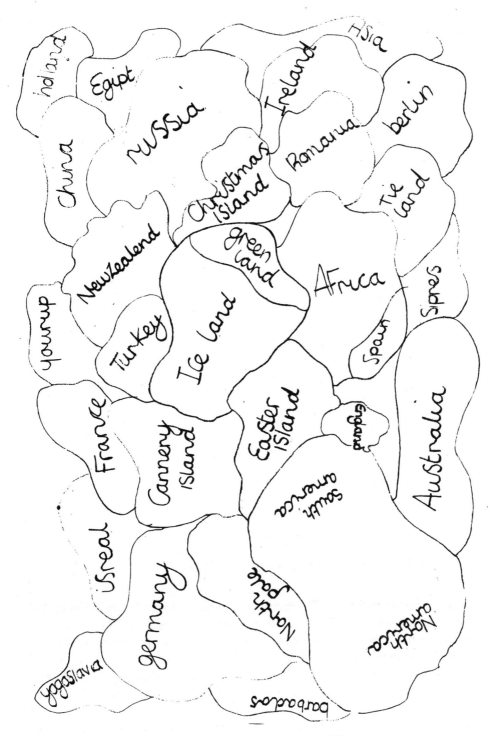

Figure 3.1(a)   *'Draw me a map of the world': Lucy (age 11).*

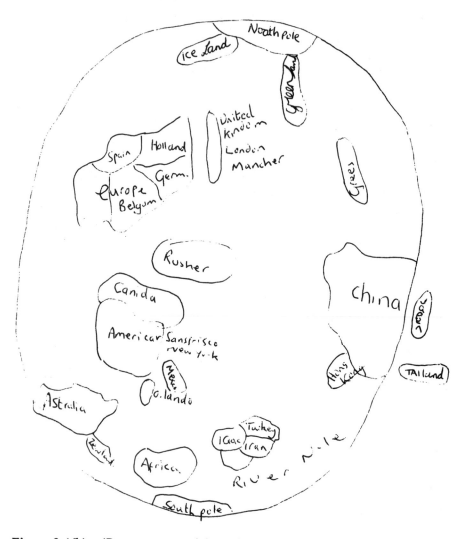

Figure 3.1(b) *'Draw me a map of the world': Steven (age 11).*

particularly useful for this. To emphasize the point that the definition of the continents is fairly arbitrary I think it is helpful to focus attention on some of the boundary zones between continents, such as Sinai (between Africa and Asia), the Caucasus Mountains (between Europe and Asia) and the island of New Guinea (usually split between Asia and Australasia/Oceania). 'Where would *you* divide Africa and Asia? At the Suez Canal or the political boundary between Egypt and Israel?' A globe is also essential for appreciating the (almost circular) shape of Antarctica and its size relative to the other continents. Labelling a blank globe as well as a series of maps with different projections is an appropriate task. Colouring the areas of the land masses on blank maps helps to reinforce recognition of their shape.

Blank wall maps of the world are flexible resources. They can be used, for example, to show food labels, stamps, postcards, currency, 'where we've been', 'where we've received letters from', etc. Teachers have used such maps as the basis for display for many years. Pupils' copies of the same blank maps are also helpful for recording the same information at a more personal level. Some children simply like to accumulate countries and to see how many names they can learn. The 'country of the week', whereby children find out as much as they can about a particular country for an information-sharing session at the end of the week, is popular too.

Much of geography is to do with 'those faraway places with strange sounding names'.[15] Some progress can be made towards geographical understanding by spending time on *sorting* the placenames that children already know. 'Make a list of 10 or 20 places that you know. Now let's sort those places into continents, countries, towns, other places, etc.' This forces children to check map and atlases and globes for meaning.

A more sophisticated form of sorting is to give titles to lists of placenames. Cornwall, Kent, Lancashire, Essex and Surrey, for example, are *counties*, but the list can be titled more accurately as *English counties*. By extending this idea (in this case to 'northern counties', 'coastal counties' or 'Home Counties', children may come to see how places are differentiated. Similar sequences of progressively more accurate titles might be: rivers, North American rivers, Canadian rivers, or countries, tropical countries, equatorial countries, etc. It is helpful for activities such as this to have the placenames written on cards so that they can be grouped and regrouped under more refined headings.

Attitudes towards people and places

Reference has already been made to children exhibiting signs of prejudice at a very early age. But do children have distinctive attitudes towards other people and places? It seems that they do. There is some evidence to indicate that children prefer places that they perceive as being more like their own homeland.[16] This accords with the more general finding in social psychology that people prefer other people they think of as being most like themselves.

At Key Stage 1, many children select their 'favourite countries' on the basis of exotic features and tend to stress the differences between themselves and foreigners. They may also deny that they themselves could ever become foreigners, not understanding that a foreigner is anyone out of his or her own country. By Key Stage 2, however, children generally seem to accept more similarities between themselves and other peoples and are increasingly able to see the point of view of others. Many researchers have reported a 'peak of favourable attitudes' towards foreigners at the age of about 10.[17]

Of course, what children *know* about other countries is closely related to their *attitudes* towards other countries. There is some, rather dated, evidence to suggest that children know most about the countries they have favourable and unfavourable attitudes towards and least about those countries towards which they feel fairly neutral.[18]

Why is this? One possibility is that children acquire information about a country and on the basis of that information develop an attitude towards it. Another is that the attitude is developed first and that thereafter children store information which confirms that attitude and filter out information which contradicts it. It seems likely that the latter sequence (i.e. that the attitude comes first) is more usual.[19] If this is so, then the primary teacher's role in building positive images towards other people and places becomes crucial and close attention needs to be paid to the way places are presented to children. This has implications for the careful selection of visual images and the use of language when talking about places.

The starting point for the development of positive attitudes to other nationalities is the development of sensitivity and thoughtfulness in the classroom. Children should have a sense of their own worth and an appreciation of their own culture, values and beliefs as well as being able to imagine the feelings and viewpoints of other people. Concepts such as co-operation, conflict, fairness and interdependence need to be built in a classroom context which provides an environment that stimulates and challenges children as well as a safe environment in which everyone is accepted. Most teachers find it helpful to establish clear rules as a background for building these positive attitudes. For example: 'Everyone listens to the person who is speaking, no one has to speak if they don't want to and no one makes fun of anyone else.' A number of books list collaborative activities designed to enable children to learn to listen to others' point of view, to be tolerant, to talk about and value their own thoughts, feelings and ideas. Collections of suitable activities can be found in:

Fountain, S. (1990) *Learning Together: Global Education 4–7.*
Cheltenham: Stanley Thornes.
Nicholas, F.M. (1987) *Coping with Conflict.* Wisbech: Learning
Development Aids.
Pike, G. and Selby, D. (1988) *Global Teacher, Global Learner.* London:
Hodder & Stoughton.
Fisher, S. and Hicks, D. (1985) *World Studies 8–13: A Teachers'
Handbook.* Edinburgh: Oliver & Boyd.

Teaching about localities

Teaching about a specific locality allows for study in depth and gives the opportunity for identification with real people and their lives. It is more likely therefore to lead to the development of 'reciprocity'; that is, the ability to see something from someone else's point of view. This, essentially, is the goal of international understanding.

A popular opening strategy is to brainstorm children's preconceptions of the locality that is to be studied. Suppose a teacher has collected information from one of the families in school about a particular village in Pakistan. Start by asking (perhaps in smallish groups with a large sheet of paper on which to record impressions): 'What would it be like to live in a village in Pakistan?' Children can be prompted after the initial flow of ideas to consider scenery, jobs, houses, school, weather, clothes, spare-time activities, and so on. It is worth recording these early impressions so that the teacher and children together can later reflect on these ideas and compare them with the results of a similar exercise after teaching has taken place. It is helpful for children to reflect along the lines: 'I used to think that . . . but now . . .'

Questions to ask in the study of localities include:

- What is this place like?
- Where is this place (in relation to where I live or other places I know)?
- What do people do there? (what work do they do?; what leisure activities do they engage in?; how do they travel?)
- How is it like/unlike *my* locality?
- How is it changing?
- What do I like about it?

To answer questions like this you need to examine *evidence*. (There are obvious parallels here with history teaching.) One of the most important sources of evidence about places is pictures.

Visual images can have a powerful effect on children. In one study,[20] a group of children initially exhibited positive attitudes towards India and negative attitudes towards Germany. After looking at a selection of pictures these results seemed to have been reversed with more negative attitudes displayed towards India and more positive ones towards Germany. It seems likely that these children had been in contact with sources of (negative) attitudes towards Germany but had themselves little evidence on which to base an opinion. The pictures seen appeared similar to their own surroundings and therefore they found them favourable. India had previously been associated in their minds with exotic images but photographs of everyday life showing crowding and poverty appeared disturbing. Photographs can therefore encourage negative and over-simplified comparisons and stress differences rather than similarities.

Good collections of pictures of places can now be obtained from general educational equipment suppliers as well as from development agencies (see addresses in Appendix 2). Some of these picture packs are well structured: for example, those in *A Tale of Two Cities* (World Wide Fund for Nature, 1992), which contains matched pairs of photographs of Calcutta and London on themes such as begging, school, homelessness, washing, street markets, water, etc. Similar paired photographs of life in Kenya and Tanzania are to be found in *New Journeys* (edited by Catherine McFarlane and Audrey Osler, Development Education Centre, Birmingham, 1991). These particularly focus on issues of tourism, self-reliance and land use.

Picture teaching strategies need to start with practice in fairly straightforward observation. It seems sensible to make sure children know what's in the picture before asking questions about the implications of what the picture shows! Young children can be helped by strategies such as simple questions requiring 'yes' or 'no' answers or statements to be answered by true or false. Observation is further encouraged by playing 'Kim's Game' with photographs. Look at a photograph for one minute then recall, with your eyes shut, all the information the photograph contained.

Information obtained from pictures can be stored in the form of grids:

	Photo 1	*Photo 2*	*Photo 3*
People	/	/	/
Trees	/		
Shops		/	
Homes	/		
Cattle		/	
Cars	/		/

Several pictures can be sorted into groups using similar criteria. For example, all the pictures that show people are put into one pile, all the pictures that show animals in another. A selection of pictures can be put into groups and classified on more difficult criteria such as:

This place could be in Britain/could not be in Britain;
This place is warmer/colder than in Britain;
This place is near where we live/far away from where we live.

It is useful to discuss with children their reasons for classifying pictures on criteria such as these. Pictures can also be matched with placename labels, or captions describing activities shown in the pictures. They can also be matched with country outline shapes.

Working in pairs, one child can describe what is seen in a photograph and the other draw what is described. This activity not only reveals the children's perceptions of what is seen and heard but encourages the use of locational vocabulary, such as 'in the foreground, behind, left', etc.

Resources for the study of localities

The availability of resources may determine to a large extent the selection of localities for study. It is worth investigating which of the following may be available for each locality being considered:

- photographs and other pictures;
- maps;
- written materials, including information from reference books;
- families in school with experience of the locality;
- possibilities of people from the locality visiting school;
- everyday items including food, clothes, artefacts;
- class-to-class links;
- (for the UK) whether the place can be visited.

The essence of the study of a locality is *authenticity*. There really does have to be some sense of contact with the place being studied. This means that if at all possible (for the study of a contrasting locality in the UK) the children should visit it. If not then their teacher should have visited it. If that isn't possible, then somebody who has been there should visit the school, and if *that* isn't possible then the best materials that are available will just have to do. But in these circumstances they must be good.

A good selection of pictures is essential. These can be taken with an ordinary 35 mm camera, printed at postcard size and laminated for class use. Enlargements are useful for display, and particularly good pictures can be enlarged relatively inexpensively to poster size by high street photo shops.

For other localities in the United Kingdom a selection of Ordnance Survey maps will be needed as well as street maps and maps from estate agents, etc. For most localities in Europe there will be maps locally available at a scale of about 1:50 000. Good map shops in Britain also sell foreign maps. For localities in economically developing countries there may be no maps available easily but a simple sketch or pictorial map of a village location (such as those provided in some of the packs published by development agencies) is sufficient.

Descriptive documentary material should cover the programmes of study. For Key Stage 1, for example, this includes: uses of buildings; how people make journeys; the goods and services needed and how they are provided; how the land is used (e.g. for farming, industry, leisure); what the landscape looks like; and so on. This is sometimes effectively presented through the medium of a 'day in the life' of one or more of the people who live in the locality.

There are a number of helpful publications available on school-to-school and class-to-class links with other localities. Especially useful are: *Making the Most of Your Partner School Abroad* (1991), from the Central Bureau for Educational Visits and Exchanges (see Appendix 2 for address) and *School Links International*, by Rex Beddis and Cherry Mares (1988) (Avon County Council and Tidy Britain Group Schools Research Project)

Contrasting localities in the United Kingdom

Children already know a good deal about their own locality. This issue is explored further in the context of environmental education in Chapter 6. Below are two examples of children studying other localities in the UK. Both incorporate some active involvement by the children, the first through pen-friends, the second through a class visit.

A class of 5- and 6-year-old children in a small market town in Yorkshire undertook a unit of work on the Post Office.[21] The activities involved are mapped onto the statements of attainment as follows:

THE POST OFFICE

AT1 Geographical skills. Pupils should be able to:

Level 1   (1b) observe and talk about a familiar place (e.g. the local post office);

Level 2   (2a) use geographical vocabulary to talk about places (e.g. features on the postcards received);

           (2b) make a pictorial representation of a real or imaginary place (e.g. draw the journey of *The Jolly Postman* by J. and A. Ahlberg, Heinemann, 1986);

           (2c) follow a route using a plan (e.g. journey to nearest post box);

           (2e) identify familiar features on photographs or pictures (e.g. familiar features on postcards sent);

AT2 Knowledge and understanding of places. Pupils should be able to:

Level 1   (1a) name familiar features of the local area (e.g. post-boxes, post office);

           (1b) identify activities carried out by people in the local area (e.g. postal deliveries);

           (1c) state where they live (writing addresses);

(1d) demonstrate awareness of the world beyond their local area (letter and postcard exchange);

(1e) name the country in which they live (locating their own school on map of Great Britain).

Level 2 (2a) name the countries of the UK (using maps to locate the origin of letters and postcards received);

(2c) identify features of a locality outside the local area and suggest how these might affect the lives of the people who live there (comparing their own experience with that of their penfriends. 'What would it be like to live in a flat compared with a house, to go to school on a bus or underground train rather than walk, etc.?' Note also similar interests and school routines of both groups of children.)

(2d) describe similarities and differences between the local area and another locality specified in the programme of study (e.g. compare photographs of cattle market, local farms, river, hills, etc. with those of motorway, factories and offices, etc. to show differences. But also compare similarities in shops (multiple retailers the same), parks and weather).

AT4 Human Geography. Pupils should be able to:

Level 1 (1a) recognize that buildings are used for different purposes (e.g. shops, schools, houses);

(1c) recognize that adults do different kinds of work (e.g. in postal service. Visit to post office and talk at school from postman);

Level 2 (2c) identify how goods and services needed in the local community are provided (e.g. sequencing stages in 'what happens to a letter once it's posted?')

The teacher concerned had a friend working in London who also taught a class of 23 first-year children. Both teachers discussed the framework of their teaching in advance by phone. Children were paired for the letter writing on the basis of their attainment. Postcards, photographs of the local area and other information was exchanged by the teachers. Later, photographs of the children were taken and exchanged as well as a videotape of them at work and play, their school and the locality. Each class located both schools on a map of Great Britain and related these to other places they knew or had visited. Distances were discussed, primarily related to time of travel. Early letters were structured by the teachers and duplicated, with gaps for the children to complete, for example:

Dear _____ ,

My name is _____ .
I am _____ years old.
My birthday is on _____ .
I live at _____ .
I go to _____ school.
At school I like to _____ .
At playtime, I play with _____ .
I would like to be your penfriend.
Please write back soon.
Love from _____ .

Later letters included a 'notelet' cut-out animal shape with a simple message, a word-processed letter printed in large characters and a freely written letter about 'what I do at school'. Each child had a folder into which were stuck the letters from the penfriend and a duplicated sheet as follows:

_____ is my penfriend.
_____ is _____ years old.
She goes to _____ school.
Her best friend is _____ .
I think my penfriend will look like this:

The folders were completed with photographs of both children and a map showing the location of both schools.

The second example is of a group of 8-year-old children from an urban school in the West Yorkshire conurbation.[22] All the children knew their addresses and postcodes and were able to say who lived nearest to and furthest from their school. They were also able to describe the buildings around the school and other similar features of the local landscape. But when it came to considering a different (rural) locality they could only speculate. They were to go to Clapham, a village in the Yorkshire Dales, for a day and their teacher asked them what they expected to see:

'There will only be a few cars.'
'No, it's in the country so people need cars to get around.'
'There's going to be less cars than in Bradford.'

'There won't be any buses.'
'Well, maybe one or two.'
'I think people might have to walk a lot.'

And what did the children think the place might look like?

'There won't be any shops and there will only be a few houses in
the village.'
'There will be millions of grass and hills.'
'There might be flowers and mud and flies.'
'There won't be any school.'

A visit is probably of more use if the children are able to see it as an opportunity for hypothesis testing – a way of confirming or denying what they
expect to see when they get there. These children from Bradford were able
to test their thoughts rather than just look and see.

Localities in Europe

The early 1990s saw substantial changes in Europe which began to be
reflected in education. A vision of the new Europe is summarized in the
Charter of Paris, adopted in November 1990 by the heads of state and
government of the then 34 countries involved in the Conference on Security
and Co-operation in Europe (CSCE):

> Ours is a time for fulfilling the hopes and expectations that our people have
> cherished for decades: steadfast commitment to democracy based on human
> rights and fundamental freedoms; prosperity through economic liberty and social
> justice; and equal security for all countries.

The political importance of the European dimension is demonstrated by the
fact that the Council of Europe's Standing Conference of the European
Ministers of Education chose it as the main theme of the Vienna meeting in
1991. The ministers pointed out that work, study and leisure in Europe are
characterized by mobility, interchange and communication and that the 'daily
lives of Europeans will increasingly take on a "living European dimension" '.
This constitutes a major focus for the attention of geography education. The
ministers recommended that in these circumstances, education should:

(i) increase awareness of the growing unity between European peoples
and countries and of the establishment of their relations on a new
basis;
(ii) foster understanding of the fact that, in many spheres of our lives,
the European perspective applies and that European decisions are
necessary.

Perhaps the clearest statement of the 'European dimension' in education and its objectives is to be found in the resolution of the Ministers of Education meeting within the European Council (European Council, 1988). This resolution set out a number of measures which were designed to:

> – strengthen in young people a sense of European identity and make clear to them the value of European civilization and of the foundations on which the European peoples intend to base their development today, that is in particular the safeguarding of the principles of democracy, social justice and respect for human rights,
>
> – prepare young people to take part in the economic and social development of the Community and in making concrete progress towards European union, as stipulated in the European Single Act,
>
> – make them aware of the advantages which the Community represents, but also of the challenges it involves, in opening up an enlarged economic and social area to them,
>
> – improve their knowledge of the Community and its member states in their historical, cultural, economic and social aspects and bring home to them the significance of the co-operation of the Member States of the European Community with other countries of Europe and the world. (European Council, 1988)

Some concerns have been raised, however, about the idea of a European dimension. One is anxiety about the possibility of imposition of uniformity. There needs to remain respect for local, national and regional diversity. Another is that by definition its scope for international understanding is limited to the continent alone and that the 'world dimension' is thereby ignored.

A label such as 'the European dimension' makes assumptions about what Europe is. What do geographers mean when they refer to Europe? There are in fact a number of different 'Europes'. A simple definition would be the Europe of the European Community, but this is increasingly far too restricted given the scale of change in central and eastern Europe.

Within the continent, there are profound economic differences. To the west is a Europe that is prosperous and efficient, yet to the east a Europe which is, despite being rich in natural and human resources, an impoverished contrast. The disparity in revenue between the extremes in Europe is greater than that between the United States and Mexico. The ratio of wealth between Switzerland and Albania for example is 25:1. Even within the west there are social and economic inequalities but it is the fundamental west–east divide which dominates. This is marked also in trade. Eastern Europe has only a 2 per cent share of the total amount of world trade whereas western Europe derives its great prosperity from intensive trade between its members.

The legacy of the political past in Europe is reflected in the human and economic landscape. The Soviet economic model has created an eastern and central European landscape of heavy industry, of huge enterprises which worked directly with the USSR, and of uniformly built cities which were at the time a solution to the acute housing shortages. This territorial heritage is not well illustrated in the school books of the new Europe.

There are also within Europe fundamental differences in society and culture. A long-standing ideological division exists between a Europe of Latin Christianity and a Europe with a Byzantine inheritance. These form two different historical rhythms, each with their own relationship to modern times. This 'frontier of faith' that runs from Tallinn to the Adriatic became a front line in Yugoslavia in 1992.

These and other differences allow Europe to be divided into several, broadly similar tracts. There is, for example, the Europe of northern capitals and decision-making centres, the Europe of western coasts, the sunny Europe of the south, the Alpine Europe of key transport networks and high-tech industry, the relatively low-populated interstitial Europe as well as the central and eastern heritage of the Soviet past.

Advice and information about the European dimension is provided by the United Kingdom Centre for European Education (UKCEE) (see Appendix 2). This is a grant-aided organization which is part of a network of centres in each Community country which seeks to promote a European perspective in education. As well as dealing with requests for information from schools and member organizations, it supports conferences, seminars and curriculum development and has published a termly bulletin called *Euroed News*, designed to disseminate information throughout the UK on teaching about Europe. This was replaced in 1991 by a new journal: *Edit* (The European Dimension in Teaching). Since 1989 the UKCEE has been part of the Central Bureau for Educational Visits and Exchanges.

Localities in an economically developing country

> For the first time it will be compulsory for all children, in all our schools, to learn about issues of world development and interdependence. What a unique opportunity this offers for all of us concerned with helping to raise public awareness of these issues. (Rt Hon. Lynda Chalker, MP, Minister for Overseas Development, 17 October 1990)

It is unlikely that most primary school teachers will have been able to visit personally a locality in an economically developing country. They will therefore have to rely principally on materials supplied by others. Some schools will be fortunate enough to have numbers of children whose families will have relatives and friends in such localities, perhaps the Caribbean or the Indian subcontinent. A collection of materials relating to the experiences of children's families would be especially valuable. A family might be asked to

85

make a record of a visit to relatives. This might include a diary of the journey, shown as a time line, photographs of the locality itself, some information about the lives and work of people who live there and so on.

If material of this sort proves difficult to obtain then the next best source is published material. At the time of writing, a number of voluntary organizations are very active in creating such materials, often using their extensive contacts in the field to develop authentic resources. *My Village, Ilesha*, for example, by Angela Holland and Nick Reggler (CWDE, 1991), has pictures, information and activities relating to Africa, Nigeria and the village of Ilesha itself. Details are provided about landscape, climate, people, work, food, health, childhood, the market and the school in the village. There are maps and stories.

If an aid or development agency resource pack such as this is used, how could it be supplemented by further information collected by the teacher and the school? Below, I have assumed that a class will be using the pack: *Chembakolli: A Village in India*. This is a pupil activity pack from Action Aid (see Appendix 2 for address). It consists of a number of photographs, a map, teacher's notes, pupil activities, etc. What additional resources might support the study of this village in southern India?

Stories help to bring localities alive. India is rich in myth, legend and fable. Many of the stories appear in the great Hindu epics (the Mahabharata and the Ramayana) and the Buddhist birth stories (the Jatakas). Ruskin Bond's *Tales and Legends from India* (Julia MacRae) includes tales from those three sources and there are useful notes on the sources themselves. Marcus Crouch's *The Ivory City* (Granada Dragon) retells many of the stories in colloquial English. This also has notes on the origins of the tales as well as a useful glossary of unfamiliar terms. *The Story of Prince Rama* (Brian Thompson, Kestrel) is the classic story from the Ramayana of the struggle between the forces of good and evil, showing the heroism of the prince, the loyalty of his brother and the love of his wife as they face Ravana, the king of all the demons.

The Stupid Tiger and Other Tales (Upendrakishore Raychaudhuri, translated by William Radice, Deutsch) is a collection of Bengali tales strongly rooted in the oral tradition. Rani Singh remembers eight of her favourite folk tales from her own Indian childhood in *The Indian Storybook* (Heinemann).

Many stories by Ruskin Bond are set in India and several of them deal with natural disasters. In *Angry River* (Antelope Books), for example, a child is stranded in a peepal tree when the river floods; *Flames in the Forest* (Blackbird) describes a forest fire encountered by Romi cycling on his way home from school; and *Earthquake* (Redwing) is set in the Cherrapunji Hills of north-eastern India. Other charming and accessible stories by Ruskin Bond include *The Cherry Tree* (Gazelle), *Tigers Forever* (Redwing) and *Big Business* (Gazelle).

Top primary fluent readers could tackle *The Village by the Sea* (Anita Desai, Puffin Plus). This award-winning book is a hugely moving story about a family living in a fishing village near Bombay. The oldest children have to take responsibility for their younger sisters in challenging circumstances: drunken father, ill mother, desperate poverty.

In Malcolm J. Bosse's *Ganesh* (Penguin, 1981), Jeffrey lives in an Indian village. Everyone calls him Ganesh after the elephant-headed Hindu god. He speaks Tamil to his friends and goes to yoga classes after school. He thinks of himself as an Indian – as Indian as his best friend Ramesh. But when his father dies, leaving Jeffrey on his own, the villagers become distrustful of his American blond hair and his blue eyes. It seems best to obey his father's instructions and leave India to live with his aunt in the USA. But will he be accepted *there*?

Soma Books Ltd (see Appendix 2 for address) stocks children's books which are produced in India. Many of these are picture books which show scenes of everyday life and can therefore be used as 'evidence' by primary school children or just enjoyed for their content. I especially like *My First Railway Journey* (Mrinal Mitra, National Book Trust, India, 1986), which through pictures alone shows a train journey from start to finish. This is a long, hot, thirsty, crowded train. Also available are comic strip books on the adventures of Krishna, tales of the Buddha, etc.

There are also published materials about visiting India, so that the country is seen, as it were, from the outside. *Nanda in India* (by Terry Furchgott, Deutsch) is a colourfully illustrated story about a young boy travelling to see his grandparents in India for the first time. Life in a bustling Indian city is seen as the boy recognizes the differences between his own home in England and where his grandparents live. The At Home and Abroad series (from Macmillan Education) also describe the types of experiences enjoyed by children in Britain visiting their parents' place of origin. *Amardip and Rema* (Steve Harrison, 1986) describes two Sikh children from Coventry who visit their family in the Punjab. In *Delhi Visit*, by Ann Morris and Heidi Larson (A. and C. Black, 1989), two girls from London stay with their mother's family in Delhi. Their father has to stay behind so they telephone home to say what they're doing: going to see a film, riding on bicycles, etc.

Sakina in India (by Tony Tigwell, A. and C. Black's Beans series, 1982) looks at a real family through the eyes of a Muslim girl in a village in northern India. *Chinnoda's School in India* by Rachel Warner (1984) in the same series also looks at daily life. The same theme is explored in *My Indian Home* (Dagmar Dasgupta, 1988, Macdonald). Tulu has been to Calcutta to visit relatives and has returned to her village. Next day she has to go to school. She does her homework on the veranda, has *rotis* (flat thin cakes) and milk for breakfast, sits on a jute mat at school, buys betel nuts on the way home and so on. Information books for children on India include *Inside India* by Prodeepta Das (Franklin Watts, 1990) and *India* by David Cummings (Wayland, 1989).

A Family in India (Jacobsen and Kristensen in the Wayland Families around the World series) and *India Is My Country* (Cliff and Bernice Moon, Wayland) look respectively at India through the experiences of one family and through a number of mini-biographies.

Books on religions (such as *I Am a Sikh*, *I Am a Moslem* and *I Am a Hindu* by Manju Aggarwal (Franklin Watts); *Hinduism* in the Our World: Life and Faith series by Hulton; *The Hindu World* in Macdonald Educational Religions of the World series) would also support the study of a locality.

In addition to using the above published materials, teachers could also make use of travel agency materials (one of the longest-established travel companies dealing with Indian travel is Cox and Kings) and guide books. These materials are quite good for helping to establish what it's like to be there. Travel guides, for example, will usually give advice on what to buy in the shops, the price of accommodation and meals, sights to visit, travel arrangements, climate, etc.

Wider resources to support the study would include clothes, food, music and videos. Details of some Indian clothes are found in P. Bahree's *Looking at Lands: India* (Macdonald, 1985). Tapes of Indian music are widely available in high street music shops, and videotapes of Indian films are also readily available in many parts of the UK. Spices such as cardamom, cumin, cinnamon, coriander, as well as root ginger, garlic, chillies, etc. are to be found in most supermarkets, and many shops in Britain now sell mooli, green bananas, coconut, mangos and sweet potatoes, so it is quite possible to investigate the taste of India too.

NOTES AND REFERENCES

1. Wiegand, P. (1992) *Places in the Primary School: Knowledge and Understanding of Places at Key Stages 1 and 2.* London: Falmer Press.
2. Wiegand, P. (1986) 'Values in geographical education.' In Tomlinson, P. and Quinton, M. (eds) *Values across the Curriculum.* London: Falmer Press, pp. 51–76.
3. Jeffcoate, R. (1977) 'Children's racial ideas and feelings.' *English in Education*, **11**, 1.
4. Jahoda, G. (1963) 'The development of children's ideas about country and nationality.' *British Journal of Educational Psychology*, **33**, 47–60, 143–53.
5. Department of Education and Science (1991) *Geography in the National Curriculum.* London: HMSO, p. 31.
6. Department of Education and Science (1991) *Geography in the National Curriculum.* London: HMSO, p. 36.
7. Wiegand, P. (1991) 'Does travel broaden the mind?' *Education 3–13*, **19**, 1.

8. Hartmann and Husband (1974) *Racism and the Mass Media*. New York: Davis-Poynter. See also Jungkunz, T. and Thomas, O. (n.d.) 'Young people's perceptions of other countries: summary of pilot study findings', mimeograph. Oxford: Oxford Development Education Unit, Westminster College. More than half the 278 children surveyed in this investigation said that television was their main source of information about economically developing countries.

9. Cullingford, C. (1984) *Children and Television*. Aldershot: Gower.

10. The value of folk tales for children has been argued by, amongst others, Bettelheim, B. (1977) *The Uses of Enchantment: The Meaning and Importance of Fairy Tales*. London: Thames & Hudson.

11. Lambert, S. and Wiegand, P. (1990) 'The beginnings of international understanding.' *The New Era in Education*, **71**, 3, 90-3.

12. Wiegand, P. (1991) 'The known world of the primary school.' *Geography*, **76**, 2, 143-9.

13. Kimble, 1951, quoted in Porter, P. W. (1987) ' "In Dunkelsten Afrika": Africa in the student mind.' *Journal of Geography*, March/April, 98-102.

14. Bateman, R. and Lloyd, K. (1980) 'Simple maps.' *Teaching Geography*, **6**, 1, 7-9.

15. The fascination of placenames does not stop at childhood. See *The Meaning of Liff* by Douglas Adams and John Lloyd (Pan Books and Faber & Faber, 1983) in which the authors apply the otherwise 'spare' words of placenames to 'the many hundreds of common experiences, feelings, situations and even objects which we all know and recognize but for which no words exist'.

16. Jaspars, J. M. F., van der Geer, J. P., Tajfel, H. and Johnson, N. B. (1983) 'On the development of international attitudes in children.' *European Journal of Social Psychology*, **2**, pp. 347-69; Stillwell, R. and Spencer, C. (1974) 'Children's early preferences for other nations and their subsequent acquisition of knowledge about those nations.' *European Journal of Social Psychology*, **3**, 3, pp. 345-9.

17. For example, Carnie, J. (1971) 'The development of junior children's ideas of people of different race and nation.' Unpublished PhD thesis, London University.

18. Grace, H. A. and Neuhaus, J. O. (1952) 'Information and social distance as predictors of hostility towards nations.' *Journal of Abnormal and Social Psychology*, **47**, 540-5; Johnson, N. B., Middleton, M. R. and Tajfel, H. (1970) 'The relationship between children's preferences for, and knowledge about, other nations.' *British Journal of Social and Clinical Psychology*, **9**, 232-40.

19. Stillwell, R. and Spencer, C. (1974) 'Children's early preferences for other nations and their subsequent acquisition of knowledge about those nations.' *European Journal of Social Psychology*, **3**, 3, pp. 345-9.

20. Stillwell, R. and Spencer, C. (1974) 'Children's early preferences for other nations and their subsequent acquisition of knowledge about those nations.' *European Journal of Social Psychology*, **3**, 3, pp. 345-9.

21. I am grateful to Pauline Ward for allowing me to reproduce her work here.

22. I am indebted here to Hilary Britton, who wrote a critical evaluation of the experiences of this class of children as part of her assessed coursework for the degree of MEd from the University of Leeds, 1991: 'The development of children's knowledge and understanding of place: a review of current research and issues.'

CHAPTER 4

Physical Geography

> Pupils should demonstrate their increasing knowledge and understanding of:
> (i) weather and climate (the atmosphere); (ii) river, river basins, seas and oceans
> (the hydrosphere); (iii) landforms (the lithosphere); and (iv) animals, plants and
> soils (the biosphere). (Attainment Target 3, Department of Education and
> Science, *Geography in the National Curriculum (England)* HMSO, March 1991, p. 13)

Some learning difficulties in physical geography

Many aspects of physical geography have important implications for teaching
and learning. Children can, for example, find it difficult to understand the
terms used to describe landscapes. One of the reasons for this is that the labels
which we give to landforms are very often not consistent. Some features of
the Earth's surface (such as hills and islands) are defined by their *form*
whereas others (such as volcanoes and deltas) are defined according to their
process of formation. Furthermore, many features that have the same or similar
form can vary greatly in *size*. Australia and Lundy are both islands although
one is about three million times bigger than the other. Other features, which
are defined principally according to how they were formed, can vary greatly
in *shape*. A river valley can be a small V-shaped feature in upland areas or
a broad flat feature in lowlands. A delta can be triangular, as in the classic
delta of the River Nile, or shaped like a bird's foot, as in the delta of the
Mississippi. Volcanoes can be steeply cone-shaped, like Mount Pelée on
Martinique in the West Indies, or can have gentle slopes, like Mauna Loa
in the Hawaiian Islands. Inconsistencies like these in the way that terminology is applied to the surface features of the Earth can make both recognition
and naming of landforms difficult for children.

Neither is it very easy to establish *definitions* of common landforms. What,
for example, is a mountain? In most people's minds it has to have at least
two properties: height and shape. But how high is a mountain? In the British
Isles we generally refer to land over 500 m as being mountainous. But in
Spain 2000 m might be more appropriate. However, it isn't just height above
sea level that's significant. There has to be some sense of a rise above the level
of the surrounding landscape, and the concept is established even more
securely if there is snow on the top and the skyline looks jagged. But not all
summits are peak-like. Compare, for example, Tryfan in north Wales,

which has a distinctly triangular shape, and Kinder Scout in Derbyshire, which is virtually flat. It is easy to see, incidentally, how some children might be misled by map symbols which show high points in the form of small triangles when the feature referred to is not an obvious 'peak'.

Human activity can mask the appearance of many landforms. A hill in the countryside is very different in the way it is experienced from a hill in town. In open countryside, hills may be more easily seen from a distance and so are more easily recognized as being three-dimensional features, whereas children's experiences of hills in towns are more linear; the three-dimensional form of the hill is obscured by buildings. Town children are therefore more likely to have a notion of a hill as merely being a 'slope'.

Many words used in the study of landforms, climate and soils have both a precise technical meaning as well as a vernacular, less clearly defined usage. 'Soil', for example, is a term which can be scientifically defined but children frequently use words such as dirt, ground, mud or earth to describe the same substance. Note also the potential confusion for children of 'earth' (soil) with 'Earth' (the planet). Words that describe topography can be especially difficult. Hills, for example, are often 'rolling', lending a rather insecure aspect to the description of landscape. Or they can form part of a 'range'. When asked what a 'range' is, children generally affirm that it has something to do with cowboys (as in 'home on the range'), or describe it as 'a place where steers are kept'.[1]

There are also substantial regional variations in the terminology used to describe features on the Earth's surface. Consider, for example: fell, alp, ben, tarn, cwm, cirque, dale, dell, coomb, strath, vale, dingle, glen, brae, gill, beck, burn, creek, knoll, down, tor and crag. (The same linguistic variety is of course found in some features of the human landscape – such as alley, path, snicket, ginnel, passage, etc.; and perhaps one way into this maze of terminology for children is to refer to the variety of terms used for more familiar phenomena, such as plimsolls, sandshoes, daps, pumps, etc.) Teachers could usefully be alert to the potential misunderstandings by children moving from one part of the country to another.

Concept development in physical geography may, therefore, pose a number of challenges for teaching. It is not surprising, in view of all the above, to find that children have some difficulty in saying what they understand by apparently fairly straightforward terms such as river, mountain, beach, desert, season, soil and cloud.[2] Their own direct experience of the landscape and examination of photographs of features on the surface of the Earth can show similar-looking features that have different names and dissimilar features called by the same name. This seems to imply that children need to be presented with a good number of instances and non-instances of phenomena both directly (i.e. in the field) and indirectly through photographs and videos. It is helpful to refer constantly to scale. Landscape pictures really do need people in them to provide a reference point for the size of the landforms shown.

Physical geographers attempt to understand forms and processes on the surface of the Earth by making measurements of phenomena, and many of the activities suggested later in this chapter involve children making their own measurements of the natural world. But measuring the real world isn't easy, even if it does apparently allow you to be more precise. There are problems not only of instrumentation but also of the genuine complexity of what it is that is being measured. Stream flow, for example, can be measured fairly accurately with a current meter. Basically this is a propeller on the end of a rod with a device to record the number of revolutions of the propeller per unit time and to convert that reading into a speed. Current meters, however, are very expensive and primary school children will almost certainly have to use other methods of measuring the flow of water in a stream. Most of these are similar to the game of 'Pooh sticks'. You throw a stick or coloured float into the stream and time its movement over a measured distance. But stream flow varies both across the *width* of the river and at different *depths* and so the process has to be repeated a number of times and an average taken. Almost all measurements in physical geography require quite complex averaging procedures, and this is particularly true of weather and climate study. A comparison of average annual rainfall in two places in the world requires a considerable conceptual grasp of what it is that is actually being compared. The average annual rainfall of Great Britain, for example, is 904 mm. However, such a figure is virtually meaningless in view of the great geographical variation in the amount of rainfall actually received in any one place.

Another feature of physical geography study is that the processes involved often appear improbable to children or, at the very least, difficult to envisage. In south Wales there is a well-known glacial erratic (a rock that has been transported from its original location by ice) called Arthur's Stone. Local legend has it that King Arthur was displeased because his shoe pinched, so in despair he threw it across the sea from Tintagel in Cornwall to the Gower peninsula where on landing it turned into stone. Now which is more probable from a child's point of view? That King Arthur threw his ill-fitting shoe away or that a great river of ice picked up this huge boulder about ten thousand years ago and dumped it where it is today?

Many children cannot distinguish between a description of a phenomenon and an explanation of that phenomenon. Young children, asked to explain how something came about, often merely describe how it is now. There seems to be very little work on children's explanation in physical geography; perhaps the nearest such evidence comes from work on understanding of ecological concepts.[3] In this context it seems to be the case that children often use anthropomorphic reasoning; that is, they attribute human characteristics to non-human organisms.

Several earlier studies appear to show that the role of God in the creation of the Earth and its landscape is frequently referred to by children, but in the light of changing religious education and attitudes this is an area of investigation that could with advantage be further explored at the present time.[4] Piaget's work on children's notions of the nature and origins of the Earth implies that children proceed from one type of explanation to another, and that this is related to their 'level of development', whereas other work suggests that children's explanations are influenced by factors such as the child's vocabulary, the nature of the questions, the interaction between the interviewer and the child and the experiential background of the child.[5]

Notwithstanding the varied explanations of the origins of Earth, the distinction between 'natural' and 'artificial' is a fundamental one for children to grasp. The recognition that water, rocks and soil are part of the natural environment is part of the first level of attainment in physical geography. Yet differentiating between natural and artificial materials is sometimes difficult. Concrete looks like rock and in many ways behaves like it, and it is used for similar purposes. Yet 'rocks' can also appear most unrocklike, because the geological use of the term includes loose, unconsolidated materials such as sand and gravel, and soft rock such as clay. The situation can be further confused for children because one of the best ways to see a variety of rocks, particularly in urban areas, is to look for their use in buildings. Almost any high street or set of public buildings will display a great range of decorative types of stone: granites, marbles, sandstones and fossil-bearing rocks. Whereas older children will appreciate that these are natural materials that have been cut and shaped by people, younger children may be less able to differentiate between them and brick, breeze-block or Tarmac. It may also be difficult for children to differentiate between natural and artificial *landforms*. Railway cuttings and motorway embankments resemble valleys and hill slopes. After all, not all 'natural' valleys have a river at the bottom.

Mention will be made below of specific examples of children's fiction dealing with themes and topics in physical geography. At this stage, however, reference can be made to Margaret S. Anderson's *Splendour of Earth* (George Philip, 1954, 1973). This is an anthology of travel containing a complete set of literary descriptions of all the standard physical features and climates of the world. Some of the extracts are too literary to be used with much success in primary school but many *can* be used or, at least, easily adapted. The book is now, sadly, out of print, but is well worth trying to obtain.

Landforms

Landscapes are made up of *landforms* such as mountain peaks, valleys and plains. The science that studies landforms is *geomorphology*. Geomorphologists are interested in the shape of landforms, the processes that make them the shape they are and how their shape has changed through time. Much greater attention is now paid by geomorphologists to the *process* of landform change.

Landscapes are the result of two major sets of processes acting on the Earth's surface. Firstly, there are the processes which *build* mountains by adding new material to the Earth's crust or by causing it to be uplifted. Secondly, there are those processes which *destroy* rocks and landforms.

The weather is primarily responsible for this destruction and so the term *weathering* is used for it. Rocks exposed to the surface are heated by the sun and then cool. Differential heating and cooling within the structure of the rock sets up stresses and strains which cause it to crack. These cracks can be further enlarged by water. Water seeps into the cracks and in some circumstances and climates may later freeze, thus expanding and splitting the rock. Water also causes rock rotting by its chemical effect. Rain-water is naturally a weak acid which reacts with many rock-forming minerals. This chemical weathering though is especially effective in urban and industrial areas where the rain is made more acidic by air pollution. Burrowing animals and plant roots may also split rocks.

Rock waste does not remain in the same position very long. Gravity, rivers, the sea, glaciers and wind all act to carry the weathered fragments away. The actual movement of these fragments further helps to erode the Earth's surface. Pebbles at the bottom of a cliff, for example, are carried away by the waves but they may also be used to wear down the cliff even more when they are hurled back at it during times of heavy seas.

All transported rock particles eventually settle. Rivers deposit silt and fine mud on the sea bed. Glacier ice dumps rock debris when the ice melts. Rocks which have broken off mountain crags collect in heaps at the foot of the mountainside. Rock particles remaining in the same place for long enough may eventually become sufficiently compressed and be cemented by the formation of new minerals in the spaces between the particles for new rock to be formed. This happens most commonly under the sea. In this way, the materials that make up the surface of the Earth have been *recycled* and it is often possible to see evidence for this recycling in the rocks themselves. Some sedimentary rocks, for example, have chunks of previously formed rocks embedded in them. The grains of sandstone that make up sedimentary rocks were once crystals of quartz in igneous rocks like granite. This cycle – of erosion, transportation and deposition – is called the *rock cycle*.

CHILDREN AND LANDFORMS

Children are required (for level 5) to 'give evidence of different types of weathering and to distinguish between weathering and erosion'. One way of doing this is to investigate how long gravestones last. Gravestones are especially good for this work because they are precisely dated. Note that the type of rock is usually marble or sandstone or granite. Children can classify the gravestones by rock type and see if there is a change in use of a preferred rock over time. Changes in stone type might be related to transport developments enabling some types of stone to be brought from further afield. Monumental masons in the neighbourhood may be able to shed light on the geographical origin of each type of stone.

It is possible to test a number of hypotheses and observe patterns. These observations can be entered into a database. Lichens may grow more readily on some rock types than others. They may also grow on the sides of slabs facing a particular direction. Sandstones may weather more rapidly from the bottom of the stone than the top. (This is in fact highly likely as moisture from the ground moves up and down by capillary action alternately wetting and drying the stone. This wetting and drying sets up chemical stresses which causes the rock to crumble.) It is also possible to assess the rate of weathering by estimating the loss of stone surface in millimetres since the date of the stone. Weathering processes in rock may also be observed in the cracks in paving stones and worn steps around the school.

Slopes are the building blocks of landforms. This was recognized by the working party which produced the draft proposals for the National Curriculum in geography. According to the first draft, children were to 'describe slopes in the local area' for Key Stage 1. This statement of attainment was later rejected on the grounds of being too technical for non-specialists, although the concept is quite simple, involving fairly straightforward terminology such as flat, steep, gentle, etc. An understanding of how slopes can vary, the terms that are used to describe them and how they are measured is central to the study of geomorphology.

Children may be familiar with road signs that describe slopes, but almost certainly not with what the figures shown on the signs mean. Road signs can show slopes in two ways: as a ratio and as a percentage. A slope of 1 in 10, for example, is shown as 10%; a slope of 1 in 4 as 25% and a slope of 1 in 2 as 50%. These figures might be translated into terms children (and teachers) would recognize as follows: It's hard to walk up a slope of 25% and hard to cycle up a slope of 7%. Most cyclists would get off and walk up a slope of 10%. A lorry driver would have to use the lowest gear going up a slope of about 15%. Trains need much gentler slopes: the steepest railway line in the United Kingdom is only 2.5%.

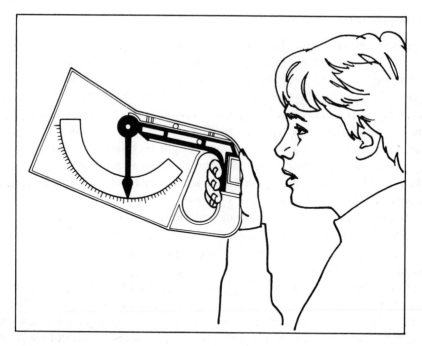

Figure 4.1 *A simple clinometer.*

Slopes can be investigated by children using simple clinometers. Highly accurate clinometers are, as you might expect, very expensive. The best sort for primary school use is probably the plastic 'handgun' type. These are available fairly cheaply from major educational equipment suppliers. The clinometer is pointed up or down the slope. When the trigger is pulled, a weighted pointer rotates. When the trigger is released, this pointer is locked and the angle of the slope may be read off from a scale at the side of the instrument. It is also possible for children to make their own clinometer with a protractor and plumb line.

An investigation of slopes in the local area might go along the following lines:

'Tell me about some slopes that you know near here. Which is the steepest?'

'Do you think Church Hill is steeper than Town Hill? How could we measure them in order to compare?'

'Our clinometer shows that Church Hill is 15 degrees and Town Hill is 20 degrees, so which one is steepest?'

'Is Church Hill the same steepness all the way up?', etc.

Children have their own direct experience of landforms and landscape. Although some will have more restricted experiences of natural environments than others, most will have climbed hills, paddled in streams or on the seashore, built sandcastles and thrown stones. Understanding landscape, however, is also a matter of looking up at the total panoramic view rather than just being engaged with the rock pool at your feet. What can children recognize of the macro-scale physical features of landscape? We know a little about what they see from photographs; rather less about what they see in 'real life'. It's one thing to recognize that you go up a hill on the way to school, quite another to realize that your whole town is built on a hill. A valley is fairly easy to spot if it takes a few minutes to run down one side and up the other. It is less easy to envisage if the valley in question is several miles wide.

In one study[6] 23 6–8-year-old children, the majority of whom had English as a second language, were shown photographs of a beach, a river, a hill with rocks, a forest, a mountain and a lake. More than 80 per cent of children could identify the sea, beach, sand and water but more children had difficulty identifying rivers and lakes. There does seem to be a real difficulty in children's minds about differentiating between bodies of water and using appropriate terminology to describe them. Children's previous experience does seem to play a large part in their recognition and understanding of physical features. A 6-year-old who had visited high mountains in Pakistan talked confidently about the mountain picture.

It is difficult to disentangle what children 'see' in the landscape of a photograph and what they *say* they see. It is more likely that they 'see' a feature when they know the name of that feature and are therefore more confident in talking about what has been observed. Perhaps the eye tends to search for items that are recognizable.[7] It also seems likely that what is seen is influenced by its location within the borders of the photograph. When looking at pictures, many children's eyes seem to 'sweep' the picture, as though 'reading' it, in a horizontal sweep from left to right or right to left. It has been claimed that details to the left of centre are more likely to be noticed than details in other parts of the picture.[8]

It seems to be the case that when children look at photographs of landscape, they attend to details, rather than to the picture as a whole or to the broad features of the landscape. When asked to write down what they saw in a photograph of an industrial landscape, a group of children referred frequently to factories, chimneys and lamp-posts but made little mention of the flatness of the land in the foreground and the hilliness of land in the distance.[9] Children seem more likely to observe, recognize and record features of *human* geography rather than physical geography. Nevertheless, children at the top of the primary school age range are generally able to recognize major landscape features such as rivers, streams, mountains, hills, cliffs, rocks and forests from photographs when there is little other distracting detail or when these features are drawn to their attention.[10]

Some photographs of landscapes are better for primary school use than others; they need to be bright and clear in order to provide interest and attract attention. Children seem to be more interested in landscape pictures if they can 'think themselves into' the scene, for example if they are able to imagine a picnic in the landscape, or think of a good game to play in that particular spot. A potentially fruitful technique for teachers to employ therefore would seem to be to engage the children's imagination when looking at pictures by asking *starter* questions such as 'Would you like to play on this beach?', rather than 'What material is the beach made of?'

Children of all ages seem to find recognition of scale from photographs, particularly aerial photographs, problematic.[11] Many children are unable to distinguish very large fields from modestly sized gardens, mountains from hills, and small patches of flat land from vast plains. Guided practice in the recognition of features and discussing what is seen are probably necessary to a considerable degree, rather than assuming that the features will immediately be recognized.

REPRESENTING LANDFORMS

It seems likely that children's conceptual grasp of the shape of landforms can be enhanced by modelling. Using a sand and water table, children can work in pairs to make models of topographical features named by the teacher. (For example: 'Show me what a valley, mountain, island, lake, etc. looks like'.) Children can also collect pictures of landforms from books and magazines and make 3D models from these pictures using a suitable modelling medium such as clay or Plasticene. This activity involves not only interpreting the shape of the landform from the two-dimensional picture but also thinking about scale. Making a model mountain, for example, might involve child and teacher discussing whether there would be climbers shown on the models and if so at what size they should be represented.

Model landforms constructed in a sand tray can be named on a sheet of clear plastic laid on top. This encourages children to look at the landforms from above (see Chapter 2). Some children may be able to experiment with drawing their own maps of the landforms they have constructed. 'How many different landforms can you make and map using the sand table?' Another challenge is to take a landform map such as that shown in Figure 4.2 and attempt to reconstruct it in the sand tray.

But models can also be used to demonstrate process as well as form, by building models in the sand and water table of streams, rivers and deltas. However, there are problems in the extent to which it is possible to scale down the effects of rivers on their valleys by using sand and water. Most difficult of all is to establish that rivers erode their valleys very slowly, as 'erosion'

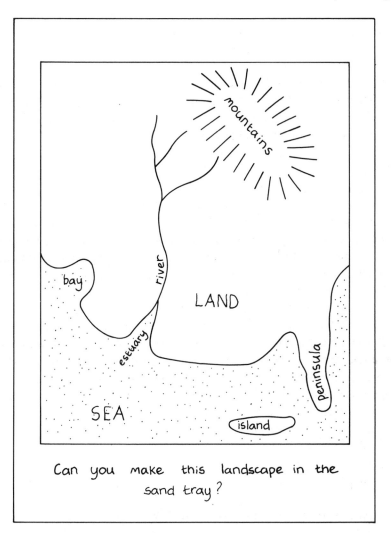

Figure 4.2 *A landform map workcard.*

in the sand tray can be very rapid. The limitation of sand as a modelling medium also quickly becomes apparent because the structures soon collapse when waterlogged. Nevertheless, a number of experiments can be carried out which attempt to model river processes and the relationships between significant factors (see below).

The role of wind in the formation of landforms (such as sand dunes) can easily be investigated in the classroom using dry sand and a hair dryer. A light sprinkling of sand is needed on a table top. By trial and error, position a hair dryer so that the air current is a light but steady flow. With patience, sand dunes can be built up. Close observation from the side (be careful of sand in eyes) shows that sand grains move in various ways, depending on their weight. The heaviest grains roll along the 'desert' floor, the lightest grains remain in the air almost permanently and the medium-sized grains bounce along the surface (desert geomorphologists call this movement 'saltation'). A sheet of sticky-backed plastic at the end of the air stream can be used to trap the sand grains and with the aid of a magnifying glass their sizes at different heights above the table top may be compared.

Rivers

The British landscape owes many of its distinctive features to the work of rivers. Rivers account for much of the variation in relief and are also of major importance to the economic and cultural landscape of Britain. They provide water for homes and industry and were at one time the principal medium for the movement of heavy goods. Most of our largest towns and cities were sited in relation to bridging points.

Children's progressive understanding of 'rivers' as a concept seems to be along the following lines:[12] firstly, they understand that rivers are 'water', then that this water is of some considerable size, then that the water moves and finally that this body of water moves along some course in its surroundings. The perceptions children have of what rivers are seem to be closely related to their local experiences of rivers. The following transcript extract[13] shows two different levels of understanding:

(i) 'What is a river?'
   'A stream.'
   'What is a stream?'
   'Water.'

(Here the child only associates 'river' with water.)

(ii) 'What is a river?'
   'A big stream that wanders in and out of hills.'
   'A *stream* you say. What is a stream?'
   'A lot of rain that collects and flows into the sea.'

(Here the child demonstrates understanding of the feature in relation to its surroundings and includes an indication of origin and destination.)

Like other features in physical geography, river characteristics need to be established in conjunction with specialized vocabulary. Words can be identified in advance by the teacher and sorted into groups. The language of rivers, for example, refers, among other things, to size, flow, shape and parts:

river size: rill, stream, river;
river flow: torrent, gurgle, whirlpool;
valley shape: gorge, floodplain;
river parts: estuary, source, tributary, spring.

A suitable starting point in river study is to establish that water flows down-hill. This is easily demonstrated in the school playground with a bucket of water. Children can predict where the water will flow and test their ideas. Compare these experiments with streams by using a float. Or make a model roof. What happens when the rain falls? Which way will the water flow on the roof? (This can also establish the principle of the landscape term 'water-shed' or 'divide'.) A large-scale map of the school's surroundings can be used to mark on the direction of water flow on the pavements either by comparison with local observations or by looking at the spot heights or contours on the map. Use a watering can on school-made relief models of landscapes.

How does the amount of water (the 'discharge') in a river affect its power to erode? Does the gradient of a river channel, or its width, have an effect on the speed of stream flow? Relationships such as these can be modelled in the classroom. Children set up a length of plastic guttering on a table so that it has a gentle slope. A length of rubber tubing from a tap provides the 'stream' and the water is caught in a bucket at the end of the gutter. Sprinkle gravel and sand in the gutter. Which material is moved first? What happens when the 'discharge' of the stream is increased (by turning the tap on more) as would happen after a rainstorm? Does this explain why large boulders in the stream bed are only moved during times of flood?

The effect of gradient on the speed of stream flow can be seen by measuring the time a drop of ink takes to reach the end of the gutter. Try this for several gradients of gutter slope, propping the gutter up on one, then two, then three bricks. The effect of varying channel width can also be investigated. Plasticene or clay is moulded into the gutter to form a gorge-like constriction. Observe what happens to the speed of flow (it increases) as the water passes through the constriction.

The behaviour of rivers can be further investigated with sand in a sand table or tray. Create a valley in the sand and allow water from the rubber tubing to flow along it. River flow, and therefore the power for erosion, is greatest on the outer bend of a river meander. It is on the outer bend that the sand grains will move the fastest. Children can carry out the experiment and make sketches of what they observe. The problem is, as was mentioned earlier, that there are limitations to the scaling down of materials used. Fairly soon the whole sand tray becomes soggy and whilst it's quite easy to see processes you know to be valid in the real world recreated in the sand, it's quite another matter to build up a clear picture of those processes, *ab initio*, from the model alone. It's probably better therefore that children undertake specific investigations such as: 'Find out on which side of a river bend the water moves sand fastest', before discussing the 'theory' of what should be seen to happen. Deltas work well in a sand table. Create a pool of water at one end of the sand table and watch the sand grains pile up as they are washed into the water. Children can also undertake investigations into civil engineering, especially dams. Compare children's models with real-world examples such as the dams of the rivers Nile, Mississippi and Colorado.

There is some good children's fiction dealing with rivers, such as the classic *The River at Green Knowe* (Puffin, 1959) by Lucy M. Boston:

> 'What a lot of islands the river makes', said Ida. 'We are on one, and I can see at least three others. We must go exploring and sail round them all.'

The children set out to make a map of the river and in the course of so doing, discover the river's secret . . . Philippa Pearce's *Minnow on the Say* (Oxford University Press, 1955; Puffin, 1978) is an adventure story about two boys and a canoe. There are some quite good incidental descriptions of the river and how it is experienced by two boys:

> When they had passed the last of the Great Barley houses and were in the open country, all lingering thoughts of the treasure left them. They tested the *Minnow* and tested their own skill and strength in her: they back-paddled, they forward-paddled; they sent her twirling in circles; they raced a squawking family of tame duck, clapping their paddles fiercely into the water with a chorus of 'One – two! One – two!' Then they changed their methods altogether, and saw how stealthy they could go: they grudged the soft whisper of water against the prow of the canoe; they slid their paddles soundlessly into the water and, as they drew them slowly out at the end of each stroke, held them so that the drops from the paddles had only a finger's breadth to fall before they were united to the river again. Their care was unexpectedly rewarded, for, as they stole round a bend of the river, they surprised a grey bird that rose and wheeled with slowly flapping wings, its legs trailing behind it, still shining wet from the river.
>
> 'A heron,' whispered Adam. 'They often fish in the Say, Aunt Dinah says; only you don't often see them. They choose lonely places.'

But perhaps the best river story of all in children's literature is Kenneth Grahame's *The Wind in the Willows* (1908; Puffin, 1983):

> The afternoon sun was getting low as the Rat sculled gently homewards in a dreamy mood, murmuring poetry-things over to himself and not paying much attention to Mole. But the Mole was very full of lunch, and self satisfaction, and pride, and already quite at home in a boat (so he thought) and was getting a bit restless besides: and presently he said, 'Ratty! Please, *I* want to row, now!'
>
> The Rat shook his head with a smile. 'Not yet, my young friend,' he said – 'wait till you've had a few lessons. It's not as easy as it looks.'
>
> The Mole was quiet for a minute or two. But he began to feel more and more

jealous of Rat, sculling so strongly and so easily along, and his pride began to whisper that he could do it every bit as well. He jumped up and seized the sculls, so suddenly, that the Rat, who was gazing out over the water and saying more poetry-things to himself, was taken by surprise and fell backwards off his seat with his legs in the air for the second time, while the triumphant Mole took his place and grabbed the sculls with entire confidence.

'Stop it, you *silly* ass!' cried the Rat, from the bottom of the boat. 'You can't do it! You'll have us over!'

The Mole flung his sculls back with a flourish, and made a great dig at the water. He missed the surface altogether, his legs flew up above his head, and he found himself lying on top of the prostrate Rat. Greatly alarmed, he made a grab at the side of the boat, and the next moment – Sploosh!

Over went the boat, and he found himself struggling in the river.

Violent Earth movements

Between 1960 and 1970 there was a revolution in geological thinking. Before that time most geologists believed that the Earth's crust was immobile. The continents and ocean floors were thought to be permanent and located in the same positions as they had been at the time of the Earth's formation. By the end of the decade, ideas which had earlier been ridiculed were accepted in the face of incontrovertible evidence. The continents we know today were once joined together in one 'supercontinent' which began to disintegrate about 200 million years ago (see Figure 4.3).

Figure 4.3 *Two hundred million years ago there was one 'supercontinent' on Earth. Reproduced from* The Times Atlas of the World: Comprehensive Edition, *by kind permission of Times Books.*

103

At first this immense land mass, to which geologists have given the name Pangea, split into two parts, corresponding roughly to today's northern and southern continents. By about 135 million years ago, South America and Africa split apart. At about the same time, India broke away from Africa and moved rapidly towards Asia, with which it was to collide only about 30 million years ago. Australia and Antarctica did not separate until about 45 million years ago. But that wasn't the end. The continents are still moving. North America, for example, did not break away from Europe until about 40 million years ago but it is still drifting away at a rate of about 8 cm per year – the rate at which fingernails grow!

The mechanism that explains the drifting continents is called the theory of plate tectonics. According to this theory the surface of the Earth is made up of about 15 major plates consisting of both continental and oceanic crust (see Figure 4.4).

These plates are rigid slabs which 'float' across the Earth's surface and jostle against each other at their edges. It is the activity at the edges of the plates that is responsible for the violent movements on the surface such as volcanoes and earthquakes. Where plates pull apart from each other – usually in the middle of oceans – new molten crust from the Earth's interior forces its way to the surface. These undersea volcanoes form great ridges indicating where the sea floor is spreading. One such ridge is located along the whole length of the Atlantic Ocean from north to south. Iceland lies

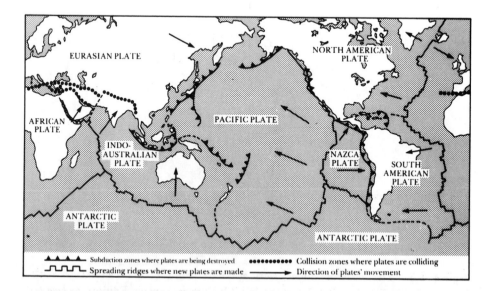

Figure 4.4 *World pattern of plates and plate boundaries.*

astride this ridge, and the volcanic eruptions at Heimaey and Surtsey were part of this process of new crust being formed where plates were splitting apart. The volcanic island of Surtsey emerged from the sea off the southern coast of Iceland in the 1970s with loud explosions and billows of ash and steam. The island now occupies two and a half square kilometres.

Where plates push together one edge of a plate is sometimes pushed under the other in a *subduction zone*. This is what happens along the western coast of South America, where the Nazca plate buckles under the South American plate, and off the coast of Japan, where the Pacific plate is pushing against the Eurasian plate. Deep ocean troughs are formed at these places and volcanoes erupt along the line of weakness in the Earth's crust.

The Earth's largest mountain ranges today – the Himalayas, Rockies, Andes and Alps – are all relatively young. They are the result of plate collisions in the last 25 million or so years. They are called fold mountains because it is clear to see how the rock strata have been massively folded and contorted by the force of the collision pressure.

Earthquakes are formed by the stresses and strains that build up along the plate boundaries. The stress builds up until the rocks can no longer bear the strain. Movement, when it comes, is therefore sudden. Earthquakes and volcanoes are located along the edges of the earth's plates, particularly at the boundaries where one plate is forced under another. This principally occurs around the rim of the Pacific Ocean (the 'Pacific ring of fire') and in a belt from central Europe to the Himalayas. Volcanoes which no longer erupt are said to be *extinct*; those which have been quiet for a very long time but which are thought likely to erupt at some point in the future are *dormant*; and volcanoes which are known to have erupted in historic time are *active*.

What do children understand of the processes of volcanism, earthquakes and mountain building? Although little attention has been paid to primary children's understanding of these phenomena, the misconceptions held by secondary school pupils may be instructive. We must not assume that landforms and processes are easy for younger children to understand. As part of the investigations of the Science Education Research Unit at the University of Waikato, John Happs[14] considered the views that children and adolescents held of the origin of two mountains in New Zealand. Mount Egmont is a volcano situated on a destructive plate margin in North Island of New Zealand. Although it last erupted in 1755, future eruptions are highly likely. By contrast, Mount Cook forms part of the Southern Alps and is situated where crustal plates are converging. The rate of compression of the plates at this point is today roughly the same as the rate of weathering and erosion but in the last 5 million years about 5 km of uplift has occurred in the Southern

Alps. Secondary school pupils were asked about the processes that led to the formation of both landforms. Their responses suggest that children are likely to hold views that differ significantly from scientifically accepted ideas. Two-thirds of the pupils interviewed were not aware that Mount Egmont has the potential to erupt again and almost all pupils were unable to connect mountain building in any way with theories that involved plate tectonics. There was also much confusion about the differences between mountains and volcanoes, with many pupils thinking that mountains could 'become' volcanoes if they were shaken by earthquakes. Many also thought that volcanoes were only found in warmer climates or that peaks could not be volcanoes if they had snow on top. The ideas that volcanoes could be active or dormant or extinct tended to be very muddled. The origins of mountains were variously attributed to the work of wind and water or creation by God. It was a common view that mountains have 'always been there'.

Despite the thousands of earthquakes and volcanic eruptions that have taken place, only a very few are well known. Knowledge of such events is generally related to the power of communications. Krakatoa, for example, is particularly famous as it was the first eruption of great size to occur after the widespread use of the electric telegraph. The abnormal red sunsets that were seen all round the world after the eruption could therefore quickly be attributed to the ejection of volcanic dust into the atmosphere. Similarly, although Mount St Helens was a relatively small eruption, it received massive publicity from the sophisticated domestic news and telecommunications systems in the United States.

It is worth considering how children receive their information about violent earth movements. They will of course receive images about volcanoes and earthquakes from the news media, but disaster movies have been shown to provide much more powerful sources of images. These images, however, may be faulty.[15] Although the *physical* characteristics of earthquakes, floods, hurricanes, etc. are generally accurately represented, the *human response* to such hazards is not. It is frequently suggested, for example, that mass panic is common, that disaster victims are incapable of responding to the crisis and that crime, often in the form of looting, is widespread. Films generally also fail to show the real nature of personal injury, with victims receiving either minor cuts and bruises or being killed outright. Little attention tends to be given to warning systems or to recovery after the event. There is also the strong implication in many such films that natural disasters are more likely to occur in the Western world, whereas in fact they predominate in the economically developing world.

Nevertheless, disaster movies are effective because they are vivid and have a strong human interest and story line. What other possibilities are there for incorporating fiction into the teaching of Earth processes? There is in fact a good choice of earthquake and volcano stories for children. Ruskin Bond's *Earthquake* (Walker Books, 1989) is set in Shillong, in the Cherrapunji Hills in north-eastern India. It's a real location and so children can look it up in an atlas. 'Whenever there was an emergency, grandfather happened to be in his bath.' He was taking a bath when the first earthquake tremors were felt. The book describes the effects of the earthquake simply and clearly. The young reader is not spared death and destruction but the book is also about hope and rebuilding afterwards. Grandfather recovers his twisted tin bathtub and hammers it back into shape.

Andrew Salkey's *Earthquake* (Oxford University Press, 1965; Puffin, 1980) is a well-crafted story of an earthquake in Jamaica. There is an exciting description not only of the earthquake itself but also of the tremors felt beforehand. The flashback to grandfather telling a story of an earthquake he experienced years before is particularly effective in establishing continuity in the story.

Paul Jacques Bonzon's *The Orphans of Simitra* (ULP) opens in Greece where a village has been destroyed by an earthquake. A brother and sister, orphaned as a result of the disaster, then wander through France, Holland and Norway.

In Rose Tremain's *Journey to the Volcano* (Hamish Hamilton, 1985; Piper, 1988), George's mother has left his father and snatches the boy from school in Britain to take him to her home on the slopes of Mount Etna. George is swimming in the sea when he sees a tiny flash of red at the top of the mountain. The volcano erupts dramatically and his grandmother is killed when lava and rubble bury her house.

There is more scientific information to be found in Willard Price's *Volcano Adventure* (Cape, 1956; Knight Books, 1973). The characters in this book are fictional but the volcanic events that are described actually happened. Hal and Roger are assistants to Dr Dan Adams, an expert on volcanoes, and they sail the Pacific from one active volcano to another. The boys constantly ask eager questions – a technique which allows Dr Dan to inform the reader about every conceivable form of volcanic eruption. Although the style is rather laboured, there is much volcano information and vocabulary transmitted through the text:

'All the things a volcano can do!' marvelled Roger. 'It buries these forty-eight villages under lava, Pompeii under ashes, Herculaneum under mud.'

'But that's not all,' said Dr Dan. 'It can destroy a city without using lava or ashes or mud. Remember how Mt Pelée killed forty thousand people in five minutes?'

'Tell us about it,' prompted Hal.

'It won't take long to tell because it didn't take long to happen. Mt Pelée – you know where it is, on the beautiful island of Martinique in the West Indies – had been growling for days . . .'

More difficult to deal with, because it is entirely fictional, is Jules Verne's *Journey to the Centre of the Earth* (1864; Puffin, 1985). Axel deciphers an old parchment which discloses a secret passage to the centre of the Earth through a volcano. Despite the fantasy of the plot, there are in fact some good descriptions of real volcanic landscapes in Iceland as the intrepid adventurers set out on their incredible voyage into the subterranean world.

Although not children's literature, there are nevertheless some vivid passages describing an undersea volcanic eruption in Desmond Bagley's *Night of Error* (Fontana paperback, 1985). Bagley's novels are authentic and detailed in the geomorphological and meteorological processes they describe. Also by Bagley are *Wyatt's Hurricane* (Fontana, 1968), describing the effects of a hurricane in the Caribbean, and *The Snow Tiger* (Fontana, 1976), which is an account of an avalanche.

Children can explore the presentation of Earth movements in the media by writing their own accounts of events using simple desk-top publishing software. The topic offers a particularly good vehicle for writing for different audiences, for example a scientific report on why an earthquake happened or a series of news bulletins describing a volcanic eruption at regular intervals or an 'eye-witness' account of the disaster. In connection with the latter, note incidentally the marvellous description from Pliny the Younger in a letter to Tacitus in which he describes his uncle's death at the eruption of Vesuvius. So curious were his uncle and companions and so eager not to miss the spectacle of the eruption that they tied pillows around their heads to protect themselves (ineffectually) from falling ash and volcanic bombs.

One way of highlighting the effects of earthquakes and making sense of news bulletins is for children to devise their own illustrations to match one of the scales of earthquake intensity. Perhaps the best scale to use for this is the Mercalli scale:

1. Detected only by instruments.
2. Detected by sensitive people at rest.
3. *Weak*. Vibrations like those of a passing lorry. Loose objects might be slightly disturbed.
4. *Moderate*. Rattling of dishes, doors and windows.
5. *Fairly strong*. Most sleepers wake. Trees and telegraph poles disturbed. Dishes broken.
6. *Strong*. Furniture overturned. Plaster cracked. People may panic.
7. *Very strong*. Some damage to buildings. Chimneys broken.
8. *Destructive*. Much damage. Walls and chimneys fall.
9. *Very destructive*. Severe damage. Many buildings collapse.
10. *Devastating*. Great damage to pipes, roads and foundations. Landslides occur.

11. *Catastrophic*. Few buildings survive. Great cracks in the ground. Underground pipelines and bridges destroyed.

12. *Major catastrophe*. Complete devastation. Ground waves occur.

'Before and after' illustrations of major Earth processes, movements and volcanic activity are brilliantly but simply shown in *Earthquakes and Volcanoes* and *Mountains and Valleys* by Imelda and Robert Updegraff (Methuen, 1980). Each open spread shows a 'before' scene, with a half-page insert that can be turned to show the 'after' effects of change. A peaceful village shelters in the shadow of a volcano. Turn the half page and the volcano has erupted sending streams of lava and clouds of ash towards the fields and houses. There is considerable scope here for recreating such 'before and after' images in the form of wall displays in class.

Note that data on highest mountains, highest volcanoes, longest rivers, largest lakes, etc. can be found in reference sources such as *Whitaker's Almanack*. There are also more specialized sources such as *The Guinness World Data Book* (Guinness Publishing, 1991) as well as the *Guinness Book of Records*. Another useful reference book is N. Blundell's *The World's Worst Disasters of the Twentieth Century* (Octopus Books, 1983).

Children may be interested to know that although earthquakes are rare in the British Isles, they do occur from time to time! One of the worst was in Colchester in 1884. Over 400 buildings were destroyed in the town and the effects of the tremor were felt over an area of 100 000 square miles.

Weather and climate

Many children appear to have substantial misconceptions about the nature of weather phenomena. Clouds, for example, are often thought to be fluffy and cottonwool-like. Rainfall is often explained as the result of clouds 'bursting' or 'disintegrating', possibly as a result of collision.[16] Winds are particularly poorly misunderstood: children sometimes report that they are formed 'by the clouds moving', or by 'aeroplanes going past'. Some children think that the moon and the stars play a part in determining the weather.

Nevertheless, despite these faulty notions, the weather is something that all children have direct experience of, and by the time they enter school they have some knowledge about how to respond to it. They know, for example, that they must wrap up warmly in winter and that they can sunbathe in summer. But this knowledge needs to be extended and developed. The starting point is usually a regular group or class discussion to build vocabulary about the weather and to encourage observation. What is the weather like today? What do we need to wear? What is the weather doing to the plants and soil? It may help to concentrate such class talk on one element of the weather at a time. Wind, for example:

> 'How does the wind feel on your face, your hair?'
> 'Does it feel different if you turn to face other directions?'
> 'Wet your finger and hold it in the wind. How does it feel?'
> 'Can you see the wind?'
> 'What does it sound like?'

Children's descriptions of the weather will probably develop from simple dichotomies (hot/cold; wet/dry; windy/calm) to more differentiated descriptions (such as: sweltering, hot, warm, mild, cool, chilly, cold, freezing). Adjectives such as these can be written on cards and matched with pictures or placed in rank order. Weather extremes can also be explored by writing headlines in the style of the tabloids ('Phew, what a scorcher!'; 'Brr, what a freeze up!'). Vocabulary for more complex concepts, such as humidity (muggy, close), needs to be developed later.

Work on weather is linked to that on rivers and oceans by the hydrological cycle. This is a system which involves water in a liquid form (oceans, rivers, rain); a solid form (snow, glacier ice); and as a gas (water vapour). There are a number of possible routes through the system. Water may evaporate from the sea, rise as water vapour, condense and fall as rain. Rain falling on the land may be returned to the atmosphere through evaporation or plant transpiration. Water may also be stored on the Earth's surface. It could, for example, be locked up for hundreds of years in glacier ice or as underground water.

Children can investigate the hydrological cycle at a number of entry points. What happens, for example, when rain-water reaches the ground? Some of it *runs off* either on the surface (as *overland flow*) or into the ground (as *through flow*), eventually, via rivers, entering the sea. The direction of overland flow has been referred to above in connection with study of relief and rivers. Infiltration into the soil, and the rate at which it happens, can be investigated with a baked bean tin and a stop-watch. Take a large tin. Open both ends and (carefully) press the tin halfway into the soil. Fill the part of the tin above the ground surface with water. Time how long the water takes to infiltrate into the soil. Repeat up to 10 times. Show the results on a graph. It takes longer and longer each time for the water to infiltrate as the soil becomes more and more waterlogged.

On hard surfaces (such as the school playground) rain-water cannot infiltrate. And if the ground is flat, little run-off occurs either. What then happens to the water? Create an artificial puddle with a bucket of water in the playground. Draw a chalk circle around the puddle. Visit the puddle at regular intervals. What is happening and why? 'Map' the shrinking of the puddle. Investigate evaporation in the playground and in the classroom by using saucers of water and timing the rate at which the water evaporates. Compare indoor saucers placed near, with those placed far, from the radiators. Note that for a fair test, there must be exactly the same amount of water in each saucer and that each saucer must be the same shape, i.e. with the same surface area exposed.

Clouds are formed when invisible particles of moisture called water vapour evaporate into the air from the surface of the seas, lakes and rivers. As the water vapour rises it cools and eventually condenses back into drops of water. A boiling kettle shows how clouds are formed. The steam cools as it leaves the kettle and forms a cloud. The problem with this as a classroom analogy is not only that clouds of steam in the classroom present obvious dangers to children but that the temperature difference is confusing. Clouds aren't hot. Water vapour from the kettle condenses because of the temperature difference between the steam and the cooler temperature of the classroom air. The same *process* occurs when clouds are formed but the *temperatures* involved are much lower. More accurate temperatures are involved when condensation is noted on the outside of a glass filled with ice, but condensation of water vapour at room temperature on a cold surface doesn't look like a cloud! Children may well find the concept of condensation elusive and it is probably necessary to revisit it several times.

It may be helpful to make sequence cards for the hydrological cycle. Pictures and text on cards can be used to illustrate (for example):

> water evaporates into the air
> water vapour is carried by the wind
> rain and snow falls from the sky
> water runs into streams and rivers
> streams and rivers run into the sea

The pictures and labels can be arranged by children to form a 'cycle'.

Children notice that the weather generally changes during each day as well as from day to day. Many teachers encourage observation by providing opportunities for weather recording. There are a number of commercially produced weather boards on the market for such records but it may be better for the children themselves to decide what and how they should record. Paired observations are helpful, such as pictures of the weather and pictures of 'what we wore to school today'. However, simply recording the weather is rather like counting cars for a traffic survey: it's a rather sterile activity unless it has some real purpose. This might be testing some hypothesis, perhaps related to weather lore. Does a red sky in the evening mean fine weather the following day? Can you predict the weather with seaweed? Do cows predict the weather by lying down (or all facing one way rather than another)? And (for a holiday project) is it true that if it rains on St Swithin's day (15 July) it rains for 40 days thereafter?

One of the problems of teaching about the weather is that even tentative conclusions about weather patterns can only be drawn after long periods of recording – too long for most children to sustain interest. Shorter spells of more intensive observation are probably more effective. Testing the accuracy of daily television or newspaper weather forecasts over a period of about a week can make a more viable short-term project. The success rate of different television stations or newspapers can be compared.

Children frequently see television weather forecasts and there have in recent years been a number of innovative attempts at making the forecasts intelligible by, for example, the use of satellite imagery. But note that you have to be able to locate your own position on a map of the British Isles if the forecast is going to make much sense, so there is a very close relationship between understanding the weather forecast and the knowledge and understanding of places required for Attainment Target 2.

From describing the weather in words and pictures, children should move to *measuring* weather phenomena. Measurements can start simply (for example: 'There's more rain in the bucket today than there was yesterday').

There are two basic types of weather study. One investigates conditions at one site for a fixed period of time, the other examines small-scale differences in the weather over a particular area at any one time. The latter is best carried out in areas that are likely to exhibit some variation, i.e. those with buildings, a lake, a group of trees, etc. You probably need at least 10 sites for recordings in order to make comparisons.

Most schools, even small primary schools, set up a great variety of micro-climatic environments. The buildings cause variations in sunshine received, the speed of wind and the amount of rain. The central heating system has a major effect on temperature and humidity of the immediate area. Some parts of the playground may receive no sunshine at all whereas others may receive 10 hours a day. The tarmac of the playground in sunshine emits more long-wave radiation than, say, the grass of the school field and children may notice that in different weather conditions certain parts of the school grounds become preferred as play areas.

Weather study needs to be related to people. People with different occupations and interests have different weather preferences. Wind is viewed differently by kite fliers and tall-crane operators. Matching exercises involving pictures of people doing different activities (such as hanging out washing, selling ice-cream, sun-bathing, skiing, wind-surfing, driving high-sided lorries, house painting, harvesting, etc.) and extracts from weather forecasts might be a suitable activity here. Children can also investigate human responses to the weather through, for example, advertisements for double glazing, paint, cavity wall insulation, rustproofing compounds, sunglasses, greenhouses, cagoules, boots, etc. Again, matching exercises contrasting weather conditions with the means by which we combat or exploit them, might form appropriate class activities.

Measuring temperature

Temperature can be measured with simple thermometers. Large wall-mounted thermometers (attractive but more expensive) are also available from educational equipment suppliers. Measurements have to be 'taken *in the shade* because it is the temperature of the air that is being measured. Thermometers are best placed therefore either on a north-facing wall or inside a cardboard tube (such as a kitchen roll tube). The readings taken need to be related to the everyday words we all use to describe temperatures. The following is a suggested list of temperatures and descriptors:

Degrees Celsius
Below −10	very cold
−10 to 0	cold
0 to 10	cool
11 to 20	warm
21 to 30	hot
over 31	very hot

Investigations into temperature might include using a maximum and minimum thermometer to find out when the hottest and coldest times of the day are. Temperatures can be taken every hour and the results shown on a graph. Ways of comparing the temperatures in two places can be discussed, for example the *hottest* temperature at each place or the *average* temperature. Comparisons can be made with other places in the world using information from newspapers.

Measuring wind

The two important elements of wind flow are direction and strength. In theory, children can investigate from which direction the wind comes most often. In practice, wind is difficult to measure because its direction and speed are rarely constant. Averaging is therefore an important part of measuring the wind. It is simplest to start with trying to record the maximum wind strength and the most consistent wind direction. Wind direction is most easily measured with a length of wool tied to the end of a stick and used with a compass. More sophisticated vanes and windsocks can be made: the trick is to find a way of allowing the instrument to rotate easily on a pivot. Note that a westerly wind *comes from* the west!

Wind strength is measured with an anemometer. The simplest sort for school use is the fairground, hand-held 'windmill'. Put a dab of bright paint on one of the sails so that the number of revolutions can be counted. A more sophisticated anemometer can be made from two laths of balsa wood and four yogurt pots. Fix the two strips of wood in the form of a cross and mount it on a vertical rod such as a knitting needle so that it will rotate freely. Fix the yogurt pots at each end of the wooden strips so that they will catch the wind. This instrument should catch the wind regardless of wind direction.

Again, it seems sensible to make links between the numerical measures of wind speed and the children's own experience. What effect do they observe when the wind blows at a speed of, say, three revolutions on their instrument? Do the top branches on trees move? Does an empty crisp packet move across the playground? Links between observed effects of the wind and measurements could be made by children's drawings to illustrate the wind descriptors in the Beaufort Wind Scale:

Beaufort Wind Scale
0 Calm
1 Light air
2 Light breeze
3 Gentle breeze
4 Moderate breeze
5 Fresh breeze
6 Strong breeze
7 Moderate gale
8 Gale
9 Strong gale
10 Storm
11 Violent storm
12 Hurricane

Measuring sunshine and cloud

Sunshine is 'officially' measured with a Campbell–Stokes sunshine recorder, a device looking rather like a crystal ball. The concentrated sun's rays burn a trace on a photosensitive paper recording strip marked in hours of the day. Without such an instrument, measuring the hours of sunlight is difficult, although as an alternative, light intensity could be measured using a photographer's light meter. It is probably better therefore to concentrate on cloud cover. Children must of course be warned not to look directly at the sun when making their estimates of how much of the sky is obscured by cloud. This estimate is usually made in *oktas* (eighths), but quarters may be more suitable for younger children.

Cloud type is a good indication of atmospheric conditions. Simple names for clouds are as effective as scientific ones and labels such as heaped, layered, wispy, thick, thin, high, low, etc. can be applied to the children's observations. A reference set of cloud pictures is useful so that children can match what they see to the photographs to help their differentiation of cloud types.

Measuring rain and snow

Rainfall is measured with a rain gauge. Here again, the technology of the instrument is an appropriate line of investigation for children. A variety of containers can be used for experiments as to their suitability. Important design factors include whether the rain will be able to evaporate before a reading is taken; whether the gauge is too light and therefore will blow away; and whether rain falling outside the gauge will splash into it and vice versa. A bucket or bowl produces a more satisfying quantity of rain-water than a jar and the larger quantity is more easily compared from day to day. The day's collected rain needs to be poured carefully into a measuring cylinder so a bucket with a pouring lip is best. A more accurate type of gauge can be easily made using a bottle (set firmly in the ground) with a funnel in the top. A thick ring of Vaseline around the bottle top helps to stabilize the funnel and prevent evaporation. The location of rain gauges is also important. They need to be well away from buildings and overhanging trees.

Children already know a lot about the properties of snow, for example that it can be squashed into snowballs. But even when it is compressed it contains air. This property of snow can be investigated by filling a beaker full of snow and allowing it to melt. Why is there a smaller volume of water than there was of snow?

Climate

Children have to be able to distinguish between weather and climate for level 5. Weather is the state of the atmosphere at any given moment or for a short period of time. Climate is 'average weather'.

The British Isles has a temperate climate, with warm summers and mild winters. It's worth finding out from an atlas what the typical January and July temperatures are for the locality of the school. They vary throughout Britain but these figures are likely to be about 2 or 3°C for January and 15 or 16°C for July. The total rainfall in a year in Britain will be between about 600 mm in the driest parts (such as East Anglia) and 2000 mm in the wettest (such as the Lake District). With just a few figures such as these it becomes easier to make comparisons with other parts of the world. It's best to make comparisons at first with places which do not have seasons – such as tropical areas, which may be hot and wet all year, or polar areas, which are dry and cold all year.

Climate maps in atlases can be difficult to interpret. Climate types are usually coloured according to a key. Look for an atlas that has descriptions that are meaningful, such as 'Very dry all year'. Children often assume that a change from one climate to another indicated on the map by a change of colour represents a sudden change on the ground, whereas the actual change is of course gradual and may happen over hundreds of miles.

Many of the stories by Jill Tomlinson deal with young animals growing up in different climates and habitats. Otto, for example, is a penguin chick who lives in the ice and snow of Antarctica.

> Otto did what he was told but it was very difficult to keep his beak shut. He wanted to know what a blizzard was.
>
> He soon found out. The wind got stronger and stronger and it felt colder and colder. Snow was driven at them harder and harder. They pressed closer and closer together to keep warm. (From *Penguin's Progress*, Methuen, 1975; Magnet, 1979)

Similar 'climate and habitat' stories are about Pongo (*The Gorilla Who Wanted to Grow Up* – Methuen, 1977; Mammoth, 1990), a young gorilla who lives in the mountains of Africa, and Pim (*The Aardvark Who Wasn't Sure* – Methuen, 1973; Mammoth, 1989), an aardvark from the African veldt.

Soils

Soil is a complex mixture of fresh and decayed rock and of fresh and decayed organic matter. It is the product of weathering of the underlying 'parent' rock and all the biological activities, such as plant growth and animal life, that take place in it. The constituent parts are reorganized by water percolating through. The whole process takes thousands of years at least and the resulting material exists in a fine balance which can be destroyed rapidly by careless farming practices. Soils vary vertically. The vertical section from ground surface to unaltered rock or sediment below is called a soil profile. It can usually be divided into a number of distinctly visible layers. Soils also vary from place to place because of differences in climate and the parent rock on which the soil is formed.

The most common misconceptions held by children about soil are that it has always been there, and that it is static rather than dynamic in nature. One child's thoughtful response to a question on the origin of soil was that it might be dinosaur manure.[17] Children are not readily able to appreciate that each soil's development is brought about by factors unique to each environment. The fact that soils take a great deal of time to form is problematic for children. They also hold widely varying notions of typical depths of soil.

Soil is best studied by digging a soil pit. You need a spade! You also need a trowel for tidying up the exposed face of the soil profile. Check that there are no underground pipes or cables and dig a clean-sided hole. The depth you dig to depends on how seriously you want to take the exercise. Ideally you should go down to the underlying rock or to a depth of about a metre. The top 'lid' of grass should be cut out so that it can be replaced afterwards. Children can then work on the exposed face. Lollipop stick markers can be used to show where the soil changes colour, appearance or feel through the exposed section. The profile will almost certainly reveal a number of layers or 'horizons'. At the very least these can be called topsoil, subsoil and parent material. Children can make rough sketches of the changing layers or an accurate scale drawing, using a metre stick.

Soil is often described by its texture, which is determined by the size of the particles it contains. There are generally three groups:

sand	2 mm–0.06 mm
silt	0.06 mm–0.002 mm
clay	less than 0.002 mm in diameter

With particles this small it is obviously impossible for children to measure their size, but a good indication of the type of soil can be gained by how it feels. If it's gritty when rubbed in the hand then it contains a good proportion of sand. If it feels smooth, soft and silky then it will have a good amount of silt, and if it is really fine and sticky then there will be a high proportion of clay. To further separate the soil sample into the different-sized particles it contains, the sample needs to be mixed with water in a jam jar. In about five minutes the sand particles will have fallen to the bottom of the jar. In about a day, the silt will have fallen on top of the sand and after a day or two the clay particles will probably still be in suspension in the water. Organic matter such as small twigs and leaves will remain floating on the surface.

Soil is more than just brown! Soil scientists use colour charts to determine colour. These are rather like home paint catalogues but are very costly. Recording soil colour by attempting to copy it using crayons is worth trying, as is simply smearing a wet sample of the soil on white paper.

Soil contains a lot of water and it is possible to investigate just how much by taking a sample, weighing it, drying it in an oven and then reweighing. You can demonstrate the amount of water by pouring out a sample of equivalent weight. The movement of water through the soil can be investigated by standing plant pots filled with dry soil in a bowl of water and seeing how long it takes for the top of the soil to become wet. Movement up the soil is by capillary action. Demonstrate this with a sugar lump suspended over a cup of tea. The tea moves up the sugar lump as the film of liquid is pulled up the lump from the wetter to drier parts. Downward movement of water through the soil can be investigated by the baked bean tin referred to in connection with infiltration as part of the hydrological cycle.

NOTES AND REFERENCES

1. The following papers contain interesting investigations into children's understanding of a number of concepts in physical geography and could usefully be replicated: Happs, J.C. (1981) 'Some aspects of student understanding of soil.' A working paper of the Learning in Science project, University of Waikato, Hamilton, New Zealand; Happs, J.C. (1982a) 'Some aspects of student understanding of rocks and minerals.' A working paper of the Learning in Science project, University of Waikato, Hamilton, New Zealand; Happs, J.C. (1982b) 'Mountains.' A working paper of the Learning in Science project, University of Waikato, Hamilton, New Zealand; Happs, J.C. (1982) 'Glaciers.' A working paper of the Learning in Science project, University of Waikato, Hamilton, New Zealand.
2. For an early investigation into children's understanding of terms in physical geography see Lunnon, A.J. (1969) 'The understanding of certain geographical concepts by primary school children.' Unpublished MEd dissertation, University of Birmingham.
3. Leach, J., Driver, R., Scott, P. and Wood-Robinson, C. (1992) *Progression and Understanding of Ecological Concepts by Pupils Aged 5-16*. Children's Learning in Science Research Group, Centre for Studies in Science and Mathematics Education, University of Leeds.
4. Moyle, R. (1980) 'Weather.' A working paper of the Learning in Science project, University of Waikato, Hamilton, New Zealand. See also Piaget, J. (1929) *The Child's Conception of the World*. London: Kegan Paul.
5. See Smith, F. and Dougherty, J.H. (1965) 'Natural phenomena as explained by children.' *Journal of Educational Research*, **59**, 3, 137-40.
6. Riley, G. (1991) 'A study of young children's understanding of physical geography and its implications for teaching practice.' Critical study submitted for the degree of MEd, Leeds University.
7. Warwick, P. (1987) 'How do children "see" geographical pictures?' *Teaching Geography*, **12**, 3, 118-19.
8. Warwick, P. (1983) 'Visual perception and geographical education: an investigation into possible visual differences between urban and rural children in viewing colour slides and methods of collecting and analysing visual perception data.' Unpublished PhD thesis, University of London.
9. Bayliss, D.G. and Renwick, T.M. (1966) 'Photograph study in a junior school.' *Geography*, **51**, 322-9.
10. Long, M. (1953) 'Children's reactions to geographical pictures.' *Geography*, **38**, 100-7.
11. Long, M. (1961) 'Research in picture study: the reaction of grammar school pupils to geographical pictures.' *Geography*, **46**, 322-37.
12. Lunnon, A.J. (1969) 'The understanding of certain geographical concepts

by primary school children.' Unpublished MEd dissertation, University of Birmingham. See also Wilson, P. and Goodwin, M. (1981) 'How do twelve and ten-year-old students perceive rivers?' *Geographical Education*, **4**, 5–16.

13. Lunnon, A.J. (1979) 'A further case for the visual.' *Geographical Education*, **3**, 331–9.
14. Happs, J.C. (1982b) 'Mountains.' A working paper of the Learning in Science project, University of Waikato, Hamilton, New Zealand.
15. Liverman, D.M. and Sherman, D.J. (1985) 'Natural hazards in novels and films: implications for hazard perception and behaviour.' In Burgess, J. and Gold, J. (eds) *Geography, the Media and Popular Culture*. Beckenham: Croom Helm.
16. Moyle, R. (1980) 'Weather.' A working paper of the Learning in Science project, University of Waikato, Hamilton, New Zealand.
17. Happs, J.C. (1981) 'Some aspects of student understanding of soil.' A working paper of the Learning in Science project, University of Waikato, Hamilton, New Zealand.

CHAPTER 5
Human Geography

Pupils should demonstrate their increasing knowledge and understanding of: (i) population; (ii) settlements; (iii) communications and movements; and (iv) economic activities – primary, secondary and tertiary. (Attainment Target 4, Department of Education and Science, *Geography in the National Curriculum (England)*. HMSO, March 1991, p. 19)

Attainment Target 4 (Human Geography) is to do with people, homes, villages and towns, journeys, work, the things we need and how the land is used. All these aspects of the social and economic world are part of children's everyday environment and experience. Most children already know a good deal about these things. So too do teachers, because topics such as these have been an important part of the primary curriculum for many years. 'People who help us' *are* geography! However, topics such as these are worth exploring further, partly because their inclusion in the *geography* statutory orders puts a slightly different emphasis on their content and partly because it is important to be as clear as we can about the nature of children's understanding of the concepts involved.

Patterns in human geography

Chapter 3 emphasized the *differences* between places by stressing what was distinctive about each locality. But modern geography is also concerned with *similarities* between places and it attempts to establish generalizations in order to discover some order and pattern in the socio-economic landscape. Although it *looks* chaotic, the distribution of houses, shops, factories, motorways, airports and so on is not in fact a random jumble. All of these familiar features depend to some extent on the physical characteristics of the surface of the Earth, such as relief, but their location is also determined by social, political and economic factors. We are aware of many of these, at least implicitly. For example, when we visit a town new to us we expect to find the largest shops clustered together in an identifiable 'shopping centre'. That's where we would expect to find the largest clothing and fashion multiples, the jewellers, furniture stores and so on. Although we would probably associate this shopping area with restaurants and fast-food outlets we would not generally expect to find supermarkets or DIY warehouses in the same place. These are generally located on the fringe of the town and in suburban areas, often near major routes such as ring roads. Industry is also generally located away from the city centre where there is more, and cheaper, space for factories. What we *would* expect to find in the town centre is office blocks – often quite tall so that the centre of the town is usually visible from some distance away. Within the office and business district we might find banks and building societies, and these also tend to cluster together.

There are a number of principles which govern this typical arrangement of urban services. One is land rent. The centre of town is (theoretically) the easiest part of the town to get to. It has the largest number of pedestrians and therefore is the place where most of the shops want to be, because that is where most potential customers are. Shops compete for space in the town centre and the cost of land is high. Therefore only the shops with the highest turnover can afford to locate there. Because the land rent is high in the centre of the town developers have to make the most of each building plot. That's why the buildings are tall. Supermarkets, on the other hand, need large car parks (a week's food shopping is heavy and the frozen peas will defrost if you don't get them home quickly) and so they have to locate on the outskirts of the town, near residential areas and where the land for the car park is cheaper. But cities change. Town centre shopping is unattractive if shoppers are battling with the traffic in crowded high streets. A high rate of car ownership and an expanding motorway network has meant that many people are now prepared to travel much further for traffic-free 'Mall'-style shopping, right away from city centres. The growth of new shopping facilities such as the Metro centre in Gateshead or Meadowhall in Sheffield is witness to completely new patterns of retailing. Maybe in the future our cities will be turned inside out – with people living in the centres (once more) and shopping on the outskirts in traffic-free and weather-free conditions.

Economic and industrial understanding

What we know about children's knowledge and understanding of human geography is patchy. We know more about children's understanding of concepts relating to industry and economics than we do about concepts relating to, say, transport or settlement. This is because a number of initiatives have led to a recent upsurge of research interest in children's economic and industrial awareness. During the 1980s there was a substantial growth in the number of agencies and initiatives that were involved in linking schools and industry in order to improve children's understanding of the 'world of work', and by the end of the decade many of them had turned their attention to primary schools. The School Curriculum Industry Partnership (SCIP), for example, was particularly influential in disseminating ideas and teaching strategies as well as making research into children's understanding of economic concepts more widely known.[1] Such initiatives also received strong support from central government. The Department of Trade and Industry's Enterprise and Education Initiative encouraged teachers to take short placements in local industrial and commercial enterprises, and Enterprise Awareness in Teacher Education (EATE) provided resources and materials on schools–industry links for institutions of initial teacher training. The materials produced by these agencies make strong links with the National Curriculum through the core and foundation subjects as well as through the cross-curricular theme of education for economic and industrial understanding. This cross-curricular theme is supported by the Educating for Economic Awareness project directed from the National Curriculum Council. Significantly, it has received far more funding than any of the other cross-curricular themes. All this activity, and more, has stimulated research into young children's understanding of concepts such as 'work', which are central to human geography, as well as concepts such as 'value' and 'exchange', which are more properly part of economics but can still shed light on children's understanding of geographical ideas. It has also done a great deal to promote and disseminate ideas and strategies for teaching. However, it has been noted[2] that primary school topic work on industry and economic awareness has often been driven by a desire to inform children about industry and *its* needs rather than starting with the *child's* needs.

Children's understanding of the concept 'work'

Exploring children's thinking about key concepts allows us to identify their different understandings and potential misunderstandings and these may in turn shed light on teaching strategies. But many concepts in human geography are in themselves diffuse. The concept of 'work', for example, is fairly ambiguous. It has different meanings in different circumstances. It can certainly be hard work cleaning a house but are you 'at work' if you're cleaning your own house, or only if you're cleaning someone else's and being paid for it? And what is the distinction between working and not working? Is it work if you enjoy it? The National Curriculum for geography usefully adopted a broad definition of work from its earliest drafts and includes amongst the examples given in the programmes of study: 'a person looking after a housebound relative'. Nevertheless children are to be taught that *adults* (not children themselves) do different kinds of work (AT4, level 1).

Some work is easy for children to envisage. It may be done by their parents at home – for example on a farm or in a shop – and they may even participate in it themselves. Other work is highly 'visible' in the community, like road mending or delivering letters. Children also have their own direct experiences of many people at work – such as dentists, health visitors and shopkeepers. They also have experience of teachers at work, although this particular activity is not actually recognized as 'work' by many children, who often ask: 'What job do you do, Miss?'! Some work is easily labelled and conceptualized, such as 'bus driver' or 'brick-layer', whereas other work can only be more vaguely expressed; either because it is in itself difficult to describe precisely or because it forms part of a much larger process or sequence of activities, the scale and complexity of which cannot yet be grasped. This sort of work might typically therefore be described by 'he works in an office' or 'she does something with computers'.

In one study of children's understanding of work it was shown that children readily recognize that work is hierarchically organized.[3] They understand that some people are 'in charge' of others. Given playing cards with pictures of people at work and labels identifying individuals' roles, this sample of children aged 7-11 showed that they were quite able to arrange them into possible organizational and management structures for a hypothetical firm. These structures included linear models of management based on job function or status as well as, by the older children, more sophisticated management hierarchies.[4] The model of hierarchical relationships that each child selected was based on his or her previous experience of school visits to industrial and commercial enterprises.

Children pick up distinct messages both from home and school about what work is like.[5] Many children's parents will 'go' to work, so that the notion of work may become associated with a remote place, from which their parents may return tired or irritable or dirty. Many children by the end of their time in primary school see a clear relationship between working hard at school and getting 'a good job' in the future. They also form rudimentary ideas about what a 'good job' is. It might, for example, be one which you enjoy, or in which you help people, or receive perks or for which you are well paid.[6]

Almost all the work on children's understanding of the social and economic world has implied that they pass through stages in their understanding. But children appear to achieve varying 'levels' of understanding across a whole range of different concepts.[7] Some children, for example those whose parents are shopkeepers, appear to understand the notion of profit in a much more sophisticated way than others. This seems to imply that experience rather than maturation is the major factor in children's understanding of such ideas. This has implications for classroom practice as children can often see another viewpoint (i.e. 'become less egocentric') when a task is presented in a way that makes sense for them. Running a mini-company at school might, for example, be an appropriate activity to develop concepts of price, value, supply and demand.

We can illustrate some of the ways children think about work by taking the example of a shop.[8] Children 'understand' what happens in a shop through their own experience from a very early age. You go to the shop. The shop has things you want. You give money in exchange for those things. Sometimes you get change. However, the precise nature of the transaction can only be interpreted by children in the light of their other experiences. Very young children may only understand that you have to give money in the shop because not to do so would be 'wrong'. (They have, after all, been told from their earliest remembered visits to shops that they cannot just 'take' things. They have to be paid for first.) This payment though is often regarded by children as a form of ritualized exchange. You give some money; you get some back; just like the earliest childhood games of pretend giving and taking. As young children are without a clear notion of number value, the 'change' from shops is often taken to be the sole source of an individual's wealth. After all, this is money you receive and therefore presumably you continue to accumulate it. The purchase itself is a form of 'swap', and understanding the nature of the exchange may depend on notions held of what makes a 'good' swap. Children frequently consider that more money is paid for objects which are more useful, more attractive (for example, 'shinier') or simply bigger than others, rather than payment being made in relation to the value added during manufacture. And what does the shop-keeper do with the money? A common belief is that it is given to charitable causes (because that is what frequently happens to money the children themselves collect – particularly in a school context). Another is that the accumulated money goes to the shopkeeper for his or her own personal use, or that it is saved (i.e. 'kept safe') in the bank or is collected by the government. Few children seem to be aware of the need to pay the shop staff or the rent or the wholesaler or of the basic 'buy for less, sell for more' principle of retailing.

How do studies such as those above shed light on children's understanding of concepts in human geography? We can detect a few, maybe unstartling, principles. Several studies in the development of children's ideas appear to have taken some notion of 'normal' adult understanding as the starting point and attempted to show how children fall short of this. But children interpret new experiences in the light of their previous learning. It is probably more productive therefore to consider what children *are* able to do as a result of their past experiences than what they can't do. We are all more adept at dealing with challenging questions when they are presented in situations which are familiar to us. If a task *means* something to us, then we understand it better and generally perform better at it. Children are more familiar with shops, for example, than banks. A task may have greater meaning if real money rather than play money is used and if children are asked to 'buy' things they really want. In an account of an infant project in which young children raised animals at school, Denise Sage[9] describes how 6- and 7-year-olds learned about economic and other concepts through being faced with the real task of feeding their animals (lambs, goats, ducks and bantams). The animals needed special food which was expensive and they had to repay a loan from the school fund. Raising money therefore became a real and urgent task for the children and they were later able to extend their own experience by considering the economics of a 'real' farm.

Understanding industrial and agricultural systems

Recognizing 'that adults do different kinds of work' (AT4, level 1c) is the first step on the road to understanding 'economic activities'. The National Curriculum for geography divides these into primary, secondary and tertiary activities. Primary industry is the process whereby natural resources are obtained from the Earth. It includes fishing, agriculture, forestry, mining and quarrying. The products are collected but not processed. Secondary industry is manufacturing industry. The raw materials are changed into goods which are used either for direct sale to consumers or to other factories so that they may use the products in their own manufacturing process. Tertiary industry is the provision of services. It includes transport, wholesaling and retailing. Tertiary industry links primary and secondary industries with each other and with their customers. Many geographers also acknowledge a further sector: that of quaternary industry. This consists of higher-order services including education, consultancy, administration and financial services. Quite young children appear to be able to discriminate between these different types of economic activity.[10] For example, given pictures of a doctor, postal worker, police officer and football player, many children are able to place the first three together in one group and justify that grouping on the basis that these were 'people that helped you'.

It is probably not necessary for children in primary school to know the terms 'primary', 'secondary' and 'tertiary' as applied to economic activity, but the differentiation of 'industry' into these three categories may be a helpful one for the teacher in selecting appropriate learning experiences for children. Office and shop work, for example, are major forms of economic activity. Two-thirds of the employed population in the UK work in service industries. But whereas the classroom shop is generally well established in primary classrooms, the classroom 'office' is less frequently seen. And yet there are substantial opportunities here for learning. Very young children can, for example, explore through play the skills of telephoning, filing and photocopying and then later do these things through the 'real' school office. Learning is rapid in situations where children have real responsibility for counting the dinner money, telephoning dinner numbers through to the central kitchens, answering the school telephone, and word processing and then duplicating circular letters to parents.

The central concept of geography is location – why are things where they are? This is what lies behind Attainment Target 4, level 4d: 'Give reasons for the ways in which the land is used, how conflict can arise because of competition over the use of the land, and for the location of different types of economic activity.' Why does this farm grow these particular crops and why is this particular factory here?

To approach these concepts it is helpful to see both farms and factories as *systems*, in the same way as the hydrological cycle was seen as a system in Chapter 4. Systems analysis is an approach which clarifies our understanding of complex relationships, and the linked elements in both industry and agriculture can be seen more clearly when put into a logical framework.

Farming is the result of a complex interaction of both physical and human factors. Among the physical factors are climate, relief, rocks and soils. All plants need warmth, sunshine and water to survive, but in different quantities – and this limits the possibilities for agriculture. A minimum temperature is necessary for crops to grow. Most crops, including grass, will grow only when the temperature reaches about 6°C. This means that farming cannot generally take place in very high latitudes. There is, for example, virtually no farming north of the Arctic Circle. Maize needs much warmer temperatures and so is rarely found above the 50 degree line of latitude. Cotton needs even warmer temperatures and is generally confined to within 35 degrees north and south of the equator. But crops also need water – and at the right time of the year. To grow cotton successfully you need between 500 and 1000 mm of rainfall per annum. Rice, on the other hand, needs much more: about 1500 mm per year.

Temperature is, however, controlled not only by latitude, but also by altitude. The higher up you go, the colder it generally becomes – by about 1°C for every 200 m. Steepness of slope is also a significant factor in determining what types of farming are possible. The steeper the gradient, the more difficult it becomes to use farm machinery. Soils are also important to farmers. The depth of the soil, the likelihood of its becoming waterlogged or too dry, together with its acidity will permit some farming practices but not others.

These and other factors set the physical limits for farming. They determine what is possible. But farmers make choices within these limits – and, if it is considered worth it, may extend those limits by using technology to overcome the physical circumstances, for example by irrigation or growing crops under glass. Changing technology has also altered the scale of production and allowed farmers in areas of high economic development to specialize in one or two products over very large areas.

126

Commercial farmers produce only those commodities which will bring enough profit to make the enterprise worthwhile. One determinant of profit is demand. There is now only a fraction of the demand for oats that there was, say, 30 years ago (mainly because farms no longer use horses) and so there has been a corresponding reduction in the acreage under oats. Demand for barley, on the other hand, as fodder for intensive livestock rearing, has increased, and so too therefore has its acreage. But it is of little use producing a crop and not being able to get it to the market in good condition. There has therefore always been a significant connection between the type of farming and the level of transport technology. Refrigerated transport, for example, allowed the development of distant parts of Argentina and Australia for the production of sheep and beef cattle. Heavy commodities which are expensive to transport, or perishable ones, have traditionally been grown close to the market, but high-value crops such as early season fruit, vegetables and flowers will even withstand the cost of international air transport. The availability of capital for investment and the controls exerted by governments through pricing policies and subsidies are further examples of 'human' factors in agriculture.

Even with quite straightforward examples it is easy to see how the question 'Why does this farm grow these particular crops?' is a complex one. Understanding industrial location ('Why is this particular factory here?') is no less complex. Manufacturing industry makes things from raw materials. But these raw materials are not available everywhere. The obvious solution therefore is for an industrialist to locate close to the source of the raw material: fish finger factories, for instance, are on the coast! But most factories require more than one basic raw material. To make steel you need iron ore, coal and limestone. In this situation, the obvious solution would be to locate nearer to the source of the raw material you need most of, or the one that is heaviest, bulkiest or most expensive to transport. But as well as making the product, you have to sell it, and sometimes the finished product is more expensive to transport than the raw materials. In this case the entrepreneur would be better advised to locate nearer to the market than the source of the raw material. A factory making fizzy drink needs to import and mix up the secret ingredients and then add water. Water is available everywhere and adds greatly to the transport costs, and so the best place for this factory might be as near to the consumers as possible – perhaps in a large town.

However, the finished product of one factory is very often the 'raw material' of another. The motor vehicle industry assembles cars from the finished products (such as windscreen wipers, tyres, carpets, headlights, etc.) of hundreds of other factories. And those factories in turn may assemble their products from dozens of further factories. (A car headlight, for example, consists of bulbs, glass, chrome, wires and so on, each in turn made from sand, iron ore, oil and minerals.) These industrial linkages are massively complex and where and how they occur may be the result of historical factors that perhaps no longer exist. Some factories are where they are because they've always been there and it would cost more to move than take advantage of some theoretically 'better' location.

Completely new industries, on the other hand, need to consider the cost of setting up a factory, and the decision to locate in a particular place may have nothing at all to do with the costs of transporting raw materials or finished products and a good deal to do with the availability of cheap land and rents in a government-sponsored 'development area'. And cutting across all these 'location factors' may be sheer chance. The motor vehicle industry in Oxford is there because that's where William Morris lived.

How can we use the idea of a system to help children understand what's going on in factories and on farms? First of all, the framework for under-standing needs to be established. Children's own homes can be viewed as systems.[11] Inputs in the form of food, energy and goods come into the home and outputs such as rubbish and waste go out. Children may need some help in separating out some of the categories of inputs such as 'things which the family bring in', 'things which other people bring in' and 'things which come in through pipes and wires' and the categories of outputs such as 'things which go out because we wear them out' and 'things which go out because we wish to get rid of them'. Other ways of categorizing inputs might be 'services that are there whenever we want them' (like electricity), 'services that come regularly' (like the milk and newspapers) and 'services that only come in an emergency' (like the fire engine). The simple system of the home can be extended to the more complex notions of the systems of water and electricity flows in houses. Through these and other services each house is seen as part of a much larger system whereby all the homes in one area are connected to each other. Each home is, for example, part of a city- or nation-wide network of water, sewage, electricity, gas and telephone services. Some of these links are physical, through pipes and wires; some are through deliveries and connections such as the postal and refuse disposal services. The same approach can be used by considering the school itself. What goes into the school? Children, teachers, electricity, water, food, paper, etc. Some-thing then goes on inside the school. And what comes out? – teachers, children (are they changed in any way?), waste paper, sewage, models and paintings to take home, etc. However, there is a problem with the analogy of the school as an industrial system. Although it has been argued[12] that schools reproduce capitalist society by developing the types of social behav-iours that are needed at work and thereby help to integrate children into the economic system, the fact remains that schools are *not* the same as factories. They do have some similarities to many workplaces; for example, there are definite hours and rules and very often there is a clear and shared perception of the difference between work and non-work (i.e. 'play', 'choosing' or 'playtimes'). But they don't have a clear 'product' or many ways of measuring 'productivity', as teachers will understand all too well in the context of pay incentives and National Curriculum testing.

Nevertheless, 'work' does go on in school and children can be engaged with issues relating to their own work and that of the adults other than teachers in the school – the caretaker, secretary, kitchen staff, cleaners and so on. Who pays these people at work? Do they have special tools or equipment for their jobs? Special work clothes? Who tells them what to do? What happens when something goes wrong? If the drains smell, or there's a gas leak, or the lights go out, who fixes it?

Understanding industrial and agricultural systems needs to start at the level of the individual enterprise: one factory or one farm. Identifying the inputs and outputs of the enterprise is a central task in studying factories and farms whether they are investigated at first hand through visits or through secondary sources such as publicity and other commercial promotional literature, or through the sorts of case study materials produced by the Association of Agriculture. Diagrams and models can be constructed for factories showing what goes in and what comes out, especially if the inputs and the outputs are easily envisaged by children. The quantities can also be added – for example in a liquorice allsort factory 12 000 000 allsorts or 200 kilometres of liquorice are produced every day (see Figure 5.1).

Actually, the separation of factory-produced and farm-produced outputs is sometimes difficult for children, not least because much food is highly processed and even in its 'raw' state is often packaged in a form that disguises its origins. Inputs for farming include the physical characteristics of the site. There is scope here for problem solving. Suppose we wanted to turn the school field into a farm. What could we grow? One starting point here would be to investigate the contents of local gardens and allotments. What *will* grow near here? What won't?

Visitors from industry to school can be helpful in developing children's understanding of economic activity but such visits have not apparently always been used to best advantage.[13] The most successful experiences seem to have been those where the visitor was fully involved at an early stage in planning activities to be later undertaken by the children.

Children's own class visits to factories, farms, shops, transport facilities and other services are not of course new but there have been a number of accounts recently of apparently successful work with very young children in connection with such visits.[14]

One teacher[15] reported not just one industrial visit as part of a project but a series of *linked* visits so that the children could see all the progressive

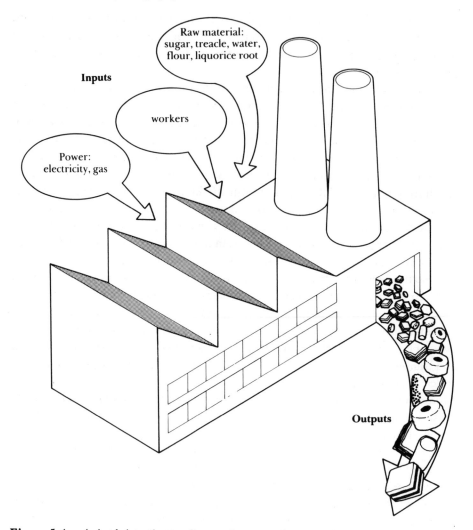

Figure 5.1 *A simple input/output diagram for a sweet factory as the basis for a class display.*

manufacturing stages in the ready-made clothing industry, from cotton mill through clothing factory to retailing in a large store. Although these visits were set up only after some tenacity on the part of the teacher concerned it is the connections and interrelatedness of industry that are the most interesting part of this work – from the raw material to displaying the finished article in the shop window. Indeed, the theme of 'geography through the shop window' has been a very long-established way into geography teaching.[16]

130

In a similar vein is an account[17] of a number of serial visits of children to different shoe factories to allow them to compare what was essentially the same process but using very different forms of technology and making different types of shoe.

An alternative to, or a development of, the industrial visit is the situation where children set up their own 'mini-enterprise' or 'kinder-economy'.[18] In the mini-enterprise the children themselves are producers. The justification for this is usually given[19] as helping children develop important interpersonal skills and to develop understanding of economic and business affairs through first-hand experience of making and selling. The aim is to involve children in a number of realistic significant steps in the development of their mini-enterprise such as planning, making a feasibility study, doing market research, raising the necessary capital, organizing the production system, advertising the product and selling it. Throughout, children need to keep accounts and records. Any profit is generally given to charity or used to buy materials or equipment for their school. Typically, children might be set up with funds from local sources in order to make products that can be sold at some school event such as a parents' evening or a summer fair. These might include Christmas decorations, key fobs, bookmarks and growing plants from seed. In one mini-enterprise,[20] primary school children bought mugs (decorated with their own design) from a local pottery company and sold them for a profit.

One of the problems of running a mini-enterprise is that although in some senses the exercise is 'real', in many others it is quite *unrealistic*. In school ventures which set out to make a profit, labour and other overheads are frequently not costed into the projects, and the enterprise may consist of parents buying back their own supplied ingredients or material in a form to which sentimental value only has been added.

There are a number of reports of industrial processes being modelled in the classroom. Ross[21] describes how class work following a factory visit attempted to replicate some of the processes the children had seen in the workplace. Some 5- and 6-year-olds made shapes out of multifix maths cubes. They did this individually (as in a craft industry) and then using a teacher-powered conveyor belt made from a large loop of wallpaper. They considered which was better and in so doing raised issues of boredom and job satisfaction. In another report, Burleton[22] describes a class making dolls' clothes on a similar production line following a visit to a clothing factory.

Other aspects of industrial life can be incorporated into work simulations. Fitzpatrick[23] describes how adults other than teachers (AOTs) took the roles of a factory inspector and a trade union official during a class-based follow-up simulation after an industrial visit. Children were asked questions about the spacing between their desks and the toxicity of the crayons they were using.

Issues such as these appear to be rarely raised in teaching about economic understanding.

Journeys

Geographers are principally interested in two aspects of journeys: why things move and how things move. Explaining *why* things move often involves ideas such as the relative attractiveness of alternative destinations. Explaining *how* things move often depends on the characteristics of alternative modes of transport, such as their speed and efficiency.

Each mode of transport has its own peculiar characteristics which lead to the use people make of it. This is what lies behind Attainment Target 4, statement 3c: 'Explain why different forms of transport are used.' Road transport, for example, is found almost everywhere although the quality of the roads themselves varies hugely. Motorways are very different from dirt tracks or roads in a local housing estate. This implies that children need language experience of various forms of road: street, highway, dual carriageway, motorway, by-pass, ring road, trunk road, minor road, cul-de-sac, etc. How are these different from each other? This experience is necessary to be able to understand maps which differentiate between types of road (such as Ordnance Survey maps).

Most roads take you from door to door. Everyone can use them and get on to them, and the cost of maintaining them is shared by a large number of people. We are all connected to roads, but there are limitations on how much can be carried by each vehicle. (The maximum number of passengers on a bus, for example, is about 50.)

Railways, by contrast, are not found everywhere. They cost a lot of money to build, but because the vehicles use tracks that can be monitored and controlled centrally, delays (in theory at least!) should be minimal. Much greater bulk cargoes can be carried in long trains than could be envisaged by road. Coal, often transported in non-stop 'merry-go-round' trains, is a good example. Railways provide fast and frequent services between large urban areas, and the trains give rise to less pollution than road vehicles. But railways are expensive to maintain whether they are used to a greater or lesser extent. They are also inflexible. Once the track is there it cannot easily be extended or moved.

Water transport is cheapest. Large vessels can be operated very economically and can handle the heaviest and bulkiest cargoes. The ocean 'networks' are also free of maintenance costs. But ships are slow. This means that water transport is generally unsuitable for perishable commodities unless there are special storage facilities, such as freezers, on board. And the increase in size of ships means that there are fewer possibilities for docking.

Very large crude-oil tankers are increasingly restricted to a small number of very large ports.

Air transport is fast but expensive. Almost all long-distance passenger transport nowadays is by air. Aeroplanes, especially helicopters, can get to places that are inaccessible by road; but air transport is not quite the unrestricted movement it sometimes seems as flights have to take place in air 'corridors'. It is also dependent to some extent on the weather, it is often noisy and the large size of modern jets means that fewer airports can accept them.

A form of transport not immediately recognized by young children, but nevertheless highly significant, is the pipeline. This method is efficient, fast and cheap. Pipelines are mostly used for transporting oil and petrochemical feedstock but also (for example in the Alps) for the movement of milk from upland pasture farms to lower-slope dairies. However, pipelines cost a lot to install and are inflexible in their use. They can be damaged by earth movements or frost. But they don't cause pollution and can operate round the clock.

Networks

All these forms of transport are connected into networks of routes. It is the characteristics of those networks that lie behind Attainment Target 4, 4d: 'Explain why roads and railways may not always take the shortest route between the places they link'; and AT 4, 5d: 'Compare road and rail networks, and explain the effects of changes to those networks'. Networks form patterns, made up of routes and end points or terminals. These patterns have different characteristics. Consider, for example, the networks illustrated in Figure 5.2.

The networks represent routes linking terminals. The 'routes' could be roads, railway lines, canals, aircraft flight paths or pipelines. The 'terminals' could be houses, towns, stations or airports. Each of the five networks in Figure 5.2 represents a different *minimization* principle. Can you work out what this principle is in each case?

Example A represents the *shortest path* that links all the terminals. This is the solution that might be adopted by a local authority wishing to minimize costs when, say, building new roads or laying sewerage pipes. Example B, on the other hand, is much more expensive for the builder as the total length of the routes is much greater, but the costs to the *user* are minimized. A passenger travelling on a public transport system constructed on this principle could do so direct to each of the towns in the system. Example C is a *hierarchical* arrangement of routes. It's cheaper than A or B to build and might represent a transport solution where only the most important point in the

133

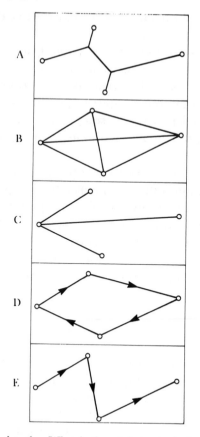

Figure 5.2 *Five minimal paths. What is the minimization principle in each case? (From Abler, R., Adams, J. S. and Gould, P. (1972)* Spatial Organization. *Englewood Cliffs, NJ: Prentice-Hall International, p. 279.)*

system has to be connected to every other point. Commuter routes to a capital city are frequently arranged in this way. The bulk of the traffic has rapid access to the principal destination at the lowest cost but user costs are very high for those wanting to travel from one suburb to another as they have to go through the city centre. Network D is often called a 'travelling sales-man' network. This form of network gives the *shortest round-trip path* through the network, as would be required by someone wanting to visit a number of towns or sales outlets, in order, in one journey. The final network, E, starts at one point and links all the others *en route to the final destination*. Geographers call this a 'Paul Revere' network, after the American patriot, famous for his midnight ride from Charleston to Lexington in 1775 to warn fellow American revolutionaries of the approach of British troops. This sort of route pattern would be adopted by people in a car pool, where the first point is the home of the car owner and the final point is the workplace.

Analyses such as these indicate that the route networks with which we are familiar in everyday life are in fact solutions to the problems of how places may best be linked and are usually determined by the need to minimize time and cost. These considerations include the physical costs of going round high points rather than bridging or making cuttings as well as maximizing accessibility and connectivity within the network. In this way there are curricular associations with many of the design and technology attainment targets. How can these principles be demonstrated in the classroom? A potentially chaotic, but effective, way is to consider the 'shortest path' to the door of the classroom from each child's seat. It involves a plan of the classroom, including the location of the furniture. The shortest path is easily drawn by ruler. But how practical is this solution in the real room? The 'least-cost' solution will require going round the furniture, but children will no doubt enjoy experimenting with the direct route and generally enjoy the anarchic approach.

This sort of experimentation can be extended to the rest of the school. It takes less effort to go round the building than it does to go through the hall when it's full of children, or less effort to go round the muddy patch than jumping over it. It is worth noting that the same principles are used in, say, planning a kitchen. An ideal plan places the cooker near the sink to prevent constant criss-crossing of the kitchen with hot pots and pans. There is scope here for observational work on movement in children's own homes and linking project work in mapping, human geography and design and technology. Associated work could include considering where to put the things we need in the classroom so that space is used to the best advantage and people are not disturbed by having, for example, noisy activities next to quiet ones. These 'mini-journeys' can be extended to an examination of the shortest paths around the school and in local parks. Short cuts across the grass and tracks in the snow show the principle of least effort in action. Children are often very familiar with short cuts in their own locality and these can be interesting when mapped. The theme can be developed by looking at routes on maps. Why do roads take the path they do? Look for the road patterns around lakes and explore the 'lowest bridging points' of rivers. These provide good reasons for the original location of settlements in many cases. The theme of detours and short cuts can also be examined at a global scale by looking at the world's great canals, such as the Suez (opened in 1869) and Panama (opened in 1914), to see what effect they had on world journeys.

How can teachers build up children's understanding of transport media? Many children are of course familiar with several forms of transport through their own travel. However, they probably have less experience of some forms of travel, such as rail, than we tend to assume. Class visits and picture book resources such as Richard Scarry's *Cars and Trucks and Things That Go* (Collins, 1976) can be used to establish the characteristics of each mode of transport. This includes developing the vocabulary of terminals (e.g. 'platform'), routes (e.g. 'junction') and process (e.g. 'arrivals') and the comparative sizes and speeds of vehicles.

It is likely that some children will have very dated images of some forms of transport. Many children's books and play materials still emphasize the 'choo-choo' image of trains with puffing steam. Notwithstanding that, however, there are useful geographical concepts to be explored in the Thomas the Tank Engine stories by the Rev. W. Awdry.[24] The big proud engine called Gordon, for example, has considerable difficulty getting to the top of the hill until he is pushed by Edward. Gradient is the central concept in the very first of the Railway Series books, *The Three Railway Engines*.[25]

It is also appropriate to focus on the different ways of carrying and types of specialized vehicles – such as containers, tankers, bulk loaders and roll-on roll-off ferries. Play with models and model layouts is valuable. A possible 'talk and play' sequence using a model layout of a town or a country might include discussion of particular loads in a simple problem-solving context: 'We have cases of avocados, bales of wool, milk in bulk, coal, passengers, fresh cream cakes, etc. Which is the best form of transport to get these from one part of the layout to another?' Problem solving starts by investigating the characteristics of each of these loads. What do they look like? How much would they weigh? How perishable are they? These answers give clues to the appropriate choice of transport.

Journey problem solving can be extended to 'real' problems in the locality. For example a person who lives in Leeds has an important meeting to attend in London. How should this person travel? There are four real-life possibilities: coach, train, car or air. There is much to be investigated here. Perhaps you start by collecting information about each of the transport types. What are the coaches like? Are they the same as local buses? How are they different? Are the intercity trains the same as the local services? Who has been to London by coach or train or by car or even by aeroplane? Which would you prefer? Next, some factual information about departure and arrival times and costs needs to be collected. There are complex issues here to be explored. Does it make a difference to the cost if you book in advance? Can you change your mind once you've booked? Does it make a difference on which day of the week you travel? Does the time of the meeting and its precise location within London affect your choice? When is the earliest time you could go and the latest time you could come back? Do those factors determine the cost? Would everyone make the same choice? What would the best choice be for a family with young children, or an elderly person travelling alone, or a foreign tourist? Which of the available possibilities allow for a stop on the way? The answers can be obtained by telephone calls, and timetables and maps. Note that the only maps that give information about routes may be topological transformations (see Chapter 2). Perhaps groups work on different options and report back. Perhaps the class 'shop' can become a travel agency . . .

How do the children make their own journeys to school? From what they know already about different types of transport they might be able to make some reasonable assumptions. Those who live furthest away probably come by car or bus. Those who live nearest probably walk. But is this true? A large-scale map of the catchment area is needed and each child has to mark on it his or her home and the route taken to school. A different colour is used for each mode of transport. Can a generalization be made from the map? Is there a relationship between distance and transport used that can be shown on a graph? How long does it take to get to school? Those who have the shortest journeys ought to get here quickest. Is that true? The map can be used to measure distance and these measurements can be compared with children's estimates of time taken. Again, these can be plotted against each other on a scatter graph. Dealing with questions like these helps to establish distances in relation to everyday experience ('My journey to school is half a kilometre'). This is clearly related closely to the mathematics Attainment Target 8 (Measures), for example, at levels 3 and 4, but is also an important pre-requisite to understanding the scale of much larger units such as the UK as a whole. Linking distance to time as well as transport mode is part of understanding scale too.

Transport is what links the farm system with the shop system. 'Tracking' the journey of one item is a fairly well-established way of teaching such links. Take the example of an apple. First you would establish the nature of the fruit itself. Children might collect several varieties and compare their colour, taste, texture and preferences, perhaps storing the information on a simple database. Next, you identify how it grows, the amount of warmth and moisture it needs, and perhaps relate the apple tree's growing season to a chart showing the whole year and differentiating between warm and cold months. You would identify a locality or specific market garden where apples are grown and look at pictures of picking and packing. The locality would be identified on a map and the apples' journey to the warehouse plotted. Then you plot the journey from the warehouse to the supermarket. A visit to the local supermarket can pick up the story and it might be possible to see the ordering of the next consignment of apples in action. Timing is quite important in this sequence. Fresh food moves fast and it's helpful to use timelines (as in history teaching) to help keep track of where commodities are on their journeys from source to shop. An orange makes a good comparison:

…urther family of fruit, contrasting climatic requirements and …s at European or perhaps world scales. Oranges, together …fruits and grapes, are grown in the Mediterranean region …parts of the world that have a Mediterranean climate. …obably already be familiar with some of their names: …ustralia, Chile, California, South Africa. The location of these places on the world map reveals another geographical pattern: they are all at about 35–40 degrees north and south of the equator and on the western side of major land masses.

Settlements

People live in settlements which vary in size and the names given to types of settlements also vary according to the number of people in them. For teacher reference the following may be taken as a rough guide to terminology:

Settlement	Number of inhabitants
house	1–10
hamlet	10–100
small village	100–500
large village	500–2000
small town	2000–10 000
large town	10 000–100 000
city	100 000–1 000 000
conurbation	over 1 000 000

Children are expected to know something about the form and function of settlements, particularly their own. It's important to know that each of the types of settlement in the table above tends to be associated with a particular set of functions. A *hamlet* may well have no services at all apart from perhaps a shop or pub. A *small village* may have a church (possibly infrequently used), a pub, a general store and perhaps a small primary school and part-time-opening bank. A *large village* may have more than one church, a number of specialist shops: a chemist, a greengrocer, newsagent, butcher, estate agent or building society or bank. *Towns*, by contrast, are characterized by the appearance of well-known multiple stores. In Britain you would expect to find branches of Marks & Spencer, Woolworths, Boots and W. H. Smith in the larger towns. Towns also have higher-order educational facilities, secondary schools and colleges of further education. Towns are also characterized by places of entertainment: theatres and cinemas. *Cities* have the highest order functions of all: universities, teaching hospitals, opera houses, major art galleries, etc. In earlier times a city had to have a cathedral. Nowadays, it's a city if it calls itself one, usually with the authority of a royal charter.

Conurbations are places where several towns and cities have merged together such as the West Midlands, or Merseyside or Greater London or West Yorkshire.

A lot of geography books describe places in terms of one function only, say as 'port' or 'resort' or 'administrative centre'. But these terms can be misleading. Cambridge, for example, is often thought of as a university city but there are significant (electronic) industries there; Oxford is also as much a manufacturing city (especially for motor vehicles) as a university one.

SETTLEMENT PATTERNS

As we have seen above, settlements vary in size and each size category (hamlet, village, town, etc.) tends to be associated with a range of particular functions. But there are also patterns to the number of settlements in each size category. There are, for example, many more villages than towns and more towns than cities and only a few conurbations. In the United Kingdom, there is only one London, but several dozen towns of the size of, say, Norwich, Plymouth or Swansea and hundreds of smaller towns such as Lyme Regis and Bridport. There are also patterns to where settlements are located. Some *sites* – the actual plots of land on which settlements were first founded – are better than others, because, for example, they are free from flooding, or can be easily defended or are near fresh water. These sites are chosen from within favourable *situations* – larger areas which offer good potential for settlement because, say, there is fertile land for agriculture or the region is crossed by trading routes.

At a world scale, the distribution of population depends mainly on where people can earn a living. More than two-thirds of the world's population lives directly by farming and so few people live where agriculture is difficult. High, cold and very wet or dry places are sparsely populated. Warm, flat regions with fertile soils are home to most of the world's people. Valleys and coasts are especially well populated because they also provide access to other areas for trade.

Children can investigate patterns such as those above for themselves, starting again from their own experience. The starting point is the home, and the possibilities of the home as a resource for teaching about systems have already been discussed. Settlement vocabulary begins with individual buildings and their uses. House types, for example, include terrace, semi-detached, detached, bungalow, flat and maisonette. This labelling includes familiarity with each part of the house – the name of each room and the functions associated with it. This may reveal interesting discrepancies between what rooms with the same function are called by different families, and that in turn might prompt discussion more generally about how space is used. Drawings and lists of what the children do in each room are helpful here.

Information about houses in the locality can be stored on a database. Setting up the database fields means that terms such as semi-detached and maisonette have to be clarified in advance. The database can include information about the building materials used, garage space, and evaluative information about the condition of the house based on a scoring system, adding points and deducting points depending on the condition of the garden, paintwork and availability of play space, etc. A particularly useful piece of software for recording information about streets in the locality is Graphic Street Profile.[26] The program allows users to input data about the width of each building (children can measure this by pacing the frontage), the number of floors and what the building is used for. The program then draws and prints a cross-section of the street.

Homes are arranged in groups and there is order in streets through the numbering of houses. Children also know about order from their visits to supermarkets. Goods are not just jumbled up together – washing powder with apples and baked beans. Sections of the supermarket are arranged so that shoppers can easily make sense of the layout and minimize time spent searching for what they want. Similar conventions in residential areas such as having even numbers on one side of the road and odd numbers on the other make the urban environment, like the supermarket, more 'legible'. How do you find your way to a particular house for the first time if you have the address? Who might need to get to a house quickly in an emergency?

During visits to local residential areas children will probably see For Sale signs. But how much does a house cost and what determines its price? Children (even more than would-be purchasers) are frequently astonished at the scale of house prices: 'The prices are a rip-off', 'What do all the 00s mean?', 'Where do people get the money from?'.[27] Older children can explore the determinants of house price such as size and accommodation, condition and location. A newspaper simulator and simple desk-top publishing program such as Front Page Special Edition (MAPE) can be used by children to write their own estate agents' property descriptions.[28] This software allows for the production of an A4 'poster' with a number of boxes that can be used for text (in six fonts and three type sizes) as well as spaces for the children's own illustrations (or even photographs) to be inserted. There is much opportunity for language work here derived from a (possibly amusing) study of existing estate agents' literature. Estate agents are, incidentally, a useful source of large-scale street maps and often provide information sheets about the local area.

The address of each child can be used as the starting point for exploration of patterns in residential areas. Children have to be able to 'state where they live' for Attainment Target 2, level 1. Take the example of a child who lives at the following, fictitious, address: 11 Village Way, Roundhay, Leeds, West Yorkshire. The address is unique. Only this child in the class has this address. But elements of the address are shared by other children in the class. We all live in West Yorkshire. All of us live in Leeds, and most of us in Roundhay (some live in Chapel Allerton and one comes from Harehills). There are three children who live in Village Way. Addresses 'fit together', like Russian nesting dolls. Village Way is in Roundhay, which is in Leeds, which is in West Yorkshire. The same nesting arrangement can be seen in postcodes. The first two letters are the region, the next number identifies a smaller area within that region. But children often experience great difficulty in understanding that you *can* be in two places at once![29] Young children will often deny that you can be in Roundhay *and* in Leeds. It's either one or the other. 'Leeds' will often be taken as the city centre, somewhere 'over there' or 'at the end of the bus route'. Indeed, in everyday conversation that's how the name is used by adults. Simple materials can be devised which will help children with these concepts. Postcodes can be collected (on cards) and sorted on the basis of common elements. It is also possible to obtain postcode maps from the Post Office which shows how they are arranged for each local area. Most local street maps have postal districts marked on and the boundaries of these can be highlighted once each child has marked his or her own address on the map. The addresses can be abstracted from the map or cards and regrouped into Venn diagrams or stored on a simple database (as in mathematics Attainment Target 12, levels 1–5). School catchment jigsaw puzzles are a further way of establishing the hierarchy of settlement form. You need some small card squares, some strips and some large circles of different sizes and colours to represent each level in the address hierarchy of a school catchment. Children each write their house number on a small square, group together to label a 'street' strip, then a 'suburb' circle, a 'town' circle and a 'county' circle. The squares are stuck onto the strips, which are stuck onto the circles. The materials need to be adapted slightly for catchments with, for example, many blocks of flats and can easily be extended to include increasingly larger spatial units such as England, the United Kingdom, Europe and the wider world. Work like this on the structure of spatial units needs to be done in conjunction with large-scale maps. The way houses are arranged on these also forms a pattern, or series of patterns. Each type of house tends to be associated with a characteristic layout. Terraced houses (especially those dating from the nineteenth century), for example, are generally in straight rows. The density of housing is high and the gardens are small. More recent housing estates, with sweeping curves and culs-de-sac, present a completely different pattern on the map.

The relationship between the number of settlements in each size category can be investigated by starting with the local school 'pyramid' structure. The principles are the same. In their preparation for school transfer, top primary pupils will be aware that they will not be the only newcomers to their secondary school. There are generally four or five primary schools that 'feed' a secondary school and perhaps several feeder secondary schools to a sixth-form college or institution of further education. Each school represents a level in the hierarchy similar to towns of varying size. Like towns, schools also offer different levels of service. A primary school may offer one science room, a small hall and a small library. A secondary school may have a swimming pool, four science laboratories, a careers room, a technology suite, a computer laboratory, etc. Children are generally quick to identify these 'services' which they themselves will use and that makes a good starting point for data collection. The services or functions can be related to the number of pupils in each school. The pyramid itself can be represented in graph and diagram form and the catchment areas of the schools involved shown on maps.

School catchments can be identified by 'desire line' maps. A sample of the school population is taken (perhaps one class or year). Each pupil marks on a large-scale map of the locality his or her address. Straight lines are drawn from each home to the school. (This could be used as the basic data for evidence about average length of journeys 'as the crow flies' and comparisons of straight line and real distance.) Joining the edges of the star-shaped set of lines that result defines the catchment. How does this catchment fit with that of a neighbouring school? There is the possibility here of comparative data collection, including the formulation of a hypothesis ('our two schools take pupils from different areas') and sending an invitation to another class to carry out the same investigation in their school with the object of pooling the results. The head of geography in the local secondary school ought to be interested in the results (and may also be interested in participating because the resultant maps can be used to illustrate a theory called 'Central Place Theory' which sets out to explain the spatial organization of settlements and their market areas).

Primary school children can investigate similar relationships between catchment areas for local services. Where, for example, do people come from to shop at the local shopping parade? Do people come from further afield to shop at the supermarket than they do to shop at the corner shop? Part of the answer depends on the numbers of each type of shop, part depends on transport opportunities.

NOTES AND REFERENCES

1. See the collection of papers, case studies and workshops from the Conference for Economic and Industrial Awareness in Primary Education held at Edge

Hill College in July 1988 and published as: Ross, A. (1990) *Economic and Industrial Awareness in the Primary School*. London: Polytechnic of North London and School Curriculum Industry Partnership.

2. Roberts, R.J. and Dolan, J. (1989) 'Children's perceptions of "work" – an exploratory study.' *Educational Review*, **41**, 1, 19-28.

3. Roberts and Dolan, op. cit.

4. Ross, A. (1990) 'Children's perceptions of industrial hierarchies.' In Ross, A. (ed.) *Economic and Industrial Awareness in the Primary School*. London: Polytechnic of North London and School Curriculum Industry Partnership.

5. Hutchings, M. 'Children's thinking about work.' In Ross, A. (1990) *Economic and Industrial Awareness in the Primary School*. London: Polytechnic of North London and School Curriculum Industry Partnership.

6. Roberts and Dolan, op. cit.

7. Holroyd, S. (1990) 'Children's development in socio-economic ideas: some psychological perspectives.' In Ross, A. *Economic and Industrial Awareness in the Primary School*. London: Polytechnic of North London and School Curriculum Industry Partnership.

8. This is a much quoted example in the National Curriculum promotional literature on enterprise. See, for example, Craft, A., Ross, A. and Hutchings, M. (1990) *Enterprise in the Curriculum*. London: Polytechnic of North London Press. There have been a number of studies on children's understanding of shops and shopping transactions. See especially: Strauss, A. (1952) 'The development and transformation of monetary meanings in the child.' *American Sociological Review*, **17**, 275-84; Furth, H. (1980) *The World of Grown-ups: Children's Conceptions of Society*. New York: Elsevier; Jahoda, G. (1979) 'The construction of economic reality by some Glaswegian children.' *European Journal of Social Psychology*, **19**, 115-27; Linton, T. 'A child's eye view of economics.' In Ross, A. *Economic and Industrial Awareness in the Primary School*. London: Polytechnic of North London and School Curriculum Industry Partnership; Schug, M. (1983) 'The development of economic thinking in children and adolescents.' *Social Education*, **47**, 2, 141-5. The points that follow are derived from those studies.

9. Sage, D. (1990) 'The mini-farm project; the experience of a Surrey First School.' Ross, A. *Economic and Industrial Awareness in the Primary School*. London: Polytechnic of North London and School Curriculum Industry Partnership.

10. Rogers, V.R. and Layton, D.E. (1966) 'An exploratory study of primary grade children's ability to conceptualize based upon content drawn from selected social studies topics.' *Journal of Educational Research*, **59**, 5, 195-7.

11. Renwick, M. and Pick, W. in *Going Places* 1, 1979, Nelson, p. 12 have a useful approach in the form of a diagram using the labels which follow in the text.

12. For example, by Bowles, S. and Gintis, H. (1976) *Schooling in Capitalist America: Educational Reform and the Contradictions of Economic Life*. London: Routledge & Kegan Paul.

13. Smith, D. (ed.) (1988) *Industry in the Primary School Curriculum*. London: Falmer Press.

14. A number of visits to industrial enterprises are fully described in Jamieson,

I. (ed.) (1984) *We Make Kettles: Studying Industry in the Primary School.* York: Longman; Smith (1988), op. cit.; Ross (1990), op. cit.

15. Burleton, S. (1988) 'The textile industry.' In Smith, D. (ed.) (1988) *Industry in the Primary School Curriculum.* London: Falmer Press.

16. Finch, R.J. (nd) *Geography through the Shop Window.* London: Evans.

17. Hales, S. (1988) 'We make shoes.' In Smith, D. (ed.) (1988) *Industry in the Primary School Curriculum.* London: Falmer Press.

18. Kourilisky, M. (1977) 'The kinder-economy: a case study of kindergarten pupils' acquisition of economic concepts.' *Elementary School Journal, 77,* 3, University of Chicago.

19. For example in EATE (Economic Awareness and Teacher Education) (1990) *Enterprise, Economic and Industrial Understanding Kit for Tomorrow's Primary Teachers.* London: Polytechnic of North London Press.

20. Fitzpatrick, S. (1988) 'The "we make" projects.' In Smith, D. (ed.) (1988) *Industry in the Primary School Curriculum.* London: Falmer Press.

21. Ross, A. (1985) 'Modelling the world of work.' *Primary Teaching Studies, 1,* 1.

22. Burleton, op. cit.

23. Fitzpatrick, op. cit.

24. Wright, D.R. (1991) 'Geographical concepts in the "Thomas the Tank Engine" stories'. *Primary Geographer, 6,* 4-5.

25. Awdry, W. (1945) *The Three Railway Engines.* London: Heinemann.

26. From the Urban Studies suite of programs produced by Science Education Software Limited, Unit 12, Marian Industrial Estate, Dolgellau, Gwynedd LL40 1UU and available for BBC B, B + , Master, Compact and Nimbus computers.

27. From comments recorded by top infant children in: Roe, A. (1990) 'Investigating housing and economic awareness at Key Stage 1.' *Economic Awareness, 3,* 1, 3-6.

28. See *Geography through Topics in Primary and Middle Schools.* Sheffield: National Council for Educational Technology/The Geographical Association, p. 15.

29. See Jahoda, G. (1963) 'The development of children's ideas about country and nationality.' *British Journal of Educational Psychology, 33,* 47-60 and 143-53.

CHAPTER 6
Environmental Geography and Environmental Education

> Pupils should demonstrate their increasing knowledge and understanding of: (i) the use and misuse of natural resources; (ii) the quality and vulnerability of different environments; (iii) the possibilities for protecting and managing environments. (Attainment Target 5, Department of Education and Science, *Geography in the National Curriculum (England)* HMSO, March 1991, p. 25)

It may be helpful at the outset to distinguish between environmental *geography* (i.e. Attainment Target 5 of the National Curriculum for geography) and environmental *education* (defined by the National Curriculum Council as a cross-curricular theme).

Environmental education views the planet as a life-support system and studies the threats that are posed to it. The attention of the world was drawn to environmental issues after publication of the declaration by the United Nations Intergovernmental Conference on Environmental Education in Tbilisi, USSR, in 1977 and the publication by the International Union for the Conservation of Nature (IUCN) of the *World Conservation Strategy* (1980). Both these documents emphasized the interdependence of human and physical systems, e.g.:

> By adopting a holistic approach rooted in a broad interdisciplinary base, it [i.e. environmental education] recreates an overall perspective which acknowledges the fact that natural environment and man-made environment are profoundly interdependent. It helps reveal the enduring continuity which links the acts of today to the consequences of tomorrow. It demonstrates the interdependencies among national communities and the need for solidarity among all mankind. (Tbilisi declaration, 1977)

Public awareness of environmental education received a further boost from the 'Earth Summit' held in Rio de Janeiro in 1992. Current approaches in environmental education in school reflect the recognition that *local* environments are part of the global ecosystem. The slogan 'Think globally, act locally' underpins a number of projects.

A traditional way of looking at environmental education is to think of it as comprising three interrelated components:

- education *about* the environment (that is, the development of a knowledge base built up through study of topics such as climate, soils, rocks, water, buildings, waste, resources);

- education *for* the environment (that is, helping children to clarify their values and attitudes towards caring for the environment as well as encouraging them to take action in solving environmental problems);
- education *through* the environment (that is, using the environment as a resource through which, by enquiry and investigation, awareness and curiosity can be stimulated).

In environmental geography, pupils are to be taught where common materials are obtained – for example, wool from sheep, rock from quarries, fish from the sea – and how they are extracted. This is education *about* the environment. They are also to be taught to discuss and explain their likes and dislikes about features of the environment; for example, what is good about the area where they live and what spoils it. They are also to be able to identify activities which have changed the environment and to consider ways in which they themselves can improve their own environment. This is education *for* the environment. Children are also expected to do geography *through* the environment – in the context of fieldwork.

The Council for Environmental Education (see Appendix 2) is a co-ordinating body for more than 50 environmental and educational organizations. It issues a regular news-sheet and publishes the *Review of Environmental Education Developments*. Friends of the Earth and the World Wide Fund for Nature (WWF) also provide support for schools on global environmental education.

There is a great deal of rhetoric about environmental education; and there are very many pressure groups concerned with environmental matters and much enthusiastic and committed activity reflecting genuine concern. But evidence about the nature of children's thinking and feeling about environmental issues is very thin indeed. It is, however, possible to make a start by examining what experiences children have of their immediate surroundings and use this as a basis for asking questions about the nature of their understanding of environmental matters. We can also distinguish between these local, direct experiences and the knowledge and attitudes children may have of wider – global – environmental concerns.

What environmental experiences do children have?

Remarkably little is known about children's use of, and relationship to, their immediate environment. One writer has claimed that we know more about the ecology of baboons![1]

Children construct their knowledge of environments from their experience. They usually know a great deal about their immediate locality through play and, especially in summer, many 10-year-old children spend as much as 10 hours per day outdoors. Childhood is our greatest period of geographical exploration. Essentially outdoor play is serendipitous (Jones, A. (1989) 'The feeling tone of childhood,' in Slater, F. *Language and Learning in the Teaching of Geography*, London, Routledge). It depends on who else is 'playing out'. Outdoor play is interrupted by other activities such as music lessons, the call to tea and bedtime. This creates a patchwork of experiences. Everyday life is also somewhat humdrum. Many places are 'boring' or at least unremarkable. This may be seen as reassuring rather than problematic.

The environmental experiences of children are different from those of adults, if only because of their difference in size. Children's eye level is closer to the ground. This is why patterns of paving stones, the texture of cobbles and tarmac, etc. assume greater significance for them. Children don't often seem to 'look up'. In a study which compared the images of the town of Harwich held by adults and children it was found that adults' freehand maps of the town showed in every case the most prominent feature of the townscape: the lighthouse. But none of the children's maps showed it. Yet many showed the public lavatory at its base.[2] Not only do children not look up, they also tend to have a rather functional view of their surroundings.

The life children lead outdoors is very different from their indoor life. Indoors is a place to be quiet, alone, private. It's supportive and secure. It's also dominated by adults. Outdoors is a complementary lifestyle. It's a public place to be explored, to meet friends, to take the opportunities presented by chance meetings and events. The role of play and place in child development has been explored by Robin Moore in one of the most stimulating books ever written on child development.[3] Moore asked children, 'Can you please make me a map or a drawing of all your favourite places – where you go after school or at weekends, including the summer – around your home, in the neighbourhood where you live.' This was followed up by interviews with children and their parents and later by accompanying children on journeys around their 'turf'.

Children's contact with their immediate environment to a large extent varies with the opinions and personalities of their parents. Access to the locality is limited by factors such as the real or perceived crime rate and social and cultural fears. This creates differences between children in the degree of freedom and independence they enjoy. Most children can generally explore freely a very limited area around their own home. But if they ask permission first, or if they are chaperoned by older children, they can usually explore a wider area. Perhaps a child of 5 can play anywhere in the garden but can go next door with permission. Or a child of 8 may be able to play in the close but must not cross the main road or go beyond the corner shop. Few children after the age of 8 restrict their play to the garden.

As children become older, they venture further from their homes. The expanding area which they experience is often termed their 'home range'. This territory expands throughout childhood.[4] Entry to primary school often marks a significant shift in children's awareness of their local area – not only because of the daily travel involved but also the increased friendship opportunities which result in visits to the homes of newfound friends. Bicycle ownership is another significant step towards increasing familiarity with the locality. Similarly, car-owning families are likely to provide children with a wider experience of their home area than those without.

There appear to be substantial variations in the local environmental experiences of boys and girls. The parentally defined limits for girls appear to be narrower than for boys – parents are more protective of girls – and it also appears that parents may be much more lenient towards sons when the rules are broken than they are towards daughters. An exception here is for girls of top primary school age, who are sent on shopping errands more often than boys.

Awareness of the local area is therefore incremental with a gradually increasing definition and negotiation of home range by parents and children. It may be initially defined by danger spots such as busy streets and other hazards. It alters in summer and winter as the length of daylight varies. Each summer may bring a leap in the area available for children to explore. By the end of the primary phase, a child's 'territory' may have a radius of about half a kilometre. Children exchange information about the local area and compare their permitted home ranges. Small friendship groups form in culs-de-sac and in the play spaces surrounding blocks of flats. Great store is set by knowing new routes and short cuts.

Children's knowledge of their locality can be used as a starting point in teaching: 'Please draw me a map of the area where you live'.[5] How are we to interpret such maps? It is worth considering what the maps themselves are likely to consist of. The marks on the page will represent a number of discrete landscape elements, of which the following will probably be significant: paths, edges, districts, nodes and landmarks.[6]

The main way children come to know a place is by making journeys through it. They are therefore very conscious of roads, streets, alleys and other routes. The other elements of the locality are arranged around this linear experience, and so routes or *paths* are usually very significant elements in children's maps. *Edges* define separate parts of the locality. They act as boundaries between places that are known and places that are not. They might be, for example, rivers, railway lines or main roads that children cannot or are not allowed to cross. Although these features are in themselves potential paths, they function in this case as barriers. Edges confine children. *Districts* are medium- to large-sized parts of the city, such as the central business district or an industrial estate. The first local districts that children differentiate between are often housing estates. These are frequently differentiated on quite subtle physical and/or social criteria. They are often named after the builder (e.g. 'the Wimpey estate') or some common denominator in the street names (e.g. 'the Cambridges', to refer to a district which contains Cambridge Road, Cambridge Terrace, Cambridge Drive, etc.). *Nodes* are small areas that can be 'entered', such as the city square, the market place or the railway station courtyard. These places are often meeting places; they are where you're going to, the end of the 'path'. *Landmarks*, in contrast, aren't entered but they serve as reference points on the journeys made through the locality. They might be monuments or distinctive buildings or particular shops.

I am not at all suggesting here that children should be introduced to this terminology for various landscape elements but that teachers use them as an agenda for discussing maps and knowledge of the immediate locality. Discussion and questions relating to a particular map might therefore include the following:

'I see you've marked and named Westgate, Kirkgate and Church Lane. What other roads do you know?' (draws attention to *paths*).

'What's on the other side of the river?' (explores an *edge* shown on the map).

'Do you know the name people often give to *this* area?' (draws attention to *district*).

'Here's the market square. Where else do people meet each other in town?' (encourages thinking about *nodes*).

'Can you add the church to your map?' (draws attention to another *landmark* to be added).

How does the environment affect children?

There is some evidence that the physical features of the home environment can affect children's development.[7] For example it seems likely that too much noise in or immediately outside the home can disadvantage children. Their early cognitive development is impaired and they appear subsequently to underachieve at school.[8] The way in which the home itself is organized may also influence development. Children from homes where furniture and toys are tidily organized and where family activities such as meals take place according to a predictable schedule apparently score more highly on IQ tests than children from untidy, haphazard homes. Perhaps when the physical and social environment is predictable children are able to concentrate more on learning about other phenomena. Children also appear to be vulnerable to the effects of household crowding. Opportunities for privacy seem to be an important part of development in fostering feelings of individuality and self sufficiency.[9]

There has been very little research on children's response to the *natural* environment. Some psychologists[10] believe that human beings *need* contact with the natural environment. Nature does, after all, seem to be important to people.[11] We plant flowers, care for house plants, donate money for the conservation of natural areas we have never seen, and so on. People also seem to have distinct and shared preferences for some sorts of landscape over others. Water, for example, is a prized landscape element. A view of the sea, the lake, the river valley is worth having, and worth paying extra for. People also seem to prefer some forms of view over others. Jay Appleton[12] has explored this under the heading 'Prospect and refuge theory'. The basis of this is that environmental preferences are related to fundamental survival instincts. Consider, for example, an analogy with the animal world. Where are good places for animals to rest? Animals generally choose places where there is shelter (the refuge) and also a clear view of surrounding area (the prospect) in order to be able to spot potential predators. Such places pose no danger from behind and offer a clear view in front. Human preferences for landscapes can be interpreted according to these principles. Views, or photographs of views, exhibiting these elements of prospect and refuge seem to be preferred by people – a view out but framed by trees, a doorway or cave entrance.

It is a well-established theme in Western thought that 'God made the country and man made the town', that life is healthier and more virtuous in the country than in the city. There is an associated belief in the existence of a sympathetic bond between children and nature that has its roots in the European romantic tradition. A common enterprise therefore is to take 'underprivileged' children who live in the city centre to the countryside as though a week or two in the country will somehow restore health and spirit. Of course it may do, but 'nature' itself is not necessarily 'good for you'. Margaret Mead challenged the belief that city children's imaginative faculties suffered because they did not live in the midst of nature by comparing Western children with those growing up in New Guinea. There are also many accounts of tough inner-city children frightened by the unfamiliar sounds and feelings of the natural environment.[13]

Nevertheless, the most valued places for suburban children do seem to be 'wasteland' areas which have been left accidentally to nature. It has therefore often been suggested that landscape planners should leave small 'unplanned' spaces next to housing areas. Ideally, there would be networks of such spaces.

How do children find their way?

Finding your way is different from using a map. When you attempt to find your way you build up information about the route in a sequential fashion and an important part is played by *landmarks* in structuring this information. Landmarks were shown by Spencer, Blades and Morsley[14] to be important in enabling 3-year-olds to retrace their steps a few days after making a trip with an adult through a previously unknown city area. Children who had landmarks casually pointed out to them (for their own sake rather than for their wayfinding potential) were all able to retrace their steps successfully. Children make use of a whole range of potential landmarks when remembering routes – many of them ephemeral and fleeting, such as writing on the pavement, parked cars and pieces of litter. They are less skilled than adults at remembering features of the landscape – not least because they are less skilled at separating the permanent features of the environment from the impermanent. Nevertheless, they *are* skilled at finding their way in their own neighbourhoods and have a large store of local environmental knowledge. There seems to be no substitute in the process of learning new areas to that of actually getting out there and finding your way. Attempts to 'teach' children an area in advance by showing slides or videotape do not appear to improve their wayfinding ability significantly.[15] This is especially true of being able to find your way back again. Reversing the sequence of landmarks in the mind seems to be especially difficult to do. You often just have to be out there and actually reorientate your body to face in the right direction to trigger the cues in order to learn a route in reverse effectively.

It is probably also true that some types of environment are easier to find one's way around than others. There are implications here for town and country planning.

Recently the suggestion has been made that wayfinding and orientation ability are innate skills rather than skills acquired by formal education. Certainly the navigational abilities and 'homing instincts' of many animals have been well documented. Do humans have an innate sense of direction and is this sense observable at the scale of finding one's way around a town? In several experiments, when people were blindfolded and driven around a circuitous route in a bus, participants did demonstrate an innate ability to sense the direction of the point of origin of the journey. Females have generally been shown to have a better ability to sense direction than males, but adults in general have been shown to have no particular advantage over children.[16]

Wayfinding is an important skill and work could usefully be done on developing ways of teaching children how to give clear directions and how they should follow such a set of directions. Verbal directions seem to be more effectively remembered and used than map information.[17] It is probably best to ask children to describe route information in a number of ways. Some children will learn better by remembering sequences such as 'second left, then first right'; others may learn better by remembering the names of roads that must be taken ('Bellevue Road, then Wood Hill, then Low Lane'). Each strategy may produce its own types of errors and successes in real wayfinding.[18]

Finding your way is an important part of adapting to the school environment, and the transition from home to school can be greatly eased by including a 'wayfinding' element in the induction programme when children transfer from nursery to first school, infants to juniors, and so on.[19] Strategies might include showing pictures of 'landmarks' around the school, as well as providing guided tours, in which these significant landmarks are pointed out.

Values in environmental geography

It was made clear at the beginning of this chapter that environmental geography and environmental education are about values and attitudes. Values enter environments in at least two main ways. Environments are determined to a large extent by decisions made by people and those decisions are taken on the basis of the values of the people who take them. Environments may be said therefore to be the physical expression of human values. Secondly, environments have value for people; that is, they are valued by them. They may therefore be conserved, developed or neglected on the basis of their perceived value.[20]

A subject of frequent discussion in education is whether teachers should only teach *about* values or should actually teach the values themselves. The obvious concern here is about indoctrination – the belief that everyone should be free to make up his or her mind. But are there values in relation to people and the environment that are so basic (substantive) that teachers should seize the responsibility of teaching those values? To my mind the situation is clear. There are at least two inescapable values that teachers must actually teach towards: firstly that the study of people's interrelationship with the environment is necessary and worthwhile; and secondly that experience of environments enriches human existence and therefore we must teach towards interest in and concern for the quality of environments.

So how can teachers develop strategies which will enable children to clarify the value positions involved in a particular environmental issue? The following approach is based on *values analysis*.[21]

An environmental issue is selected for study. For example: should the main runway at the local airport be extended?[22] The teacher provides source material so that the children are thoroughly familiar with the issue itself and the background to it. In this case resources might consist of maps, photographs, newspaper articles and letters, pamphlets from pressure groups, talks from interested parties, a visit to the airport, etc. Once there is a basis of factual information, the values implicit in the issue can be addressed. Children firstly list positive and negative statements about the issue. For example:

Positive: 'Why is the runway extension a good thing?'

Because building it will make more jobs.
Because bigger and faster aeroplanes can use the airport so journeys will be quicker.
Because a longer runway will be safer.

Negative: 'Why is the runway extension a bad thing?'

Because it will use up farm land.
Because more aeroplanes will be noisier for people who live nearby.
Because more passengers will mean more traffic locally.

These statements about positive and negative aspects of the development are then grouped and ranked in order of importance during class discussion. It is helpful during this stage to write each of the statements on cards so that they can be easily moved around and put into order.

Each of the negative statements is then analysed. For example, in the case of the issue of noise solutions are found to this problem, such as:

Don't allow aeroplanes to use the airport at night.
Give people who live nearby compensation so that they can buy double glazing.

Each of these statements can in turn be examined for their positive and negative aspects. Double glazing, for example, brings further benefits to householders because it increases the value of their property and keeps homes warmer as well as quieter. More work for double glazing companies also means more jobs. On the other hand, there is still the problem of noise out of doors and it may be difficult to decide who lives 'nearby' enough to qualify for the compensation.

All these pros and cons could be plotted onto a large wall display, colour coded for the 'good news' and the 'bad news' about the issue as a starting point for the children's own decision about what they think should happen. Once they have chosen, they can further clarify their own values by having to defend them. This could be in the form of a brief announcement to the rest of the group or class. 'I think the runway should be extended because . . .' A further step would be to consider what they could do to progress the issue.[23] What could they do, for example, to prevent the extension happening? (Write to the local newspaper, their MP or join a group of people who think the same way.) This focus on action is an obvious link to education for citizenship through which children are introduced to their rights as citizens: the civil rights necessary for individual freedom, the right to participate in the exercise of political power and a range of social rights ranging from welfare to sharing in the cultural heritage of society.[24]

Children's environmental preferences

Children like areas with natural materials, especially those which offer opportunities for collecting and observing (for example, leaves, seeds, insects, acorns, conkers, sticky buds, sycamore helicopters, stones, etc.) and those areas which permit a certain amount of destruction – such as throwing sticks or breaking branches. They like places that allow for activity such as climbing and jumping. They like rivers, lakes and woods (although young children rarely penetrate beyond a few trees deep). Children also enjoy getting into or making small places, such as pretend shelters and houses.

But the built environment offers possibilities too. Shops are attractive, especially those containing items of interest for children such as sweets and ice-creams, videos, magazines and comics. Children appear to be greatly attracted to the *street* as a place to meet and play. It is a constantly changing public space which allows groups of children to interact. There's an element of chance in these encounters – you never know who will be 'playing out' at any one time and the physical characteristics of the street usually allow play with wheeled toys and vehicles. (There are restricted opportunities for roller boots and bikes in gardens.) Colin Ward has explored the feelings of growing up in the city through a very rich range of references and reminiscences which evokes the great variety of ways in which city children have used the street and how they continue to do so today.[25]

Children are also aware of dangerous and scary places. These are 'landscapes of fear'[26] – places where there are bullies, gangs and children who get into trouble. They include abandoned buildings and places in the dark, places warned against (busy roads, the canal . . .), where there are strangers, places where there are thought to be bad influences.

To what extent is there a 'shared view' of the potential of places for childhood play? Children from a large post-war council housing estate in Leeds[27] were asked about their locality. Two groups of four 9-year-old boys from the same area but who attended different schools and did not know each other were asked what they considered to be the most important features of their environment. They were invited to select places to be photographed in their neighbourhood. Each group was shown its own set of photographs and were asked later why they had chosen that particular feature and what was the most important aspect of it. In several cases the two groups chose the same or nearly the same sites and for those sites that were not the same there was a remarkable degree of agreement as to the play potential of the location. 'Dares' and testing yourself to the limit were important features of play. A row of lock-up garages provided play potential:

Pupil: 'Best place for duffs and running and jumping off 'top, garages.'
Teacher: 'Can you explain what a "duff" is?'
Pupil: 'A duff is when 'first person does a duff or summat like that – gerring on 'top of garages and jumping off – and uvver ones – uvver people have got to copy off what he does – and if they can't do it, they're out o' game'.

Children's outdoor play varies with the surroundings and what is provided for them. The equipment in a playground seems to determine what age groups use it and what they do when they're there. Traditional play areas with swings, slides and roundabouts as well as contemporary play areas with mounds and tunnels seem to be preferred by very young children, who play 'in parallel' rather than interactively. 'Adventure' playgrounds, on the other hand, are frequented much more by older children who play together, form gangs and develop extensive and elaborate imaginative play.[28]

However, children appear to spend relatively little time unaccompanied in these 'safe' playground areas, preferring instead the reality of the streets or waste ground.[29] Some children seem to prefer anywhere to play *but* the conventional playground with roundabout and swings:

A child's play is most satisfactory when it allows him the opportunity to manipulate the environment according to his needs: to image, create and hide, a well differentiated world and one that is plastic to his hands and mind.[30]

This is often a source of conflict with adults, who frequently prefer children not to 'hang around' stairwells, car parks, phone boxes, railings or street lights. But it is from those types of location that children can more readily observe what is going on around them and are enabled to interact with a wider range of age groups.

Adaptations can therefore be built into the 'draw a map of where you live' exercise, discussed above; that is, for the children to show places that have personal significance. Maps like this are called 'turf' maps.[31] Children produce maps which show their favourite places, places that are dangerous or out of bounds and changes or improvements they would like to see. Each child's map can be displayed without the author's name and other children can guess whose map is whose.

Safety out of doors

Road safety statistics point to an apparent paradox: the roads are becoming safer, yet they're also becoming more dangerous.[32] Judged by road traffic statistics, Britain has become safer. Half as many children are now killed in road accidents as were killed in 1922, despite the fact that there are now twenty-five times more cars on the road. (Nevertheless, some 400 children are killed on the roads each year. There are also some 3000 pedestrian casualties under the age of 5 and nearly 17 000 pedestrian casualties between the ages of 5 and 14 each year.) But the roads have also become more dangerous. In 1922 the streets were considered safe for children; almost all children would walk to school and to see a motor-car was something to be talked about. The fall in accident statistics simply means that children are now forbidden to go near main roads. The last 20 years has shown a drastic reduction in children's independence. In a 1969 survey, 90% of 7-year-olds were judged capable of crossing the roads outside their homes by themselves.[33] By 1989 the Secretary of State for Transport declared himself appalled that one in three children claimed to be crossing roads on their own at this age.[34] In 1971, 80% of 7- and 8-year-olds were allowed to go to school on their own. By 1990, this figure had dropped to 9%. In part this retreat from street-based activity has been due not only to parental opposition from children playing in the street with all its attractions as described above, but also to the rise in home-based leisure opportunities such as televisions, videos, computers, etc., as well as more comfortable homes in which to enjoy these diversions.

There have been various attempts to teach children safety procedures for dealing with road traffic. Kerb Drill was introduced in 1942. It was clear and simple. Yet its simplicity and the fact that it was learned by rote led to little functional application by children in the real situations in which it was designed to help them. Many children, for example, have real difficulties in discriminating between right and left. In 1971 it was replaced by the Green Cross Code and local authorities were required to fulfil a road safety function.

Notwithstanding the endeavours to teach children about road safety, the prevailing view of road traffic accidents involving children remains that the accidents are caused by the children themselves being 'careless'. The assumption has been that children's behaviour can be shaped to match that of adults and that it is the fault of the children if they do not match those expectations. A major Swedish research study into road safety[35] adopted a different approach: that children can only operate at a level of competence commensurate with their age and degree of development and that as adults we have failed to appreciate the situations children find themselves in and failed to adapt our behaviour to reasonable expectations of theirs. Children *need* to be active and if there is nowhere else to play then they play on the street – and as we have seen, the street is in any case preferable as a play environment to some of the places provided by adults for them.

Children are also *physically* different. Their eye level is lower than adults': they cannot look over the tops of parked cars but have to go to the edge to see round them. Neither do they notice signs that are placed at 'adult' height. Children also find it difficult to do several things at once – such as crossing the road whilst keeping an eye out for traffic. They may look first, then walk, but during the walking do not continue to look. In any case young children's visual systems are not as well developed as adults'. It takes them longer to focus and their peripheral vision is not as efficient. Traffic flow changes more rapidly than children can think. The 'shape of movement' is difficult to recognize. When a person or animal runs, their shape is changed – but cars stay the same shape. Neither can children adequately estimate distances or realize just how fast a moving car can reach them. Many children appear to believe that the best way to avoid an accident is to *run* across the road on the principle that if you are on the road for less time then there is less likelihood that you will be run over. Judging walking speed is difficult, even for adults.

The responsibility for children's safety therefore has to be fully shouldered by planners and drivers as well as parents and teachers. Nevertheless, some excellent material has been produced for road safety education for children from the Royal Society for the Prevention of Accidents (RoSPA). There is also good material produced for pre-school playgroups.[36] Key ideas for under-5s are:

Always go out with a grown up; never play on the road.
Before you cross the road: Stop, Look, Listen.
Roads are for traffic; pavements are for people.

The Safe Routes to School planning project is worth describing because it may prompt some local investigations that could be useful in keeping children safe on the roads.[37] The project is based on the principle that you need to find out which routes children take to school and make *them* safe. Children's journeys are plotted on a map and then sites where accidents or near-accidents have occurred, as well as places that the children themselves identify as potentially dangerous, are added. A picture should then begin to emerge as to where there are dangerous roads, corners or junctions that need to be made safer. It is often the case that areas around schools are used as short cuts or 'rat runs' by motorists. Strategies to combat this might include slowing traffic speed (for example by speed humps), or prohibiting through traffic. The data for traffic modifications such as these could easily and

usefully be collected by schools themselves and presented to the local responsible authority.

As well as traffic education, note also the recent moves towards 'street-
proofing' children – how to say 'no' to strangers. This should also be seen
as an important part of environmental education. 'Good sense defence' has
been widely promulgated by Kidscape – a campaign which provides practical ways for all children, with the help of their parents, teachers and others,
to keep safe from dangers, particularly from sexual assault. The 'environmental' implications of this approach can be highlighted by the following
selective extracts from the advice given by the campaign.[38]

> Don't answer the door if you're at home on your own.
> If you get lost, go to a shop or place with lots of people, and ask for help or find
> a policeman or policewoman to ask.
> When you're out on your own, keep far enough away from other people you don't
> know so that you can't be grabbed and so can run away.
> Never play in deserted or dark places.

Helping children to experience the environment

Children are to 'express their personal likes and dislikes about features of the
local area' (AT 1 1b). What activities can teachers provide in order to give
them a basis upon which to make a judgement? Experience of the environment depends on looking for and processing information about it. The aim
is to establish critical awareness. This is the basis of being able to participate
in local decisions about planning and development. Children therefore need
to be helped to experience their own environment. But they are not all
budding Betjemans and potential Pevsners. A real danger is that only the
carefully conserved historic attractions will be seen as having value. In fact,
'most of us spend our lives in the backwaters of the environment'[39] and so
we need to sensitize children to the detail of ordinariness which makes their
surroundings special.

A starting point is to focus on the ways in which environmental information is received: via the senses.[40] It is instructive to start a consideration of
the use of the senses in environmental education with a description of the
experimental work of Steve van Matre at the Towering Pines nature camp,
Eagle River, Wisconsin.[41] This work was initially described as a 'new kind
of nature study'. It is based on the assumption that people have distanced
themselves from nature – that people view rather than participate in the
natural world and that children have therefore to be put back into touch with
the natural world. The purpose of the one-week programme as run at the
Towering Pines nature camp in Wisconsin is to create a greater degree of
involvement with nature in the belief that once you have felt unity with the

environment you are more reluctant to destroy it – because to destroy nature would be to destroy yourself. This process, called acclimatization, is a set of sensory experiences. Children attending the week's camp spend a day in each of a series of different environments – forest, lakeshore, wetland, etc. – and are engaged in activities explicitly designed to heighten their sensory awareness. They go on blindfold trails, crawl through marsh, lie like logs in the forest and scrabble in the earth.

Many teachers find it helpful to structure environmental activities around the senses. For example:

> Children *listen* to the environment. 'Sit in a circle and close your eyes. What sounds did you hear? Where do the sounds come from? Which sounds are natural (wind in the trees) and which are not (cars, aeroplanes)? Which was the loudest sound?' Repeat the activity at different times of the day. 'Would the sounds be the same in summer or winter? What would you prefer to hear less/more of? Listen to one of the sounds now. Does it come and go or is it there all the time (i.e. intermittent or continuous)? Is there an echo? Can you tell the difference between similar sounds, e.g. a motor mower and a motor-cycle; a lorry and a bus?'

> Children *touch* the environment. 'Feel the texture of the brick, stone, asphalt. Which is smooth? Which feels gritty? Feel the movement of the air – on your face, on your clothes. Run your hand along the railings. Feel which surface warms up more quickly in the sunshine. Can you balance by walking on the cracks in the pavement?'

> Children *smell* the environment. 'Does the place have a characteristic smell? What does it smell like outside the baker's? The fish and chip shop? The factory? Can you smell the flowers, the new-mown hay?'

Sensory impressions such as these can be recorded. Words and phrases only may be better at first. These may if desired be grouped onto postcards so that the impressions of the whole group or class can be sorted and classified as the basis for discussion.

The 'sensory walk' is a popular strategy. It consists of a slow walk in which children concentrate on one sense at a time. Some have suggested the use of (playing) cards, marked with 'Look down', 'Look up', 'Look behind you', 'Listen', etc. The cards are shuffled and then taken from the pack at strategic stops on the walk. Activities such as these may be worth while but in view of the discussion above it is of course essential to maintain the greatest degree of supervision when they are undertaken. Each teacher or adult can really supervise only a few children at a time.

Above all, environmental experience is visual. Children's attention can be focused on light (natural and artificial), colours, shapes (straight edges, rounded edges, regular and irregular), repeating-shape patterns, and the breaks in them (like the gaps in railings), the volume of the spaces observed (large, small, narrow, wide). Questions on the 'geometry' of the environment

('How many triangles can you see?') help to give some structure to observation in order to pick out the constituent parts of a mass or detail. Visual discrimination may be developed by questions such as 'Which is the odd front door, or chimney, or roof, out of the others?' Colours in the environment form a good focus. 'What colours can you see around you? Try to describe the colours. Who likes which colour? What is your favourite colour? Where can you find that colour in the environment? (Look for liked colours in the built environment especially.) What colour is the sky, sea, grass? Are these things always those colours? When and why do they change? When is the sky red, when is the sea silver?'

Town trails

The 'Town trail' movement developed in the 1970s. It was based on the principle that one of the best ways to get to 'know' your town is to take a walk through it! A town trail is an open-ended exercise in informal environmental education which should lead the tracker to ask questions and evaluate the experiences gained on the trail. It is to do with qualitative appraisal, not a quantitative survey. A town trail doesn't take the child from point to point to identify key historic buildings but tries instead to point out unusual detail or contrasts or relationships between buildings, or in the glimpses between buildings, or in distant and near views. It is a kinaesthetic experience which attempts to develop a sense of place.

What would such a trail look like for primary children? The following structure could be adapted for different ages. A walk might last from half an hour to an hour. It might cover half to three-quarters of a mile. It would be safe from traffic and other potential dangers so that children could concentrate on the environment. It would be undertaken by small groups with effective supervision and enough access to the teacher or adult to discuss what was experienced. The trail would first have been carefully prepared by the teacher in order to provide varying 'texture' of experience. Children would stop at particular points which had been carefully thought out in advance. It might be best if, say, 20 features that would be noted on the trail were previously photographed so that they could have been discussed beforehand or afterwards. Each pupil probably has a map of the route. They are all clear about what the symbols used mean. The stopping points would be marked on the map. At each stopping point there would be tasks, questions, etc. Children would use a variety of recording methods (written, drawing, completing a part-drawing, checklist, tape recording, table completion, photograph, etc.). The stopping points would focus on a precise list of features that are selected in order to simplify the complexity of the urban environment. Children might be encouraged to look at different eye levels.

A selection of features to be highlighted might come from a list such as the following:

- a typical house or houses in the locality (include old and new);
- a shop;
- a public house;
- a church;
- a public building (e.g. library or clinic);
- items of street furniture;
- a traffic-orientated feature (car park, garage);
- a 'natural' area (park, garden, wilderness area);
- a hazard.

Attention to detail helps. Examine windows, doors, trees, seats, gates, railings, bins, chimneys. Look especially for pattern and shape in brickwork, wire netting, ironwork, and so on. How do the shapes fit together? But a broader view is also important. Children more easily see detail in landscape and often find the broader shape of the 'lie of the land' more difficult to perceive. The idea of silhouette can be helpful here. Note the pattern of buildings and roof tops against the sky. Supply them with boxes into which to draw their skylines, from four compass directions. (Use a compass to get the orientation correct.)

Activities in town trails are as open-ended as possible:

- list the different ways in which people are using this open space;
- list the eyesores here;
- draw one of the carvings on this building;
- how many different types of lettering are there in this notice?
- would you like to live in this house?
- is there any danger here?
- what evidence is there that this is the business centre of the town?
- how could the environment in this street be improved?
- choose six things that make the place better to look at; six things that make it worse to look at.

Children can also *score* each stopping point on a five-point scale for its attractiveness. Scores can be compared later.

The following words could apply to buildings, traffic, the street or the environment generally. Places can be scored on a five-point scale between the following extremes:

boring	interesting
old	new
ordered	chaotic

neglected	cared for
clean	dirty
ugly	beautiful
busy	quiet
slow	fast
colourful	drab
ornate	plain
safe	dangerous

There have been some reports of teachers constructing town trails especially for parents to use with (young) children.[42]

Environmental preferences can be discussed in class: 'Where do you like to be in the school? At playtime? Where don't you like to be? Where is your favourite place?' Again, the idea of sharing preferences with others is important. It is also possible to map these places. Use a large-scale plan of the school and its grounds. 'Place your (self-adhesive) dot on the place you like.' Talk about the pattern of dots from the whole class. Compare with similar data from another class. Do older children prefer different places? Is there a difference in preferences between boys and girls? Is that related to their activities?

Visit the places shown on the map of the school. Record impressions, draw pictures. Ask children what is their 'second best' place? Do the two favourite places have something in common? (The idea here is to try to get at the characteristics of preferred places – some generalization or criterion that links the places together.) Ask children what they could do to places they don't like in order to make them better.

Other open-ended investigations into the environment might include:[43]

- Make a list of all the things in the environment that are impossible to count. How would you design a way of estimating how many of them were in the locality?
- Find two things in the environment one of which is responsible for the other. How could you prove this?
- Find something in the environment that you think isn't really very desirable. Make a plan to make it more desirable.
- Make a collection of materials in the immediate environment and make a collage to represent the local environment.
- Create an advertisement for some aspect of the environment in the locality.
- Find evidence of good change and bad change in the locality. Collect information on what people locally think about these changes.
- Write down the names of three or four places that you like. For each one: make drawings of the place, labelling things that you think are

important. Write down any special things that you can't draw such as special sounds, feelings and so on. Why did you choose these places? Can you say what makes them special to *you*? What is your favourite time for visiting each place? Who do you think owns these places? Have they changed since you first visited them? Have they changed for the better? Can you find out what your special places used to be like? Do other people (parents, grandparents) have special places?

Understanding of the immediate locality can be enriched by awareness of environmental language.[44] The written word is an important part of our surroundings. It is subject to changing form and meaning and can be difficult to decode because of the need for rapid impact on the reader for information (such as road signs and instructions) as well as advertising. There are also many symbols in the environment, at least partly as a response to the need to cater for people who do not read (English) easily. Children may be familiar with many of these already, such as fire hydrant signs, the British Rail logo, Keep off the Grass and anti-litter symbols, etc. There is also much meaning to be found in the names of houses and streets and many of these make connections with distant places; for example, London Road, Blenheim Terrace, Trafalgar Street, etc. Note also 'foreign' shop types (such as coiffure, boutique, cafe, delicatessen) as well as shops and services that refer to specific places (such as foreign restaurants). The language of suburban structure can also be discussed. What *is* the difference between an avenue and a street, a close and a parade, a crescent and a mews?

Language in towns can be classified. There are instructions, persuasions, warnings, protests, etc. One category of language in the environment is rules, such as: No Smoking, Keep off the Grass, No Entry, One Way Street. There are also symbols for rules. But who makes the rules in the environment? Are they good rules? Are they written down somewhere? How do they get changed? Who enforces the rules? What happens if you don't obey them? Collect rules that apply to school. Collect rules that apply outside school about how the area is used. Can these rules be put into a rank order of importance?

Another dimension of first-hand place experience is the notion of boundaries. Geographers are of course interested in places but when does one place become another place? Some definitions are easy. You know when you're in one country and not another when you've crossed the border. Some borders are scarcely noticeable (like the border between the Netherlands and Belgium), others are very obvious (for example the former Berlin Wall). Internal administrative areas such as counties or urban districts also have boundaries which may be clearly marked on maps but are usually less visible on the ground. For older children boundaries form an excellent way of linking mapping with thinking about the nature of space and place. Consider the school. The most obvious boundary as you enter the school grounds will be a fence or wall. (What is this boundary for? Why do we need it? It keeps young children safe, keeps the footballs in, etc.) There may be boundaries marked on the playground, for example, games pitches. Why do we need these? The outer wall of the school building is another boundary. You need that for shelter. But is there an unnoticed boundary at the doorway? A small stair or step might be unnoticed by most children but could form a significant boundary for people in wheelchairs. Are there other boundaries within the building that define where people can and can't go? Are there places where only the teachers are allowed to go or places where only the dinner staff or caretaker can go? Why do we need places that are 'out of bounds'? Discussion of the nature of boundaries, mapping them and classifying them for the map key is a powerful way of thinking about the ways in which space is used by people.

Exploring how the school and local area might be perceived by others is a related theme. Assess the school and its immediate surroundings from the point of view of visually impaired or hearing-impaired visitors. Are there clear signs that show visitors which way to go? Interview visitors with a view to making the school more 'visitor friendly'. How could the school cater for visitors who did not read English well? Do elderly people or visitors with very young children have particular needs when visiting the school?

Where do we put things? The notion of mapping the classroom as a way of making better arrangements for the location of items within it was mentioned in Chapter 2. This idea can be broadened to include the whole school and then to the immediate neighbourhood. Plot, for example, the location of street furniture (such as litter bins, telephone boxes, bus stops, street lights, post-boxes, public lavatories). Describe where these things are. Are they in the best place? If the council wanted to put another of these in the locality, where would be the best place for it?

Sensitivity to and awareness of the locality are closely related to art education.[45] This and environmental education share some common goals: for example, they both wish to develop children's perception and give pupils a 'feel' for their surroundings as well as to enhance their capacity for discrimination between environments and their competence in the visual appraisal of environments. There is often so much to see in the locality that children don't know where to start in their recording of it. One possible way to start is to use pre-prepared sheets with the outline of a place already marked by the teacher, to which the children add detail or colour. This can be of a building or the background shapes of landscape.

There are a number of significant 'out-of-school' projects aimed at developing children's experience of their environment. A helpful guide has been produced by the Earthkids project,[46] which aims to develop the natural environmental awareness of young children from a wide cross-section of the community, especially in urban areas, of pre-school age to age 11, by working through playschemes, playgroups and play opportunities.

Improving the environment

Litter is an issue that is readily understood by children. It is a bigger problem now than previously because there is more packaging, much of it doesn't rot and money made available for street cleaning has not generally kept pace with the increase of litter. The number of fast-food outlets is also rising and it appears to be more acceptable for people to eat food in the street. Litter is also dangerous: broken glass causes fires, and discarded polythene bags are a potential source of damage to animals.

Litter is a very 'geographical' phenomenon. It has a distribution and therefore you can ask questions of it such as 'Where does it come from? How does it get to be where it is now?' It can be plotted and mapped and graphed. The role of the wind can be investigated. Draw a large chalk circle in the playground. Leave some rubbish there such as crisp packets, soft-drink tins, sweet wrappers. After a while look again and see if the rubbish has moved. Plot where the rubbish has ended up. What sort of litter is susceptible to wind transport, what sort of litter stays put? Litter investigations could usefully lead to analysis of issues of responsibility. A litter map shows a large radius of packaging around a fast-food outlet. Is this the responsibility of the shopkeeper or the customer? Who makes the profit? Who enjoys the food? Should shopkeepers be encouraged to have responsibility for their shop frontage? Should they be punished if they don't?

Every week 250 000 tonnes of rubbish is put into household dustbins, 90 per cent of which is eventually conveyed to landfill sites. These are usually old quarries or low-lying valleys or marshy ground. Landfill sites need careful management to avoid pollution. Every day the waste is compacted and sealed with a thin layer of soil or rubble, and when the site is full it can be covered with a thicker layer and eventually used for farming or recreation or forestry. Such sites are rarely stable enough for rebuilding.

Landfill sites are an acceptable form of waste disposal but there are problems associated with them such as the toxic liquids and gases created by rotting rubbish. Some of the characteristics of landfill sites are explored through David Leney's book (1987; Puffin, 1988) *The Landfill.*

Danny loves to play at the landfill – a council rubbish tip. His father has told him (rightly) that it's a dangerous place to play. 'About the most dangerous place I can think of. You carry on like this and you're going to end up cutting your leg open, or splashing yourself with toxic waste or, quite simply, buried alive.' However, danger of a different sort emerges in the subsequent adventure. The tip and the tip workers form the framework to the story.

More whimsical is the ever-popular *Stig of the Dump* by Clive King (Penguin, 1963). Barney is a solitary 8-year old, given to wandering off by himself. One day he is lying on the edge of a disused chalk pit when he tumbles over, to land face to face with Stig – a cave man. Together they raid the rubbish dump at the bottom of the pit to improve Stig's cave dwelling. It's an endearing story, not least because of its pervasive tolerance. Both Stig and Barney accept each other's way of life unquestioningly and uncritically.

In *The Books for Keeps Green Guide to Children's Books* (1991) Pat Thomson in the introduction indicates that 'green' fiction for children is a new idea in a campaigning sense, yet there is a long tradition of children's books which celebrate the natural world. Most of the classic nostalgic books of childhood (*Swallows and Amazons*, *The Famous Five*, *The Wind in the Willows*, and so on), she says, are set in green and pleasant England. 'God made the country but man made the town' is evident in children's literature.

Wider environmental issues

The planet Earth is showing signs of gradually becoming warmer in a process known as the *greenhouse effect*. This is because of a substantial increase in the atmosphere of gases such as carbon dioxide, methane, nitrous oxide and chlorofluorocarbons (CFCs) – the so-called greenhouse gases. The Earth's atmosphere allows energy from the sun to reach the lower layers, warming the planet. This incoming energy is eventually reflected back into space in the form of long-wave radiation. In this way the temperature of the Earth is kept constant. The build-up of greenhouse gases, however, prevents the loss of the outgoing long-wave radiation and the planet is therefore gradually warming. Predictions of the rate of temperature increase vary but some scientists indicate that an eventual rise of 5°C is likely. For those living in the British Isles this seems at first sight to be quite attractive (a recent letter to *The Guardian* stated simply: 'I *like* the greenhouse effect'). However, the more sinister outcome is the melting of polar ice, causing a rise in sea levels of up to a metre around the globe. This would threaten many of the coastal low-lying areas of the world which are heavily populated. Much of Bangladesh and parts of major cities such as New York, London, Rotterdam and Venice would be inundated.

Other atmospheric changes are effected by gases such as CFCs and other highly stable synthetic chemicals produced by the petrochemical industry. The ozone layer in the upper atmosphere acts as a shield against ultraviolet radiations from the sun. CFCs and similar gases rise into the upper atmosphere, partially decompose and destroy the molecules of ozone protecting the Earth. Increased ultraviolet light reaches the ground, causing damage to crops, killing plankton and giving rise to an increase in carcinogenic sunburn to humans. Despite world- and government-scale initiatives to reduce the use of CFCs the existing concentration of such gases will probably continue to affect global warming and the ozone layer for some decades.

Emissions of sulphur dioxide and nitrogen oxides from coal-fired power-stations and other industrial processes create acid rain (dilute sulphuric acid or nitric acid). This has seriously damaged the forests of central and northern Europe and poisoned large fish in many of Europe's lakes. The absence of these fish causes knock-on effects throughout the food chain as the entire lake ecosystem, formerly in critical balance, is destabilized. Acid rain also damages the soil by killing bacteria and fungi that break down organic matter into nutrients for plants. The fitting of catalytic converters to cars and scrubbers on industrial chimneys is an attempt to reduce the emissions of acid-rain-forming pollutants.

Other global environmental problems include pollution of drinking water through radioactivity and synthetic chemicals, the loss of oil from tankers and radioactivity from nuclear power stations.

What do children know and feel about large-scale environmental issues such as these? Despite the increasing media attention to such issues we have very little hard evidence about children's knowledge or attitudes to such matters. Two sources of information are significant, however: a research study conducted for the World Wildlife Fund on children's attitudes to the environment in 1986 by MORI[47]; and a few years later a report commissioned by British Telecom from the Henley Centre for Forecasting on children's vision of the environment in the future.[48]

The environment seems to be an issue of concern among primary school children. One-third of children say they are very interested in the environment and half say they are slightly interested.[49] Most children also appear to believe that environmental problems are urgent: they believe that unless something is done, they themselves will have to suffer the consequences. After all, today's children will live to beyond the middle of the twenty-first century. Primary school children appear also to have, by and large, a good understanding of environmental issues, even complex ones such as the ozone hole, deforestation and CFCs, even though they may not be able to understand the interrelationships or implications. The principal source of most children's information about these macro-issues is school lessons and projects. Television is the second most important source. It is also significant that many children's pop idols and soap actor heroes have identified them-selves with environmental issues. Nevertheless, it is the local environment which appears to them to be the arena in which they themselves can effect change, particularly through recycling schemes, tree planting and litter collections. The local environment therefore seems to be an important star-ting point for environmental awareness.

The Henley Centre study identified 'a profound change in the environ-mental debate'.[50] Whereas previously 'being green' and maintaining Western levels of consumption were seen as being contradictory, there appears today to be little inconsistency between being a consumer and being concerned about the environment. Even when discussing steps that govern-ment should take in protecting the environment children talked only about banning sales of some goods when alternatives were already available. Children thought that people should buy lead-free petrol instead of leaded but were resistant to the idea that private cars should be used less. Whilst expressing environmental concern, they clearly indicated great reluctance to change their lifestyles. They also expect industry to be proactive in producing environmentally friendly products to replace existing products and, although they don't mind paying more, do not expect to be inconvenienced as a result.

Consumer issues such as these are explored in a very lively way for children in *Buy Now, Pay Later: Be a Careful Shopper* by Thompson Yardley (Cassell, 1990). The text has simple explanations, energetic cartoons and tips for what children can do.

The MORI survey asked 524 children between the ages of 6 and 15 about environmental issues. The term 'environment' was most highly associated in children's minds with people and animals (rather than, for example, physical characteristics). Children appeared to obtain most of their environmental information from teachers (39% of the primary-age children quoted this as the main source). Television was a further important source of information. Geography was seen as the most important subject through which environ-mental information was delivered. Two-thirds of the children interviewed claimed to have heard of the survey's sponsor: the World Wide Fund for Nature.

Natural resources

Natural resources are those products or properties of the physical environ-ment which human beings are technically capable of utilizing and which provide desired goods and services.[51] Resources are therefore defined by what people want or need and their ability to access them. They are deter-mined by culture and therefore the definition of whether a substance is a resource or not will change in time and space.

For level 5, children have to be able to distinguish between renewable and non-renewable resources. This is a conventional division but one that is not quite accurate. *All* resources are renewable – even coal and oil and metals, but these over a period of time lasting millions of years. It may be better therefore to regard renewability as a continuum. At one end are the fossil fuels, which are effectively non-renewable. These are being steadily depleted and unless substitutes are found the depletion will eventually lead to scarcity. At the other end of the scale are solar energy, water and wind power, which in theory are available indefinitely. Most resources are in between, and the extent to which they remain available depends on choices people make. A balance needs to be found between the rates at which supplies are being depleted and the investment needed to replenish. The continued availability of timber, for example, depends on replanting programmes. The continued availability of metals depends on recycling policies. Water and air quality depends on investment in anti-pollution measures.

Several issues relating to obtaining materials from the Earth are explored in Frederick Grice's *The Bonnie Pit Laddie* (Oxford University Press, 1960; Puffin, 1980). All his life Dick Ullathorne had expected to follow his father and brother into the coal mine. But as a result of a strike and pit accident he comes to question the disparity between the mine owner's living conditions and those of his family. The story is historically accurate, there are credible characters and the author demonstrates the ability to bring to life the story of ordinary people.

Good non-fiction sources of stimulus and information include the following guides to 'saving the Earth', all of which are written very directly for the young reader and all are action-orientated: Early Times, *Environmentally Yours: A Green Handbook for Young People* (Puffin, 1991); The Earth Works Group, *50 Simple Things You Can Do to Save the Earth* (Hodder & Stoughton, 1989); Debbie Silver and Bernadette Vallely, *The Young Person's Guide to Saving the Planet* (Virago, 1990); John Elkington and Julia Hailes, *The Young Green Consumer Guide* (Gollancz, 1990).

Some will find it a bit over the top, but there is good material for raising issues and starting environmental teaching in *The Ozone Friendly Joke Book* by Kim Harris and others (Red Fox, 1990).

A personal favourite is Jonathon Porritt's *Captain Eco and the Fate of the Earth* (Dorling Kindersley, 1991). 'Your planet needs you right now! Enough talk, let's get on with it!' Thus warns super-hero Captain Eco, friend of the Earth and champion of the planet's fragile ecosystem. Together with two Earthlings, Michelle and Clive, Captain Eco sets off on his remarkable mission to save the Earth. The cartoons by Ellis Nadler are striking and the emphasis throughout the book is on commitment on the part of the reader. I also like the beautifully illustrated *Brother Eagle, Sister Sky* (Hamish

169

Hamilton, 1992), which consists of paintings by Susan Jeffers to accompany the environmental message from Chief Seattle, spoken when the American government forced his exhausted and dispirited people to sell the lands of the North-west Indian nations in the mid-1850s. 'To all of the Native American people, every creature and every part of the Earth was sacred; it was their belief that to waste or destroy nature and its wonders was to destroy life itself. Their words were not understood at the time. Now they haunt us. Now they have come true and before it is too late we must listen.'

NOTES AND REFERENCES

1. Hart, R. (1983) 'Wildlands for children'. *Bulletin of Environmental Education,* **141**, 5.
2. Bishop, J. and Foulsham, J. (1973) *Children's Images of Harwich.* Kingston: Kingston Polytechnic Architectural Psychology Research Unit, Environmental Education Research Report No. 3.
3. Moore, R.C. (1986) *Childhood's Domain.* Beckenham; Croom Helm.
4. The most often quoted study here is: Hart, R. (1979) *Children's Experience of Place.* New York: Irvington. But see also bibliography in Moore, R. and Young, D. (1978) 'Childhood outdoors.' In Altman, I. and Wohlwill, J.F. (eds) *Children and the Environment.* New York: Plenum.
5. The methodology used by Downton, P.J. (1973) *Children's Perception of Space Project: Melbourne Study.* Preliminary draft Report, School of Architecture and Building, UNESCO.
6. Lynch, K. (1960) *The Image of the City.* Boston, Mass: MIT Press.
7. See a broad review in Poag, C.K. *et al.* (1985) 'The environments of children: from home to school.' In Cohen, R. (ed.) *The Development of Spatial Cognition.* Hillsdale, New Jersey: Lawrence Erlbaum Associates.
8. See, for example, Wohlwill, J.F. and Heft, H. (1977) 'Environments fit for the developing child.' In McGurk, H. (ed.) *Ecological Factors in Human Development.* Amsterdam: North-Holland.
9. The seminal work on children's privacy is Plant, J. (1930) 'Some psychiatric aspects of crowded living conditions.' *American Journal of Psychiatry,* **9**, 849–60; a more recent review is found in Wolfe, M. (1978) 'Childhood and privacy.' In Altman, J. and Wohlwill, J.F. (eds) *Children and the Environment.* New York: Plenum Press.
10. E.g. Olivegren, J. (1974) 'A better socio-psychological climate in our housing estates'. In Canter, D. and Lee, T. (eds) *Psychology and the Built Environment.* London: Architectural Press.
11. Kaplan, R. and Kaplan, S. (1989) *The Experience of Nature.* Cambridge: Cambridge University Press.
12. Appleton, J. (1975) *The Experience of Landscape.* London: John Wiley.
13. For a review of these themes see Tuan, Yi-Fu (1978) 'Children and the natural environment.' In Altman, J. and Wohlwill, J.F. (eds) *Children and the Environment.* New York: Plenum Press.
14. Spencer, C., Blades, M. and Morsley, K. (1989) *The Child in the Physical Environment,* Chichester: Wiley, pp. 97–8.

15. Cornell, E.H. and Hay, D.H. (1984) 'Children's acquisition of a route via different media.' *Environment and Behaviour*, **16**, 5, 627–41.
16. Baker, R.R. (1981) *Human Navigation and the Sixth Sense*. New York: Simon & Schuster; Walmsley, D.J. and Epps, W.R. (1988) 'Do humans have an innate sense of direction?' *Geography*, **73**, 1, 31–40.
17. Petchenik, B.B. (1985) 'Facts or values: basic methodological issues in research for educational mapping'. *Cartographica*, **22**, 20–42.
18. Blades, M. and Spencer, C. (1986a) 'Map use in the environment and educating children to use maps'. *Environmental Education and Information*, **5**, 4, 187–204.
19. Cohen, R. *et al.* (1986) 'Easing the transition to kindergarten: the affective and cognitive effects of different spatial familiarization experiences'. *Environment and Behaviour*, **18**, 3, 330–45.
20. For a fuller discussion of values in geography and geographical education, see Wiegand, P. (1986) 'Values in geographical education.' In Tomlinson, P.D. and Quinton, M. *Values across the Curriculum*. Brighton: Falmer Press.
21. Chadwick and Meux, M. (1971) 'Procedures for values analysis.' In Metcalfe, L.E. (ed.) *Values Education* (41st Yearbook of the National Council for Social Studies). Washington, DC: National Council for the Social Studies.
22. This example was used in Wiegand, P. (1984) *Introducing Geography*. London: BBC Publications. Based on the then topical issue of the extension of Leeds–Bradford airport.
23. This is a version of the *values clarification* strategy devised by Raths, L. *et al.* (1966) *Values and Teaching*. New York: Merrill.
24. See Marshall, T.H. (1950) *Citizenship and Social Class*. Cambridge: Cambridge University Press.
25. Ward, C. (1978) *The Child in the City*. London: The Architectural Press. See also Ward, C. and Fyson, A. (1973) *Streetwork: The Exploding Schools*. London: Routledge.
26. Tuan, Yi-Fu (1978) *Landscapes of Fear*. Oxford: Basil Blackwell.
27. Pick, W. and Beer, E. (1978) 'Children's perception of their environment: a tape slide sequence.' *Bulletin of Environmental Education*, **86**, 5–127.
28. Haywood, D.G., Rothenburg, M. and Beasley, R.R. (1974) 'Children's play and urban playground environments: a comparison of traditional, contemporary and adventure playground types.' *Environment and Behaviour*, **6**, 131–68.
29. Playboard, *Make Way for Children's Play*. Association for Children's Play and Recreation Ltd, Birmingham, 1985.
30. From one of the most influential environmental books of the 1970s: Jacobs, J. (1972) *The Death and Life of Great American Cities*. Harmondsworth: Penguin.
31. See Anderson, J. (1985) 'Teaching map skills: an inductive approach, Part 3.' *Journal of Geography*, May/June.
32. Hillmann, M., Adams, J. and Whitelegg, J. (1990) *One False Move*. London: Policy Studies Institute.
33. Sadler, J. (1972) *Children and Road Safety: A Survey amongst Mothers*. London: HMSO, OPCS Social Survey Division.
34. Rt Hon. Paul Channon, Press notice, Department of Transport, 26 June 1989.

35. Sandels, S. (1975) *Children in Traffic*. London: Elek.
36. One such is: *Road Safety through Play: Activities for Use with Pre-school Play Groups*. Produced by the County Road Safety Officers' Association in co-operation with the Pre-school Playgroups Association and available from LEA Road Safety Officers.
37. A report of the project is to be found in: Clarke, A. (1986) 'Safe routes to school.' *Bulletin of Environmental Education*, **178**, 10–13.
38. See Elliott, M. (1986) *Keeping Safe: A Practical Guide to Talking with Children*. London: Kidscape.
39. Wheeler, K. and Waites, B. (1971) *Bulletin of Environmental Education*, **16/17**, 3.
40. I acknowledge here the very valuable collection of ideas, many of which are repeated or developed below, in Farbstein, J. and Kantrowitz, M. (1978) *People in Places: Experiencing, Using and Changing the Built Environment*. Englewood Cliffs, NJ: Prentice-Hall. See also the *Bulletin of Environmental Education* as a highly stimulating collection of teaching ideas.
41. Van Matre, S. (1972) *Acclimatization*. American Camping Association, Martinsville, Indiana.
42. See Docherty, R. (1983) 'Stony Stratford: a study with first school children.' *Bulletin of Environmental Education*, **144**, pp. 22–3.
43. Taken from Fien, J. (1985) 'Geography as environmental experience.' *Teaching Geography*, **10**, 4, 148–51; see also Leesan, P. and Agyeman, J. (1986) 'A sense of place? A place of our own.' *Bulletin of Environmental Education*, **183**, 4–18.
44. See the Town Teacher materials. In Boon, G.S. (1973) 'Language in towns.' *Bulletin of Environmental Education*, **22**.
45. See, for example, the Schools Council project Art and the Built Environment, and the book of that title by Eileen Adams and Colin Ward, published (1982) by Longman for the Schools Council.
46. *I Know Someone Who's Afraid of Sunflowers* (n.d.) London: Earthkids Project.
47. Market and Opinion Research International Ltd (1986) *Children's Attitudes to the Environment*. August–September, London: MORI.
48. The Henley Centre for Forecasting (n.d. but *c.* 1991) *Young Eyes: Children's Vision of the Future Environment: A Report Commissioned by British Telecom*.
49. The Henley Centre, op. cit., p. 3.
50. The Henley Centre, op. cit., p. 3.
51. Rees, J. (1991) in Bennett, R. and Estall, R. (eds) *Global Change and Challenge: Geography for the 1990s*. London: Routledge, p. 6.

A Guide to Choice of Maps for Primary School Use

The Ordnance Survey

This is the principal organization supplying large-scale maps and associated products and services. The address of the Ordnance Survey is: Romsey Road, Maybush, Southampton SO9 4DH. Telephone (central switchboard): (0703) 792000.

The Ordnance Survey produces a range of maps and atlases including motoring atlases, leisure guides, world maps and town plans. There are also extracts from maps available for projects and videos about map making and map using.

Copyright subsists in all Ordnance Survey products for a period of 50 years from the end of the year in which the map was made. It is therefore essential that teachers wishing to copy maps do not do so without prior permission of the Ordnance Survey. Local education authorities usually hold Ordnance Survey copyright licences which enable schools which they support or maintain to make map reproductions on their premises from Ordnance Survey maps purchased by the school. Alternatively the local education authority may make copies on its premises on behalf of an educational establishment which it funds. If a school is independently funded or 'opted out', the Ordnance Survey copyright section will be happy to issue the school with a licence which enables teachers to copy maps on basically the same terms as schools funded by local educational authorities.

Large-scale Ordnance Survey maps

1:50 000 (2 cm on the map represents 1 km on the ground)

This is the most popular Ordnance Survey map and will be familiar to most readers. It is sold folded as the Landranger map series in magenta covers. These maps are most useful for seeing the general features of the region in which the school is located. Each of the Landranger maps covers an area of 40 km by 40 km and so a whole city or conurbation can be seen on one sheet. It is possible to see where you live but houses are not marked individually although each road is shown. The maps show contours and conventional symbols. They are at too small a scale for children to use when walking – but could be used effectively when travelling by car or coach. They are good for seeing the relationships of nearby towns and villages and how to get there.

1:25 000 (4 cm on the map represents 1 km on the ground)

This series of maps is known as the Pathfinder series and is also available widely in high street booksellers. It shows all the features of the 1:50 000 maps but in more detail. You can see each building, gardens and field boundaries. These features and the larger scale make it suitable for primary children to follow when walking as well as for seeing the relationships described above but in more detail. The new Pathfinder maps cover an area 20 km from west to east by 10 km from north to south. They are twice the size of the first-series maps, which showed an area 10 km by 10 km.

1:10 000 (1 cm on the map represents 100 m on the ground)

This is the largest-scale OS map available for the whole country although some areas still only have its pre-metric predecessor (1:10 560, i.e. 6 inches to the mile). It is the largest map scale to show contours. These are printed in brown; the rest of the map is black and white only. These maps are ideal for seeing patterns in urban streets such as the straight rows of Victorian terraces and the curving sweeps of modern housing estates. Assuming the school was located centrally on the map (which of course it is unlikely to be!), you might expect to find the whole of a primary school catchment area on one map at this scale. Each map covers an area of 5 km by 5 km.

1:2 500 (1 cm on the map represents 25 m on the ground)

Most of the country is covered at this scale, apart from remote upland areas. This map is really a 'plan', as every feature shown on the map is truly to scale, for example road and pavement widths. The exact outlines of buildings are shown (i.e. they are not just represented by conventional squares and rectangles) and outbuildings are also shown. All road names and most house numbers are marked. Each sheet covers an area of 1 square kilometre.

1:1 250 (1 cm on the map represents 12.5 m on the ground)

This is the largest-scale map published by the OS and is available only for large urban areas. The generous scale makes it possible to plot accurately the location of features such as post-boxes and lamp-posts, although it has no more detail than the 1:25 000 map. This series of maps is useful for very young children to relate features of the local environment. Each sheet covers an area of 500 m by 500 m; that is, a quarter of a square kilometre.

The latter two scales are available either in thick paper versions sold from stock or as printouts from digitized data held by OS agents. A list of Ordnance Survey agents who can supply printouts is available from the OS.

Goad plans

Charles Goad first published fire insurance plans for Canadian cities in 1878. The company grew by making plans of shopping centres showing, at a scale of 1:1056 (1 inch to 88 feet), the name and trade of each retailer, street names, pedestrian areas, service roads and car parks, bus stops, the location of banks, building societies, hotels and restaurants, early closing and market days, road distance from London and details of new developments, vacant properties and sites. These maps are valuable for project work and are available from Chas E. Goad Ltd, 8–12 Salisbury Square, Old Hatfield, Hertfordshire AL9 5BJ. An education pack for primary schools gives details of how the plans might be used in school. The Goad map shop (an official OS agent) has a wider range of publications and maps.

Street maps

Street maps of most towns in the United Kingdom are available from companies such as Geographers A to Z, Geographia, Barnett, Estate Publications and the Automobile Association.

A Guide to Sources of Further Information Referred to in the Text

Many of the organizations listed below are voluntary agencies who welcome new members and financial support. It would be appropriate to enclose a large (A4) stamped addressed envelope when contacting them.

Action Aid, The Old Church House, Church Steps, Frome, Somerset BA11 1PL. *Good range of resources for primary schools, including photo resource pack about Chembakolli – a village in India.*

Aerofilms Ltd, Gate Studios, Station Road, Borehamwood, Hertfordshire WD6 1EJ. *Vertical and oblique aerial photographs in colour and black and white.*

Air Fotos Ltd, 23 Ingram Avenue, Fawdon, Newcastle upon Tyne NE3 2BR. *Take aerial photos to clients' instructions and have a library covering the north of England. Publish postcards and intend to develop schools market for aerial photography.*

Catholic Fund for Overseas Development, 2 Romero Close, Stockwell Road, London SW9 9TY. *A church mission which works to combat poverty, hunger, ignorance, disease and suffering. Education programmes and publications. Resources catalogue.*

Central Bureau for Educational Visits and Exchanges, Seymour Mews House, Seymour Mews, London W1H 9PE. *Provide guidance and contacts in school-to-school links.*

Centre for Alternative Technology, Machynlleth, Powys SY20 9AZ. *Display and education centre offering practical ideas and information on environmentally sound ideas. Catalogue of books and products.*

Centre for World Development Education, Regent's College, Inner Circle, Regent's Park, London NW1 4NS. *An independent educational agency which promotes education in Britain about world development issues and Britain's interdependence with developing countries. Very comprehensive catalogue of primary school publications. Good starting point in the hunt for resources.*

Christian Aid, PO Box 100, London SE1 7RT. *A major relief and development agency, committed to strengthening the poor. Catalogue with many and varied educational materials.*

Commonwealth Institute, Kensington High Street, London W8 6NQ. *Exhibitions, speakers and educational materials.*

Council for Environmental Education, School of Education, University of Reading, London Road, Reading RG1 5AQ. *Co-ordinates and develops environmental education in England, Wales and Northern Ireland. A focal point for the environmental education movement. News-sheet, annual review and environmental education resource sheets in addition to a range of other publications. The complete set of resource sheets provides almost all you ever need to know about environmental materials and organizations.*

Council for National Parks, 45 Shelton Street, London WC2H 9HJ. *An independent charity which campaigns to keep the national parks beautiful and promotes their quiet enjoyment by everyone. General fact sheets and charts on each national park.*

Countryside Commission (Publications), Printworks Lane, Levenshulme, Manchester M19 3JP. *A variety of leaflets, booklets, reports, guides and periodicals on countryside conservation and recreation. Free children's pack.*

Development Education Centre, Selly Oak Colleges, Bristol Road, Birmingham B29 6LE. *Particularly impressive centre with a good range of materials for children and teachers.*

Earthkids Project, The Urban Wildlife Trust, Unit 213, Jubilee Trade Centre, 130 Pershore Street, Birmingham B5 6ND. *Aims to develop the natural environmental awareness of young children from a wide cross-section of the community, especially in urban areas, of pre-school age to age eleven, by working through playschemes, playgroups and play opportunities.*

Friends of the Earth, 26–28 Underwood Street, London N1 7JQ. *A range of environmental resources and information.*

The Geographical Association, 343 Fulwood Road, Sheffield S10 3BP. *The largest subject teaching association representing the interests of geography education in the UK. Journal, Primary Geographer; free annual conference and publishers' exhibition at Easter has a primary day. Local branches, competitions, working groups.*

Geonex, 92–94 Church Road, Mitcham, Surrey CR4 3TD. *Aerial photographs and a resource pack with teacher's guide for using aerial photographs in the classroom.*

Greenpeace, 30–31 Islington Green, London N1 8XE. *International organization campaigning on matters such as commercial whaling, seal culling, nuclear power, the fur trade and marine pollution.*

Information and Documentation Centre for the Geography of the Netherlands, Heidelberglaan 2, Postbus 80115, 3508 TC Utrecht, The Netherlands. *A national foundation whose objective is to provide information about the Netherlands*

177

to teachers, textbook authors and others. Brochures, wall maps, guides, bulletins and slide series.

Kidscape, Third floor, Europe House, World Trade Centre, London E1 9AA. *Exists to develop and provide a comprehensive range of materials and services to assist all those interested in the protection of children and the prevention of child sexual abuse in particular.*

Learning through Landscapes, Third floor, Southside Offices, The Law Courts, Winchester, Hampshire. *An organization aiming to transform the quality and use of school grounds. Newsletter, conferences and a range of publications.*

National Association for Environmental Education, University of Wolverhampton, Walsall Campus, Gorway, Walsall, West Midlands WS1 3BD. *An association of teachers, lecturers and others who are concerned with education and the environment. Conferences, courses and publications.*

The National Trust, 36 Queen Anne's Gate, London SW1H 9AS. *Teaching packs, trails, documentary and visual primary sources, activities and ideas related to the Trust's properties. Schools' corporate membership gives free access to all Trust properties.*

Pictorial Charts Educational Trust, 27 Kirchen Road, London W13 0UD. *A range of full-colour wallcharts including volcanoes, earthquakes, air pollution, energy and mapping at local and global scales.*

Royal Society for the Prevention of Accidents (RoSPA), Cannon House, Priory Queensway, Birmingham B4 6BS. *See especially road safety material and links with geography through map-based safety activities.*

Save the Children, Mary Datchelor House, 17 Grove Lane, London SE5 8RD. *The UK's largest international voluntary agency concerned with child health and welfare. Catalogue with posters, information sheets and country reports, leaflets, educational materials including videos.*

Soma Books Ltd, 38 Kennington Lane, London SE11 4LS. *Stocks books and materials from India.*

The Tidy Britain Group, The Pier, Wigan WN3 4EX. *A campaigning organization 'working to create a litter-free and beautiful Britain'. Produces a programme of materials designed to support teachers of environmental education throughout the curriculum.*

United Kingdom Centre for European Education (UKCEE), Seymour Mews House, Seymour Mews, London W1H 9PE. *Seeks to promote a European perspective in education. Supports conferences, seminars and curriculum development and publishes EDIT (The European Dimension in Teaching).*

Unicef UK, 55 Lincoln's Inn Fields, London WC2A 3NB. *Books, leaflets, slides, videos, posters. Games, songs and stories from around the world. Teachers' materials and activity packs.*

World Wide Fund For Nature (WWF), Panda House, Wayside Park, Godalming, Surrey GU7 1XR. *Working to save endangered species and habitats. Comprehensive education catalogue.*

Index

'acclimatization' 158–60
addresses, children's understanding of
 140–1
aerial photographs 55–7, 98
agriculture 125–7, 129
atlases 11, 51, 58–61; *see also* road
 atlases
attitudes towards people and places
 75–6

climate 115
cognitive maps 22–5
comparitor maps 52
continents 72
contours 36–8
cross-curricular themes 8–9

development education 8–9
direction 46–8
distance 48–51

Earth movements 103–9
economic and industrial understanding
 8, 121–2; *see also* industry
environment and children's
 development 149–50
environmental education 8, 145–70
environmental preferences of children
 154–5, 162
ethnocentrism 46

fiction (children's) 53–5, 69–70, 86–8,
 93, 102–3, 107–8, 116, 136, 165, 169

gazetteer 60
Geographical Association, the 10–11
Geography in the Primary School
 Curriculum Project (GIPP) 11
geomorphology 94
globes 42, 58, 72, 74
graphicacy 16
greenhouse effect 166

Her Majesty's Inspectorate of Schools
 2, 4
home range 148

industry 125–32; *see also* economic and
 industrial understanding
international understanding 8

journeys 132

'known world' of primary school
 children 71–2

landforms 90–109
language in towns 163–4
latitude and longitude 41–6, 59
Leeds City Council, Primary Needs
 Programme 2, 3
Lego 33
localities 77–88
location 39–42

map projections 43–6

Index